WRITERS, PLUMBERS, AND ANARCHISTS

WRITERS, PLUMBERS, AND ANARCHISTS

The WPA Writers' Project in Massachusetts

Christine Bold

UNIVERSITY OF MASSACHUSETTS PRESS *Amherst and Boston*

Printed in the United States of America

LC 2006003178
ISBN 1-55849-539-8 (paper) ISBN 1-55849-538-X (library cloth ed.)

Designed by Sally Nichols
Set in Berkeley OldStyle Book
Printed and bound by The Maple-Vail Book Manufacturing Group., Inc,

Library of Congress Cataloging-in-Publication Data

Bold, Christine, 1955–
Writers, plumbers, and anarchists : the WPA writers' project in Massachusetts / Christine Bold.
p. cm.
Includes bibliographical references and index.
ISBN 1-55849-539-8 (pbk. : alk. paper)—ISBN 1-55849-538-X (library cloth : alk. paper)
1. Federal Writers' Project of the Works Progress Administration of Massachusetts—History. 2. Writers' Program (Mass.)—History. 3. Massachusetts—Historiography. 4. American guide series. 5. New Deal, 1933–1939—Massachusetts. 6. Massachusetts—Politics and government—1865–1950. 7. Massachusetts—Ethnic relations—History—20th century. I. Title.
F63.2.B65 2006
974.4'04—dc22
2006003178

British Library Cataloguing in Publication data are available.

To Ric
for everything

CONTENTS

ILLUSTRATIONS

ACKNOWLEDGMENTS

"An adventure in co-operation" is how the Massachusetts state editors described their work on the writers' project. I would like to borrow their phrase to express my great gratitude for all the support—financial, collegial, and personal—which I have received in the course of working on this book.

My research was generously supported by grants from the Social Sciences and Humanities Research Council of Canada. Invaluable expertise and assistance were provided by archivists and librarians at the following institutions: Rare Books and Manuscripts, Boston Public Library; National Archives and Records Administration, Washington, D.C., and College Park, Md.; Manuscripts Division, Library of Congress; New Bedford Free Public Library; New Bedford Whaling Museum; Millicent Library, Fairhaven; and Department of Rare Books and Special Collections, University of Rochester Library. I appreciated the opportunity to present my research and receive helpful feedback from colleagues at conferences hosted by the Canadian Association for American

Studies, the American Studies Association, and the New England American Studies Association. Earlier versions of chapters 3 and 5 appeared in *The Massachusetts Historical Review* 5 (2003) and *Prospects: An Annual of American Cultural Studies* 28 (2003).

Some individuals deserve particular thanks: Ondine Le Blanc and Donald Yacovone of the Massachusetts Historical Society for their editorial wizardry; Eugene Zepp of the Boston Public Library, Paul Cyr of the New Bedford Free Library, Joseph Thomas and Jay Avila of Spinner Publications, Gail Couture of the *New Bedford Standard-Times* clippings file, and Debbie Charpentier of the Millicent Library for their very helpful leads; Amy Appleford, Morgan Dennis, George Grinnell, and Mark Schwandt for their sterling work as graduate research assistants at the University of Guelph; Martin Schwalbe for his consistently inventive photographic support; and Kevin Millham for his first-rate work on the index. Paul Wright, Carol Betsch, Jack Harrison, and other staff members of the University of Massachusetts Press have provided invaluable professional guidance. Kay Scheuer is a magnificent copy editor.

I am personally indebted to my dear colleague Harry Lane, my one-time codirector in the School of Literatures and Performance Studies at the University of Guelph, who gamely struggled on through the administrative quagmire, allowing me to escape intermittently on research trips. Lewis Bold Wark has gone to the limits of teenage tolerance in pretending interest in my archival adventures and contributing his general *joie de vivre* to the enterprise. And Ric Knowles deserves a medal for his unique combination of perspicacity, engagement, support, and willingness to chauffeur me endlessly around the more obscure highways and byways of Massachusetts. An adventure indeed.

WRITERS, PLUMBERS, AND ANARCHISTS

INTRODUCTION

My title gives new meaning to the initials WPA. The Works Progress Administration housed America's largest arts funding program ever, part of the New Deal's foray into nationwide work relief. In the 1930s, hostile commentators jeered that the organization's acronym stood for Wet Pants Administration, We Piddle Around, We Poke Along; government administrators retorted, Work Pays America. In Massachusetts the acronym could well stand for Writers, Plumbers, and Anarchists, in tribute to the state's distinctive contribution to the writers' wing of the program. The Massachusetts Writers' Project attempted to implement an inclusive definition of authorship which took a huge range of white- and blue-collar workers off the breadlines to be government writers—to the point that WPA worker-writers in the state were routinely accused of being "plumbers" and, after publication of the state guide, the project was accused of supporting anarchists and other subversives. Its innovative arrangements did indeed present new opportunities for minority and politically oppositional voices, whose input into the WPA guides rattled several "skeletons in the Bay state cupboard" (Nicholas 89). This book pursues the WPA writers' project in a single state, exploring Massachusetts to discover the consequences of New Deal patronage for writers-in-the-making, for community image-making, and for minority groups attempting to achieve cultural citizenship in America.

Of the fifty state offices that made up the nationwide experiment from 1935 to 1943, Massachusetts stands out as a risk-taker, testing the limits of what public funding allowed.[1] Its story shows how the federal met the local, as government sponsorship bore down on communities' cultural identities and memory-making strategies, and WPA guide-makers struggled to resolve New Deal pragmatism, state left-liberalism, and varieties of local boosterism. The results left a distinct mark on the state's public culture, shifting its image away from an ethnically homogeneous "cradle of the nation" to a much more culturally diverse and politically volatile society. The guides offered thoroughgoing coverage of the "316 towns and 39 cities of the Commonwealth," and they took on the challenge of the state's changing population—"65% of foreign birth or of foreign or foreign-mixed parentage," the second-largest percentage of any state (*Massachusetts* 7; *Armenians* n.pag.). This shift in representation was neither easy nor complete: while the project's hiring practices and research priorities flushed out Euro-American diversity in Massachusetts, it took them much longer to—much more incompletely—cross the color line. The Massachusetts project's surviving records also allow a unique glimpse into what New Deal pieties meant in practice for the "worker-writers" (as the left dubbed them) in its employ. In short, Massachusetts dramatizes what was at stake in the writers' project: the perception of who belonged to the state's cultural polity, who would get remembered, and in what terms.

Searching for evidence of the writers' project in Massachusetts today, however, is a bit like using a road map with half the names erased. In Boston, home of the project's state office and some of its liveliest controversies, it remains a great deal easier to reconstruct the biographies of writers from three hundred years ago than to find the smallest trace of some of the men and women—especially the women—who staffed the Boston office in the 1930s. Down in New Bedford, public display and archival records lavish attention on the history of its whaling community. The New Bedford Writers' Project office gets little billing. Combing municipal records for the fifty-odd employees, trudging around town matching names to addresses, searching for sites long demolished, I felt like a vaguely furtive private eye on the coldest of trails. My warm welcome from the Sudbury Historical Society dropped several degrees when the custodian discovered that I was after unemployed writers from the thirties, not the military records of colonial and revolutionary engagement. Even the best-known story about the Massachusetts project—the scandal surrounding its state guide—forgets half the truth.

Why the reticence? In many ways, Massachusetts' involvement in the writers' project could figure as one of the state's finest cultural moments. When the New Deal initiated the four Federal Arts Projects—for theater people, visual artists, musicians, and writers—under the umbrella of the vast Works Progress Administration, it classified artists as socially useful workers.[2] This act initiated the most inclusive experiment in public arts funding that America has ever seen—one which promised to cut across the privileges of class, race, ethnicity, region, political affiliation, and artistic training. The Massachusetts project came to commit to this inclusiveness with a fervor outpacing many other states. At a time when people in Massachusetts "faced disastrous levels of unemployment—twenty, thirty, even forty percent in some localities" (Richard Brown 228), the project took hundreds of writers from the relief rolls and off the breadlines, not through some competitive process of selection but with a capacious definition that welcomed everyone with an interest in writing who proved financial need. The Boston office hired published authors on the left and right (mainly clustered in Boston and Cape Cod), ex-newspapermen, new college graduates, diverse white-collar workers, people who had lost their life savings—destitute applicants of all stripes, one third of them twenty- to thirty-year-olds (Mangione, *Dream* 107).

This motley group produced approximately two dozen state, regional, and community guides whose stories run the gamut from the quirky to the disturbing.[3] One guide to the Berkshires tells of the resourceful tavern-owner in State Line who, discovering that his establishment straddled the Massachusetts–New York border, mounted his bar on casters and pushed it in one direction or another during Prohibition whenever there were—fortunately, alternating—state liquor raids. The guide to Massachusetts addresses one of the state's darkest moments when it condemns the execution of the Italian American laborers and anarchists Nicola Sacco and Bartolomeo Vanzetti. By and large, the project's publications supported the progressive onslaught against "Yankee hegemony" by recording and celebrating the state's ethnic diversity (Richard Brown 227).The guides also conserved the state's heritage in forms alternative to Henry Ford's proto-theme parks or chamber of commerce puffery. The assistant state director in Massachusetts claimed that guidebook activity was reshaping historical consciousness across the state: "One of the most significant results . . . of our projected studies has been the formation of historical societies dedicated to the preservation of racial records and encouragement of historical research."[4] Project writers in Massachusetts also captured in book form events —such as the New England hurricane of 1938—otherwise consigned to ephemera. They produced, in short—as one member of the national staff wrote to another—"a story that has never been told, and couldn't have been told without the amazing set-up known technically as the Writers Project."[5]

Part of the reluctance to celebrate this 1930s experiment may be born in the contradictions thrown up by its effort at inclusivity. The Massachusetts Writers' Project demonstrates the best and the worst of how the public funding experiment played out in practice, with experiences ranging from cultural inclusion to political suppression. On the one hand, Massachusetts produced the most politically provocative writing of the nationwide project and some of its most innovative charting of hitherto unacknowledged ethnic communities. On the other, there were failures of vision and nerve. For a long time, the project denied equitable representation to the state's Native and African American populations—both as project employees and as guidebook subjects. And the Boston state office conspired in one of the most deeply buried acts of censorship in the project's history when it secretly excised the controversial entries on Sacco and Vanzetti and on labor struggles from the state guide. The project's most inclusive initiatives—those dedicated to the state's workers—got going only in 1938, and their publication was prevented when Congress closed down the writers' project as a federal operation in 1939, and the State Department of Education became the sponsor of the Massachusetts project.

Public embarrassment may also linger. Dependence on a government job creation program was an uncomfortable experience for many project employees. The famous example is author John Cheever, whose Republican family strongly disapproved of his employment on the writers' project in New York City and Washington, D.C. Many less famous writers on the project experienced a similar discomfort. My search in New Bedford and Fairhaven, for example, was thwarted by the fact that numerous employees camouflaged their project standing in the public record. In the Millicent Library in Fairhaven, where I sat scrolling through microfilm reels of local newspapers from the period, trying to piece together fragments of information, I encountered a woman who still laughed apologetically as she spoke of family members "on the WPA" who were publicly branded "shovel-leaners" and "boondogglers" in the community.[6]

It is important to recover the local impact of this experiment in government funding, not in a spirit of uncritical celebration or apologetic embarrassment, but with questions about its achievements and limitations. The New Deal programs reached into the cultural lives of the citizenry with a breadth and depth not experienced before or since in the United States. The writers' project organized the first large-scale charting of America, thereby serving as the discursive edge of the New Deal plan to refashion the public landscape. As multiple agencies reworked the physical landscape to create the infrastructure of modernity—the Works Progress Administration and Public Works Administration overhauling the built environment, the Civilian Conservation Corps and Tennessee Valley Authority transforming natural areas—so the writers' project reshaped the cultural landscape with travel guides which served as a conceptual baseline for modern representations and perceptions of America.[7] Daniel Aaron argues that "the re-examination after the war of what Whitman called 'the large unconscious scenery of my land,' embodied, for example, in a book like F. O. Matthiessen's *American Renaissance*, was a cultural spin-off of the guides" ("Guide-books" 837). Aaron's observation is particularly pertinent for Massachusetts, given how many of Matthiessen's subjects had previously appeared in the state's project publications.

At the time, the guides were disputed as powerful arbiters of cultural citizenship. Massachusetts project publications consistently provoked struggles over cultural access, representation, and memory-making. The combination of the guides' factual rhetoric, their status as America's first indigenous travel guides, their claim to be collectively authored by representative Americans, and the imprimatur of government sponsorship positioned them as powerful cultural gatekeepers, mapping the lines of cultural belonging and exclusion. The guides also fed the great appetite of Depression and New Deal America for constructed traditions, memorials, and monuments that bolstered communities against an uncertain future—an appetite exhaustively documented by Michael Kammen. He calls it the "perversely symbiotic" condition of "nostalgic modernism" and considers it a hallmark of the thirties (300).

Several scholarly books have taken the measure of the Federal Writers'

Project in its national reach. Jerrold Hirsch values the nationwide experiment for its attempt to reconcile romantic nationalism and cultural pluralism, a powerful riposte to 1930s' totalitarianism in Europe and 1920s' xenophobia and racism in "an America that defined itself as white, Protestant, middle-class, and rural" (*Portrait* 39). Petra Schindler-Carter argues that the project's publications were central to the 1930s' "search for a usable past" and the development of a "rhetoric of cultural enthusiasm" (46, 83). My own earlier book situates the American Guide Series within its production and reception history, reading selected guides for what they tell us about the New Deal's attempts to broker cultural citizenship across the country and to map "American" identities onto the nation's landscape. An earlier generation of books offered institutional history. Monty Noam Penkower documented the organization and administration of the writers' project, while Jerre Mangione produced a wonderfully rich memoir of project personalities and procedures from his perspective as national coordinating editor. When the Massachusetts project appears in these works, it does so predominantly in terms of the controversy which greeted its state guide. (Indeed, Penkower reads that controversy as so momentous that it led other states to water down the language of their publications.) This book argues that there is more to Massachusetts than scandal, that this project offers a particularly powerful case study of how federal promises about public funding played out in practice at the state and local levels.

Writers, Plumbers, and Anarchists excavates the cultural power of the Massachusetts Writers' Project in three sections. The first section provides an overview of the project's organization and personnel (in chapter 1) and of the full range of the state's publications (in chapter 2). These chapters pay particular attention to the ways in which relations among federal, state, and local levels shaped the project's cultural production. The statewide and Boston guides aspired to a kind of history writing that espouses critical distance and professional authority. Local community guides seem closer to collective memory-making which values continuity, lived experience, and group identity.[8] The few works dedicated to minority ethnic and racial groups sit somewhere between, pulled in different directions by the different models of cultural recovery dominating the project at different moments.

The second section explores the political fallout from these three-way negotiations, as it affected acts of representation and conditions of employment. Chapter 3 reconstructs the censorship of Sacco and Vanzetti material in *Massachusetts: A Guide to Its Places and People* (1937), the full story of which has remained secret for over sixty years. It is a key demonstration of the project's capacity to contribute to (or challenge) governing notions of citizenship and exclusion. Chapter 4 demonstrates how the hardening color line of the 1930s ran through project publications, sidelining African Americans and Native Americans as living presences in the state's contemporary scene. A more inclusive turn came in 1938, when new series of workers' life histories and social-ethnic interviews recognized the richness of the state's citizens of color. Chapter 5 focuses on how the project's equation of art and work impacted on some of its writers' lives, social relations, and literary productions. Government patronage repositioned worker-writers in their communities—with quite different effects in New Bedford, with its depressed blue-collar industries, compared to Provincetown, with its established artists' colony.

The third section explores some local and specialized guides for the ways in which they replay these preoccupations with minority groups, local memory-making, and worker-writers. Chapter 6 reads the idiosyncratic guide *Cape Cod Pilot* (1937) by Josef Berger as an innovative appreciation of racial difference and hybrid identities in the state's contemporary culture—a model of inclusive representation which helped to lead the project in more progressive directions. Chapter 7 explores two volumes dedicated to immigrant groups—*The Armenians in Massachusetts* (1937) and *The Albanian Struggle in the Old World and New* (1939)—showing how different models of cultural recovery in the project's national office produced different visions of ethnic difference. Chapter 8 reads three local guides—*A Brief History of the Towne of Sudbury* (1939), *A Historical Sketch of Auburn* (1937), and *Springfield, Massachusetts* (1941)—for the varieties of memory work they mount in the face of threatening modernity. Chapter 9 shows how the project finally honed its equation of writers with other essential workers in the innovative photojournalist text *New England Hurricane* (1938), one of the project's bestselling publications. The epilogue explores the legacies of the writers' project, as they can be traced in subsequent publications, employees' future careers, and the government-sponsored tourism adopted in Lawrence and Lowell forty years later and still on show today.

The Boston state editors called the voluminous cultural activity generated by the Massachusetts Writers' Project "an adventure in co-operation"

(*Massachusetts* x). The adventure drew in writers of many stripes and agencies at many levels, and it produced hugely diverse images and stories, historical and contemporary, of the state. Yet one central principle did emerge: access, representation—ultimately, a sense of cultural citizenship—were most inclusive when bureaucrats, writers, and their subjects most closely shared an identification as workers.

SECTION ONE

THE FEDERAL WRITERS' PROJECT IN MASSACHUSETTS

1

WRITERS, PLUMBERS, AND ADMINISTRATORS

> The by-line, "unemployed writers," is actually in this state a libel on this class of workers. The book apparently is to be written, at least in Massachusetts, by unemployed plumbers or men of any other qualification.
>
> Josef Berger to Mary Heaton Vorse, December 17, 1935

> Blame for the present state of the guidebook in no way attaches to local writers on the project. Its misinformation is in despite of their best efforts to instill some degree of accuracy into the tome, which was written and edited by Boston writers, nee plumbers.
>
> *Fairhaven Star* August 26, 1937

> In one State headquarters . . . a toilet over-flowed one day and four journeyman plumbers on the editorial staff volunteered to repair it.
>
> Bernard De Voto, "New England via W.P.A." *Saturday Review of Literature* May 14, 1938

Throughout the life of the Massachusetts Writers' Project, commentators of all ideological stripes threw around the term "plumber" as the ultimate disparagement of project writers. The epithet serves as a nice litmus test of the WPA experiment's ambitions and limitations, where the project succeeded and where its nerve failed, aesthetically and politically. When the New Deal administration classified literature as labor, it breached traditional class lines in ways that were at once exhilarating and fraught, even to its strongest supporters (Fig. 1). Writers on the left celebrated governmental recognition as socially useful workers and support for solidarity with the working classes. However, some of the same writers—especially the likes of Josef Berger, quoted above, who had already achieved publication and had a stake in individual authorship—worried that the classification would de-skill writers, downgrading them to the lowest of workers, i.e., "plumbers." Berger's complaint to Vorse (penned when the project

Fig. 1. WPA poster designed by the Federal Art Project. Library of Congress, Prints and Photographs Division, WPA Poster Collection (LC-USZ62-59986 DLC).

initially refused to recognize his qualifications) continued: "This seems doubly unfair because the writers have waited so long for their one opportunity. . . . men who have by their training the right to do this work."[1] The structure of the writers' project exacerbated this tension. Employees in Massachusetts—as in the other forty-seven states—found themselves at the bottom of an administrative and editorial hierarchy which reserved one level of decision-making to a state office in Boston and another to the national office in Washington, D.C. Twenty years later, John Steinbeck casually characterized the WPA guidebook writers as "the best writers in America" (103). At the time, however, being a project writer in Massachusetts did not carry with it anything like that level of cultural confidence.

At the inception of the Federal Writers' Project, national director Henry Alsberg boasted that it embraced the most democratic company of writers that America had ever seen and that it put literature and other forms of labor into unusually close conjunction. With approximately 10,000 employees across the country, it stretched the qualifications for artistic, in this case writerly, status more broadly than any other project (and than any public-funding program since). Massachusetts, a state rich in the history of labor organization and struggle, saw that commitment through. The Massachusetts project did not have any actual plumbers on its payroll (as far as I can ascertain), but it did employ women and men whom the Depression had turned into manual laborers. Merle Colby, assistant state director, reported: "Llewlellyn B.'s doctorate makes him valuable to us, although not of much use to him when he swung a pick 'in the ditch' out in Randolph. George G., shovelling dirt on frozen Fisher Hill last winter, is now of more use to himself and to the community as a member of the writing project."[2] Employing people from many walks of life meant that the project included writers with deep working relations with multiple social classes and ethnic communities—Albanian, Armenian, Irish, Portuguese, and African American, among others. Only late in the day, after its state guide came out, did the project direct its writers to chart the state's working-class cultures, contemporary and historical: the conditions, organizations, attitudes, politics, and ethnic alliances of porters, garment workers, whalers, fishing people, factory workers, mill workers, hotel workers, munitions workers, teachers. In the process, the project played out a major trope of solidarity within the thirties' left—what Jack Conroy dubbed the "worker-writer" at the American Writers' Congress in 1935—and produced its most innovative and culturally inclusive writing.

But there were distinct limits to the experiment, at both the federal and state levels. While Alsberg prated about the virtues of a capacious definition of writer, neither he nor his colleagues in Washington trusted project employees to write up their own localities in their own terms for the state guides. The central office developed a massively detailed American Guide Manual, which attempted to control everything from writers' conceptual parameters to the details of their style. At the same time, Alsberg was prone to reach into the mass of employees, pluck out those he considered the most promising writers, and give them special work conditions. On the Massachusetts project, these conditions exacerbated a center-periphery mentality, with employees across the state voicing suspicions of administrators, editors, and union organizers in Boston and Washington. The *Fairhaven Star*'s characterization of "Boston writers, nee plumbers," for example, resulted from disgruntled employees in the New Bedford district office leaking their suspicions of Boston editors to the local press.

This chapter introduces some of the structures and key people—at several levels—who shaped the work of the Massachusetts Writers' Project. Project employees generated guidebook material within a chain of authority which devolved from the federal to the state to local levels. Each level had a different political complexion. New Dealers dominated the central office in Washington, D.C. Left-leaning Harvard academics dominated the Massachusetts state office in Boston, at least for a period. And more educationally diverse and politically conservative groups staffed the five district offices across the state. There was a direct correlation between who—by gender, race, ethnicity, class—staffed these positions and the project's insights and blind spots. Alsberg, for example, rarely identified a woman writer for special treatment. Women were much more likely to make their mark by coming up through project ranks. There were no African Americans or Native Americans in positions of authority in the Boston office, and the Massachusetts project—at least in its early years—had a notably bad record on African American representation (in employment and textual coverage) and on recognizing Native peoples as living presences in the contemporary scene. And, of course, the state's larger political landscape brought its own pressures, as appointed project officers struggled to accommodate the demands of elected government officials who ultimately held the fate of the project in their hands.

CENTRAL OFFICE, WASHINGTON, D.C.

New Dealers—some with close links to Roosevelt's cabinet—headed up the central office in Washington. By and large, they were not relief clients, but reform-minded social workers, writers, and academics who believed in the project's capacity to reeducate the nation. They set about producing guidelines and templates to make this vision a practical reality, assuming the right to cultural leadership over the dispossessed farther down the project hierarchy.[3]

The most passionate figure, and the one who looms largest in the Massachusetts story, was Henry Alsberg. When he accepted the position of national director, Alsberg was a fifty-seven-year-old Jewish bachelor who was economically comfortable enough to have sustained a nomadic lifestyle in law, journalism, foreign service (including providing emergency famine relief in Russia in 1922 and 1923) and theater (at one time he was a director of the Provincetown Playhouse in New York City, for which he adapted the Yiddish play *The Dybbuk*). A self-identified "philosophical anarchist," Alsberg believed that the project would bring about a democratic renaissance of American letters, first by energizing literature with the vigor of labor, then by uncovering a wealth of cultural detail hitherto invisible to the nation's people (Mangione, *Dream* 56). He went before the Second American Writers' Congress in 1937 to argue: "We must get over the idea that every writer must be an artist of the first class, and that the artist of the second or third class has no function. I think we have invested art with this sort of sacrosanct, ivory-tower atmosphere too much. . . . I think the conceit of the average writer and the average painter separates him from the average worker. I have experienced it myself" (Hart, *Changing* 245).

Alsberg had two lieutenants who translated his vision into administrative practice. Reed Harris, his assistant director, said, "Henry, in addition to being a philosophical anarchist, was a sort of anarchist about the way he ran an office."[4] Harris, still in his twenties, was a diplomatic and principled administrator. A few years earlier, he had been expelled from Columbia University for his investigative journalism, and he went on to publish an exposé of corrupt university football and to work in New York City journalism. In 1934 he joined the publicity arm of the Federal Emergency Relief Administration, where he hooked up with Alsberg. George Cronyn, associate director in the national office, oversaw editorial structures. A little younger than Alsberg, Cronyn was a rover of a different sort: he had been a cowboy in New Mexico, a rancher in Oregon, then an instructor at the University of Montana, as well as magazine and encyclopedia editor and best-selling novelist. His style was more autocratic and blunter than Alsberg's, and it made manifest the assumptions of educational and cultural superiority which dominated the central office.

Next to Alsberg, Katharine Kellock, national tours editor, made the greatest impact on Massachusetts. Like the others, she came to the project through a mixture of social work, travel, and scholarship. She had worked for Lillian Wald's Henry Street Settlement House in New York City and with Quaker relief groups in western and eastern Europe and Russia, as well as in research and writing positions. Her travel abroad had convinced her of the cultural efficacy of tour descriptions as a concrete way to draw attention to current social conditions. On occasion, for example, she smuggled into tours sections word of labor disputes that state administrations were trying to sweep under the rug. Throughout the life of the project, she policed and edited tours copy with missionary zeal. In the dominantly homosocial community of the central office, Kellock's gender set her apart. Her male colleagues' resentment of women in authority remained palpable for decades. In 1973, Harold Rosenberg, who had worked on the national editorial staff, still talked of "the contemptuous self-assurance of the head of the 'tours' section of the Guides . . . this lady . . . was to become the dominant editorial power on the Washington staff" (99–100).

The national director and his advisors decided on an innovative scheme: project writers would collectively produce a nationwide series of state guidebooks, the first in the United States (Fig. 2). Particular in local details but conforming to a uniform tripartite design, each guide would consist of research essays on the state's cultural and physical properties, followed by city and town descriptions, then mile-by-mile highway tours. The central office circulated the American Guide Manual—a template for guidebook production—to state directors, who in turn coordinated the efforts of district offices and field workers across each state.[5] The American Guide Manual was a massively detailed document, eighty-six pages long. It directed state editors in the classification of writers as "intermediate," "skilled," or "professional"—the first of which categories, in particular, the American Writers' Union consistently resisted. The manual also divided every community, large or small, into thirty-three categories which covered contemporary, historical, natural, social, political, and cultural topics: from "Flora and Fauna" to "Army and Navy." In effect, those categories framed writers'

Fig. 2. Federal Writers' Project display, *New York Times* National Book Fair. Photograph No. 69-N-11508-C, Work Projects Administration, Record Group 69, National Archives at College Park, Md.

perspectives on their own locales, and they inadvertently encouraged blind spots—around race in particular. The manual omitted African Americans from its taxonomy and aligned "Indian Tribes and Reservations" with "Archeology." The manual even dictated minutiae of style, the rules for tour copy forbidding the passive voice and the second-person pronoun, for example. As the national editors took stock of the results of their guidelines, they continually adapted the instructions—ultimately to the tune of twenty supplements, anywhere from three to forty-five pages long, much to the frustration of project employees across the country. Miriam Allen deFord, working on the California guide, expressed the frustrations of many at "the maze of conflicting instructions" emanating from the central office:

> I think that I have never tried
> A job as painful as the guide.
> A guide which changes every day
> Because our betters feel that way.
> A guide whose deadlines come so fast
> Yet no one lives to see the last
> A guide to which we give our best
> To hear: "This stinks like all the rest!"
>
> There's no way out but suicide
> For only God can end the Guide. (qtd. in Mangione, *Dream* 138, 140)

Something of a sea-change came over the national office when Alsberg added three national editors who all passionately valued and sought to encourage culturally diverse voices. Separately and together, they initiated Black and ethnic studies that greatly enhanced the solidarity between project writers and other workers. Sterling Brown, African American writer, critic, and university professor, became national Negro Affairs editor in 1936. He assembled a tiny office of 2.5 employees who strove to heighten employment equity and visibility for African Americans all across the country, partly by monitoring guidebook content and partly by setting African American writers to record their communities by archival and oral history methods. Benjamin A. Botkin replaced John Lomax as national folklore editor in summer 1938. A first-generation Jewish American folklorist, Botkin developed an innovative approach which valued folklore as a dynamic, multicultural part of urban and rural modern life. He worked closely with Morton Royse, who also joined the central office in summer 1938, as social-ethnic studies editor. Royse had studied with Franz Boas and John Dewey, researched and written on European ethnic groups, and came most recently from the Workers' Education Bureau of America. Botkin and Royse guided project workers in gathering folklore and life histories, preferably from their own ethnic communities. In these oral histories, working people (interviewers and interviewees) were key creators of America as a "composite of cultures" (qtd. in J. Hirsch, *Portrait* 31).[6] Supporting these efforts in New England were two regional administrators: at first Joseph Gaer, a student of Jewish folklore, as field supervisor, then from August 1938 Frank Manuel, hailed as one of the most brilliant men of his year at Harvard and author of a book on Spain, as regional editor. Although Alsberg appointees, these men came to align themselves strongly with the Boston office perspectives. At one point, in the white heat of getting the Massachusetts guide to press, for example, Gaer wrote exasperatedly to Alsberg: "There are just about a million details to attend to at the last moment and I am trying to get the books off the press as early as is physically possible but frankly I do not find the Washington editorial inquiries, requests and suggestions in the least helpful."[7]

In 1939, this regime disintegrated. Under Colonel Francis C. Harrington—"a military being to the core"who replaced Harry Hopkins as WPA administrator—the writers' project devolved from federal to state control, and Alsberg was dismissed (Mangione, *Dream* 329). In 1938, Martin Dies's Committee on Un-American Activities and Clifton A. Woodrum's subcommittee of the House Committee on Appropriations had initiated investigations into the politics of the four federal arts projects. The ensuing witch-hunt led to the closure of the Federal Theatre Project in August 1939, while the music, art, and writers' programs survived only in those states—including Massachusetts—which agreed to fund 25 percent of their operations. At this point, Harrington promoted John Newsom from state director of the Michigan office to national director of the renamed writers' program. Newsom, who had also seen armed service, was considerably more managerial, more conservative, and less fervent about cultural renaissance than Alsberg. Brown, Royse, Cronyn, and Harris soon left the project. Botkin moved to a more organizational role, collecting project material for the Library of Congress, while Kellock remained in a greatly diminished version of the central office. Newsom survived in the scaled-down position until he joined the navy in February 1942.

MASSACHUSETTS STATE OFFICE, BOSTON

Harvard-educated academics dominated the Massachusetts state office in Boston, an emphasis also evident in the guide's volunteer consultants. Although Clifford K. Shipton—the first, short-lived director—was conservative, the most vocal presence in the state office identified with the political left. The second state director, Ray Allen Billington, estimated that "between one half and one third of the personnel either were members of the Communist party or were fellow travelers."[8] These young men had the confidence of their training, their class, and their gender. They felt, on the one hand, more currently informed than the Washington, D.C., editors (some of whom were themselves "Harvard men") and, on the other, more sophisticated in perspective than the local writers with their home-bound loyalties.

The key editorial team consisted of the state director and two assistant directors. Shipton began his appointment in October 1935. Editor of *Sibley's Harvard Graduates*, he came with the backing of the Harvard faculty of history and the Massachusetts Historical Society, but the rest of the staff soon deemed him obstructive, uninterested in the aims of the guidebook, and unsympathetic to unemployed writers. "DIRECTOR SHIPTONS HARVARD ACCENT DROWNS OUT PROTESTS OF DESPERATE WRITERS," complained one telegram from the Artists and Writers Union of Massachusetts to Alsberg, who soon arranged Shipton's transfer to the post of regional supervisor on the historical records survey.[9] Early in 1936, Billington, also a Harvard-trained historian and an assistant professor at Clark University, assumed the state directorship on a part-time basis, an arrangement allowed under the quota for project personnel not off the relief rolls. Washington editors valued Billington for his scholarly profile, his Harvard backers, and his personal qualities: "alert, intelligent, very personable and tactful," according to Roderick Seidenberg, architecture editor in the central office. Alsberg later said that "we needed him for a long time as a front to the project."[10]

Two assistant directors had been part of the state editorial team from its inception. Bert J. Loewenberg, another historian with a Harvard Ph.D., would have assumed the directorship after Shipton, according to Billington, but for the prejudices of the day: "I was selected instead, only because the Washington officials feared that Loewenberg's appointment would fan flames of anti-Semitism that were already directed against the New Deal, and have some influence on the election of 1936."[11] Billington's and Loewenberg's politics veered to the left of Shipton's: he was a registered Republican while they "considered themselves liberals."[12]

Further left again, Merle Colby, the other assistant director, functioned as spokesperson for the radical contingent in the state office. Yet another Harvard graduate, Colby was already, as Shipton wrote to Cronyn, "a novelist of some standing" in 1935.[13] He turned out to be the great political chameleon of the state office. His political savvy first appeared in his story of how he secured employment on the Massachusetts project:

> While standing in a long line of applicants, waiting to be interviewed and afraid there would be no jobs left by the time he reached the head of the line, his knowledge of Boston politics inspired him to scribble a note which read: "Take care of Merle Colby." He signed it with the first obviously Irish name that came to mind, and instructed a passing boy to deliver the note to the WPA interviewer. Within moments he was taken out of line, ushered into the presence of the official, and hired as soon as he had identified himself as a certified pauper and published novelist. (Mangione, *Dream* 101)

The Artists and Writers Union of Massachusetts also endorsed Colby as its first choice for assistant state director in 1935, and he became spokesman for the left-wing contingent. Yet he escaped political purge, first rescued from controversy in Massachusetts by Alsberg in 1937, then taken under the wing of national director John D. Newsom in 1939. He survived one cut after another, taking over from Newsom as director of the newly restructured writers' unit of the war services subdivision in March 1942. One of the very few employees on the payroll on the project's last day, he submitted the "Final Report on Disposition of Unpublished Materials of W.P.A. Writers Program" to the Library of Congress in April 1943.[14]

In later life, Billington remembered the Massachusetts project as a place of perpetual turmoil. He described the Boston office when he arrived early in 1936: "All reason and order seemed to have fled as writers converted reams of copy paper into the manuscripts that would justify their continued employment, as each day's mail from Washington brought orders that contradicted those of the day before, as district supervisors shouted their opposition to each procedural change and the state director helped keep the telephone company alive by relaying their invective to his superiors in Washington" (470). Billington championed his state's rights within the federal system, lobbying to retain Massachusetts' employment quota (beginning at 350, it dipped to 146 in 1937, then 139 in 1938) and its distinctive cultural properties.[15] A long-running struggle developed with Katharine Kellock in the central office over the template for tour descriptions. The Boston editors insisted that Massachusetts' distinctive township structure should provide the guidebook's organizational principle, so that visitors gleaned an accurate sense of the disposition of settlement—with its political and cultural implications—within the state. Joseph Gaer sided with the Boston editors, confirming that Washington's insistence on standardization ran counter to "local knowledge" and local practice—in other words, the lived texture of communities and collectivities.[16] Kellock (with the support of Alsberg and Cronyn) insisted that the state office use the centrally mandated system of route descriptions, one more familiar to travelers from outside Massachusetts, "who have no clue to the township administrative arrangement on any highway map, including the one put out by the Massachusetts State Highway Department."[17] The Boston editors also resisted Kellock's template for tours, which insisted on a north-to-south and east-to-west direction. They pointed out that starting a tour at Provincetown, on the tip of Cape Cod, for example, made no sense. As the publication deadline for the guide loomed in 1937, the rhetoric heated up. Billington sent several long, angry telegrams to Alsberg, threatening to resign. Correspondence from Kellock and Cronyn became so "drastic in its verbiage" that Alsberg had to divert and in some cases destroy their letters. A broadening network of editors in Washington and Boston became drawn into the attempt to de-escalate "the unnecessary personal feelings of grievance that seem to exist between the two offices."[18] Eventually, Massachusetts wrung some concessions from the central office, but the centrally mandated structure did dominate the published guide.

Billington also mediated disagreements within the Boston office. The one which most visibly marked the state guide erupted when Conrad Aiken, the Pulitzer Prize–winning poet fallen on hard times, produced an essay on Massachusetts literature which characterized it as quintessentially individualist in its genius, thereby inflaming the left-leaning writers on the project. Billington's version of events is as follows:

> [Aiken] was assigned the task of fashioning an essay on the state's literary history from the masses of research notes gathered by workers. The result was a literary gem, so perfect in composition and styling that all concerned agreed not to change a single word. This decision posed a dilemma for the

> more outspoken Marxists on the project, for Aiken had made individualism his theme—"that profound individualism," as he put it, "which has so deeply marked the American character ever since, and of which Massachusetts—especially in the field of letters—has been the most prodigal and brilliant source." This was heresy to our communist and near-communist friends who held that everything good in America's past had stemmed from collective action. But what to do? Their answer, foisted on the project after weeks of bitter debate, was to insist on a second essay describing the Commonwealth's literary history in terms of group movements. Thus the Massachusetts guide appeared with two essays on literature, with each in effect arguing against the other. The volume was hardly strengthened by this compromise, but given the political divisions existing, no other solution was possible. ("Government and the Arts" 475)

Billington also had a conflicted relationship with Grace Kellogg, a state editor in the Boston office and another of the feisty female workers who played essential roles in the project's output of material yet were characterized as thorns in various (male) editors' sides. Author of two novels—*Windyjinn* and *The Drum*—when she joined the project, Kellogg initially functioned as a district supervisor. She took so much responsibility for shaping tour copy into forms acceptable to the state and central offices that soon the male editors—more interested in the academic essays in the front half of the guide—recommended to Alsberg that she be promoted to state editor. In time, she also spearheaded a script unit for radio productions, and she initiated her own project, "A Documentary and Narrative History of New England Women," for which she managed to win both the backing of the Boston local of the American Writers' Union and Billington's approval.[19] The paucity of women in both versions of the guide's "Literature" essay suggests that such a project was timely. Throughout 1937, however, as Kellogg took on additional responsibility, she sought both a salary raise and a reporting structure which bypassed Loewenberg and Colby to make her directly responsible to Billington. When she received no satisfaction from the state director, she traveled to Washington to confront Alsberg directly, a move that Billington called insubordinate; Reed Harris in the central office, labeled it "hysterical behavior" and threatened her with dismissal.[20] Eventually, Alsberg negotiated an agreement between Kellogg and the three male editors in Boston, but the label of irritant stuck to her, and in 1939 Alsberg succeeded in removing her from the payroll.[21] Kellogg never did publish her history of New England women.

After 1937, in the wake of the public controversy surrounding the entries on Sacco and Vanzetti in the WPA guide to Massachusetts, the makeup of the Boston office changed dramatically. Billington resigned in January 1938 to take up a full-time professorial position at Smith College, further west in the state. By this time, Loewenberg had already departed for a teaching position at the University of South Dakota, and Alsberg had spirited Colby out of the state, deeming that he would be safer working on the guide to Alaska. Muriel Hawks, another outsider to the circle of Harvard men, picked up the slack left by these departures. In the early days of the project, Hawks worked as district supervisor for Essex County, where she demonstrated a flair for producing collaborative work. Billington brought her into the Boston office to replace Loewenberg in late 1937; then she replaced Billington himself in an acting capacity. Later in 1938, she became state director proper, surviving in that position (and its variants) until the project ended. Hawks was a different political animal from the officers she replaced—and, perhaps for that reason, not Alsberg's first choice as third state director.[22] A resident of Cambridge with considerable social standing, she functioned much more as a professional administrator and paid much more attention to public relations across the state than had the academic editors.[23] She needed these qualities in abundance when she was left to clean up the fallout from the Sacco-Vanzetti controversy. Looking back on this period, she sounded weary of her role as compromiser and peace-maker: "It has been a long pull, since the Guidebook storm, to restore friendly relations with the press and conservative public."[24] As she became more confident in her position, she also became more assertive about her employee rights, insisting on a raise and confirmation of her position as state director in 1938.[25] Later that year, she also coordinated one of the most innovative and successful works to come out of the project—*New England Hurricane*, which she and Frank Manuel pulled together at top speed, to rave reviews.

DISTRICT OFFICES ACROSS MASSACHUSETTS

Most of the approximately three hundred project employees in Massachusetts were attached to district offices across the state: in Salem, Boston, New Bedford, Worcester, and Springfield.[26] District offices differed markedly from the state office in the diversity of local employees' educational and employment backgrounds, the range of their political affiliations, and their wage scales. While Massachusetts' first state director received $300 per month, project writers in the state's farther reaches could earn as little as $69 per month.[27] Almost all field workers came off the relief rolls: former newspaper people, fledgling writers, unemployed white-collar workers, recent high school graduates, the likes of "Llewlellyn B." with his doctorate swinging a pick in Randolph. This was the motley group whom Josef Berger, in his letter to Vorse quoted above, dubbed "unemployed plumbers or men of any other qualification." Ray Billington vividly described the effect of WPA employment on these people at the end of their rope:

> To interview such men and women for employment as I did time and time again, to watch their bleak, downcast eyes, their broken spirit, their air of sullen defiance, was a heart-rending experience. But this was more than offset by the transformation that occurred as their first paychecks brought a modicum of financial security and a wealth of renewed confidence. To watch the physical rehabilitation as new shoes replaced tattered footgear or a warm coat was added against Boston's winter blasts was pure joy, but even this was surpassed by the sight of raised heads, squared shoulders, eyes that had lost their look of haunting fear, and smiles that were radiant rather than depreciating [*sic*]. (471)

For some employees, being labeled a writer was a familiar experience, for some a long-sought dream, for some simply a means of surviving the Depression. Some regarded themselves as skilled writers whom the government owed a living. Others thought of themselves, rather apologetically, as government dependents. All wrote up their own localities—the hierarchies of township governance, cultural organization, and social status in which they were most deeply implicated. Field workers, then, were subject to community pressures which did not touch the state and national editors directing their work.

Boston's district office (for Greater Boston and Essex County, at first a physically separate building from the state office in Boston) had the greatest concentration of published writers and the most visible union activity, centered around the American Writers' Union and the Workers' Alliance (Fig. 3). Probably the best known writer was Conrad Aiken, whose essay on Massachusetts literature so enraged his colleagues on the left. Aiken communicated his blunt perspective in a letter to Jerre Mangione thirty years later: "in Boston they were a bunch of Commies, hopelessly incompetent, except for the photographers, and I learned to stay away from meetings as every time I appeared they dumped a new job on me: after I found that out, and that the meetings were Commie soirees, I sent my wife round with the completed work. Left after five months."[28] African American writers on the project also congregated mainly in Boston. Always few in number and insecure in employment status, they included Zylpha O. Mapp, Harry O. Bowles, and Ernest Ormsby, secretary to the Boston local of the American Writers' Union. Edythe Mae Gordon, a member of the Harlem Renaissance who had subsequently moved to Roxbury, found herself threatened with termination in the project cuts of 1937. She fought to retain the project wage that was her only means of survival with a direct (and successful) appeal to Alsberg and other upper-level administrators. William E. Harrison, an African American doctoral candidate at Harvard and winner of the Julius Rosenwald scholarship, was also cut and then reemployed after intercession from Alsberg.

The other district offices held more mixed constituencies. The New Bedford office (discussed in chapter 5) was typical. Its supervisor, G. Leroy Bradford, was an ex-newspaperman, as was its oldest employee: Clarence Ryder, over 80 at the time of his project employment, whose fifty-odd-year journalistic career included the *Boston Herald* and the *New York World*.[29] Field worker Evelyn Silveira was newly graduated from Fairhaven High School and still lived with her parents in Fairhaven. By 1937, Charles Goldenberg, who headed up the state's racial surveys (subsequently reconceptualized as social-ethnic studies) had identified her as a talented interviewer of Portuguese Americans.[30] Julia Keane, a clerical worker, and Elsie Moeller, a secretary, earned promotion to "professional writer" status on the project. The latter went on to become a published author. Also attached to the New Bedford office was a group from Provincetown, a long-standing artists' colony which had attracted writers from across the country. WPA officials at first rejected three writers from there—Josef Berger, George Willison, and Carl Malmberg—because, although in desperate economic circumstances, they were not "certified paupers."Alsberg identified this group as the most pronounced cluster of talent in the state outside Boston. He intervened directly to secure them positions, a wage scale of $94 per month (considerably higher than the Provincetown WPA rate of $69 per month), and an unconventional reporting structure which bypassed the district supervisor and gave Berger in particular a degree of authorial autonomy.[31] Shipton resented the intervention throughout his time as state director, maintaining a high level of suspicion about the "loafing" Provincetown contingent.[32]

Fig. 3. "WPA Boston writers' project, hard at work 1937." Courtesy of Spinner Publications.

The different perspectives of local, state, and federal employees frequently clashed as guidebook copy passed up the chain of command. Tensions and negotiations regularly surrounded the apportionment of space to a topic or place and the merits of local knowledge versus scholarly authority: local experts distrusted the scholarly authority of state editors, while Boston academics considered their Washington counterparts out of date. Sometimes the issue was manifestly ideological. Throughout the composition of the Massachusetts guide, editors in Washington pushed for increased attention to the contemporary scene. Cronyn and Kellock hammered away at the need to document manufacturing plants, trade unions, contemporary architecture and livelihoods, against the tendency of the first state director and many local writers to escape into the "minute details of early pre-revolutionary history."[33] The central office also had a hand in foregrounding the guide's treatment of Sacco and Vanzetti, while Boston editors produced a notably left-wing account of the state's labor history. When controversy exploded around this material, local project writers—at least as far as they were represented in their local press—scrambled to distance themselves from these editorial decisions.

The different degrees of cultural confidence accompanying these different levels of employment come across strongly in the voicing of editorial disagreement. When Cronyn complained to the Boston office about the Cambridge city description, he adopted the haughty tone of the Harvard alumnus: "Altogether, I cannot see that it would greatly please other Harvard men."[34] When J. Henry King, a field writer living in Cambridge, did the same, his obsequious tone gives some sense of the insecurity which reigned further down the hierarchy. His letter opens, "If I might be permitted to make an observation on what seems left behind on Cambridge, I would like to name the following Subjects." After a long list of hospitals, churches, forts, art and music schools, museums, industrial institutions, societies, clubs, and associations omitted from the city description, he concludes: "You of course know best about all I have named, and I have only done so, thinking you would like to know a little more of the situation, as I have been observing it in my travels from point to point."[35]

By 1943, this richest, quirkiest collection of writers the state had ever seen had collectively produced somewhere between twenty-three and thirty-three publications (depending on whose figures you trust) and initiated a dozen more works with the potential to discover a Massachusetts hitherto hidden from the public record (Fig. 4).

THE PROJECT AND THE POLITICIANS

Whatever plans were developed in theory, the practice was always affected by political climates—national, state, and local. Although the writers' project was tiny in budgetary terms—in 1943, *Time* Magazine estimated that its total expenditure was approximately one-fifth of 1 percent of all WPA appropriations—like all the federal arts projects it was highly visible and controversial as the cultural face of the New Deal (K. McKinzie 23). From Martin Dies's House Committee on Un-American Activities in Washington to Governor Charles Hurley's "little HUAC" in Massachusetts—established in 1937 "to Investigate the Activities within this Commonwealth of Communistic, Fascist, Nazi and Other Subversive Organizations"—to municipal power struggles, the writers' project was always available as a whipping post.[36] The effects showed at times in editorial and publishing decisions.

Throughout the life of the Massachusetts Writers' Project, its officials in the Boston office had an uneasy relationship with state WPA administrators, elected state officials, and congressmen who belonged to the Massachusetts

Fig. 4. WPA poster for American Guide Week, 1941. Library of Congress, Prints and Photographs Division, WPA Poster Collection (LC-USZ62-78002 DLC).

Democratic machine, itself a recent political realignment and shaky coalition.[37] On the one hand, long-standing suspicions—between, for example, "Al Smith" Democrats and Roosevelt's New Dealers, Irish politicos and Ivy League Brahmins—made state and municipal officers skeptical about writers' project personnel and activities. (Clifford Shipton most explicitly reciprocated that feeling with his haughty statement that "it is difficult for a respectable man to vote the Democratic ticket in local politics."[38]) On the other hand, local politicians wanted to participate in the benefits of patronage, and the project needed state backing—specifically, the sponsorship of Governor Hurley and Secretary of the Commonwealth Frederic W. Cook—to enable the guidebook's publication. The circulation of the finished product came under equal political pressure. The press trumpeted objections from local cultural and political representatives who found the guidebook's representations of their towns unacceptable. Outraged constituents also lobbied their congressmen and senators, who turned up the political heat on the Roosevelt administration. Clearly, a wide range of constituencies in Massachusetts had much at stake in how, or whether, the WPA guidebooks represented them, and—as subsequent chapters demonstrate—the pressures of these investments showed.

2

WPA GUIDES TO MASSACHUSETTS

> All over the Commonwealth, field workers began to interview local historians, consult town records, talk with oldest inhabitants, tramp miles of country roads. In district offices, research workers checked and re-checked data against all available sources. Officials of State and local governmental agencies were pressed into service; volunteer consultants—geologists, architects, historians, anthropologists, travel experts, critics—read, criticized, and corrected copy. Photographers clicked cameras, cartographers wrought maps, tour checkers clocked mileage.
>
> Ray Allen Billington, Bert James Loewenberg, Merle Colby, "One Moment, Please!" *Massachusetts*

The Massachusetts project produced a cornucopia of little-known stories, statistics, and information which it shaped into guides designed to preserve and promote the state's distinctive identities. Under the prevailing conditions of economic and cultural crisis, these publications offered a lifeline to struggling communities. The form the guides took also left a lasting mark on the state's image-making. The writers' project sat on the cusp of two important cultural shifts: the onset of the tourist industry, which took off after the Second World War, and large-scale government involvement in public memory-making. Project publications subsequently became templates of sorts for federal and state heritage projects which attempted to bring tourist dollars to depressed communities. In Massachusetts, for example, the makeover of selected locations into "living history" displays in the 1970s closely echoed the strategies of representation in the WPA guides from the 1930s. This chapter surveys the output of the Massachusetts Writers' Project.

It charts broad patterns of representation emerging from Boston, selected local communities, and a few minority groups; glances at some illustrative publications; and points to further exploration of others in subsequent chapters.

The Massachusetts project's efforts at inclusive employment produced broad geographical coverage of the state—indeed, a degree of coverage that it has not enjoyed before or since. In 1996, one guidebook began to sell itself on the complaint that Massachusetts tourism clustered around Boston and Cape Cod, with the other three-quarters of the state sadly undervalued (Tree and Davis). In the 1930s, in contrast, the writers' project produced guides across the length and breadth of the state: four to the state as a whole; three to the Berkshires; two to Boston; one each to Auburn, Cape Cod, Fairhaven, Old Newbury, Springfield, and Sudbury; as well as special guides to Massachusetts Albanians and Armenians, New Bedford whalers, Westfield Teachers' College, and a bibliography of the works of Horace Mann. Massachusetts also figured prominently in two regional guides to New England—*Here's New England!* and *New England Hurricane* (both directed by Frank Manuel, regional editor)—and less extensively in the cross-regional guides *U.S. One: Maine to Florida* (overseen by Katharine Kellock, national tours editor) and *Skiing in the East* (by the New York Writers' Project). The project's personnel uncovered myriad details, from employees' own local knowledge, their interviews with oldtimers, consultation with professional and amateur historians, archives, and out-of-print local publications. Despite the fact that much of this material never made it into print, the accumulated publications mapped the state with a thoroughness never before produced. The Massachusetts state guide alone plotted this information mile by mile for over 9,000 miles—"more than half the total mileage of all types in the State of Massachusetts," according to Kellock.[1]

This comprehensive mapping of the state's cultural and natural landscapes fell into three main patterns. Statewide guides and those to the city of Boston came most closely under the control of the Boston office and reflected its fortunes in their deep structure. The first publication to come out of the state office—the guide to Massachusetts—visibly struggles to accommodate incompatible perspectives, the direct imprint of disagreements within the state office and between state and national editors. After the controversy which greeted this guide, then the personnel reshuffle of 1938, and finally the devolution of the project to state control in 1939,

Boston publications spoke more univocally for state organizations. Local guides to smaller towns and more rural communities across the state were more heavily influenced by district offices. These publications read, to different degrees, like bids for cultural survival, communities shaping distinctive forms of cultural memory-making to ensure their continuity from past to future. Finally, a small number of guides targeted ethnic and racial minorities. The result of cooperation between the project and members of minority groups, these guides seek state recognition for communities struggling for cultural citizenship. While all the Massachusetts guides implicitly or explicitly argue the distinctive value of a community—whether the state at large or localities within it, urban ("the metropolis") or rural ("the hinterland"), immigrant or "old-stock American"—those that stress ethnic heritage most vividly demonstrate the stakes in the guidebook project.

STATEWIDE AND BOSTON GUIDES

The first publication to emerge from the Boston office fulfilled the New Deal vision of seamless cooperation among federal, state, municipal, and community forces, albeit in modest form. In June 1937, the well-received pamphlet *Selective and Critical Bibliography of Horace Mann* appeared, overseen by assistant state director Bert Loewenberg. Project writers compiled this work for the Horace Mann Centennial, in cooperation with the State Department of Education, the Boston School Department, and pupils of the Roxbury Memorial High School for Boys, who designed and printed the fifty-odd-page pamphlet. Modest as the outcome was, state editors celebrated it as the first proof of the project's cultural value: reviving public awareness of a nationally significant figure, central to the American public school and public library systems, and cooperating with organizations at many levels.

Two months later, cultural cooperation looked much more difficult. The second publication to be heavily influenced by the Boston office was also the project's most compendious, most complex, and most contentious production: *Massachusetts: A Guide to Its Places and People*, which appeared in August 1937 (Fig. 5). In several ways, the 700-page tome comes closer to the realities of the New Deal juggling act (as opposed to the pieties of its pronouncements), bringing together state and federal interests in a structure visibly straining at the seams. The compromises among federal, state,

Fig. 5. *Massachusetts* guide book photographed for Federal Writers' Project. Photograph No. 69-N-17109, Work Projects Administration, Record Group 69, National Archives at College Park, Md.

and district offices, and within the Boston office, produced a guide incorporating both conservative celebrations of the state's individualism and left-wing collectivist critiques of its power structures; sites marking traditional local color and others marking industrial collapse; and—especially along race lines—some glaring gaps.

Following Washington's template for state guides, *Massachusetts* was divided into three sections. Only the first, "Massachusetts: The General Background," with essays on the state's topography, history, government, and culture, deeply engaged the Boston directorate. Like Alsberg, state director Billington and his assistant directors, Loewenberg and Colby, believed that the essay format offered the opportunity to reeducate the citizenry with little-known information about the state and some analysis of its implications. In the opening essay, "Clues to Its Character," they fastened on the east wind as symbol of Massachusetts's intermittent radicalism: "Time and again a salty breeze has blown through this most conservative of commonwealths" (*Massachusetts* [3]). Clearly, these Harvard boys saw themselves as that east wind. They put together essays informed by public figures of different ideological stripes (Republican Leverett Saltonstall—soon to be governor—wrote much of the essay "Government," while the liberal academic Arthur M.

Schlesinger acted as primary consultant on "Enough of Its History to Explain Its People"). The editors' own interventions were more to the left. When left-wing writers in the Boston office set up a howl of protest at Conrad Aiken's conservative vision of American individualism in "Literature," Billington brokered a second essay, "Literary Groups and Movements," to represent a more collectivist and—at least in terms of class and gender—more inclusive version. Merle Colby, with the support of Billington and Loewenberg, wrote the essay "Labor," which heavily critiques triumphalist narratives of the state and nation and includes some of the inflammatory references to Nicola Sacco and Bartolomeo Vanzetti, the Italian Americans executed by the state in 1927. The east wind blew harder, perhaps, than the Boston editors had reckoned: such was the outcry by state authorities that the federal office eventually had to step in, reshuffling the Boston personnel and covertly suppressing some of the controversial material (the full story is told in chapter 3). The book that was known as the Massachusetts guide from 1938 to 1983 (when the first edition was finally reissued) was, consequently, a rather tamer affair.

Sections two and three of the state guide were less explosive, but contain equally incompatible conjunctions. The city and town descriptions in "Main Street and Village Green" and the mile-by-mile tours of the state's highways in "High Roads and Low Roads" run the gamut from traditional legends and ghost stories, through the colonial heritage that was typically a source of local pride, to the marks of industrial progress and failure that the Boston and Washington offices insisted be included. A Boston foot tour, for example, moves directly from Louisburg Square—"the epitome of Beacon Hill style" whose exclusiveness extends even to its Christmas carolers, "selected from musical groups with sufficient social prestige"—to Pinckney Street, "the border-line between wealth and poverty" (151, 152). The entry on Fall River juxtaposes on the same page a revolutionary battle site, the "haunted hut" of "an old hag reputed to be in league with the Devil," and the Bradford Durfee Textile School, designed to counter the contemporary industrial decline of New England mills (231). The entry on Cambridge insists on detailing "the Industrial City," "a city of workers," alongside its more famous historical, literary, and academic sites (184, 191). Meanwhile, the photographs—mainly by W. Lincoln Highton of the WPA and anonymous staff photographers of the Massachusetts Writers' Project—methodically separate out these trends into "Historical Landmarks," "Industry Early and Late," Architectural Milestones," "Centers of Learning," and the like.

To a contemporary reader, the most troubling aspect of the guide is not its thought-provoking conjunctions but its gaps, particularly glaring in its attention to racial difference. In all three sections, Native Americans rarely appear as living presences. The essay in section one dedicated to "First Americans" is all about a vanished past. The immediately succeeding essay, "Enough of Its History to Explain Its People," further consigns Aboriginal inhabitants to prehistory with its opening: "Massachusetts' history begins not with the landing of the Pilgrims at Plymouth but when Martin Luther dramatically nailed his ninety-five theses to the church door at Wittenberg" (28). In city descriptions and tours, Native figures make stock appearances in captivity tales, colonial battles, and legends of doomed lovers. That a different, more vibrant and complex vision of Native peoples in present-day Massachusetts was possible is proven by Josef Berger's *Cape Cod Pilot*.

The state guide renders African Americans even more invisible. There is no essay dedicated to Blacks in Massachusetts, and they remain statistics without individuation, names, or narrative presence. The long Boston entry, for example, denounces "the legend of ethnic homogeneity" as "so much pernicious twaddle" (136), yet proceeds to demonstrate diversity exclusively in terms of Euro-American inhabitants. Three of the briefest notes on African Americans appear in 41 closely printed pages on the city: "20,574 Negroes" live in Boston (136), "Negro troopers" appear in the Civil War sculpture known as the Robert Gould Shaw Memorial (153), and the Old South Meeting House contained galleries for "Negro slaves" (156). This absent presence sets the tone for the guide as a whole—a conundrum, given the state office's liberal and left-wing leanings. All in all, the state guide is at once lively and fissured, innovative and contained—a recognizable product of New Deal pragmatism, progressivism, and compromise.

After the sea changes of 1938 and 1939 at the state and federal levels, Massachusetts publications avoided controversy. Alsberg put Muriel Hawks into the state director's position in 1938 with a clear directive to calm troubled political waters. The first publication to appear under her leadership was *An Almanack for Bostonians 1939* (1938), a whimsical compilation modeled on the successful New York City almanacs issued by the New York Writers' Project. The almanac layers climatological, cultural, and historical information in a day-by-day format, interspersed with witticisms. On New Year's Day, for example, we are told that it is the Jewish Feast of the Circumcision, that New Year's Day was not a legal holiday in Massachusetts until

1918, that the flag of the "United Colonies" was first raised by General Washington at Cambridge in 1776, that William Lloyd Garrison released the first issue of *The Liberator* on this day in 1831, and that—"Sad, but true"—no one has ever discovered a cure for the hangover:

> Breathes there a man with soul so dead
> As never to have had a whopping head? (10)

Odd conjunctions again, but now explicitly aimed at entertainment.

Once Alsberg was ousted as national director, and the project largely devolved to the control of state administrations, project publications became more direct and more utilitarian mouthpieces of their sponsoring agencies. The Department of Conservation sponsored *State Forests and Parks of Massachusetts: A Recreation Guide* (1941), the State Librarian sponsored *The Origin of Massachusetts Place Names of the State, Counties, Cities, and Towns* (1941), and the Boston Port Authority sponsored *Boston Looks Seaward: The Story of the Port 1630– 1940* (1941). All these publications are thick with informational details, but the last is the most substantial in terms of narrative content. It exemplifies the workings of agency advocacy, not as crude propaganda but in a more subtle organization of information.

The whole shape of *Boston Looks Seaward* is geared toward making the port's future a matter of national urgency. The joint prefaces—by Richard Parkhurst, vice-chairman of the Boston Port Authority, and by Muriel Hawks—connect the port to the larger body politic. Parkhurst insists that the city's future depends on its port, while Hawks makes a larger, explicitly patriotic, claim: "The Massachusetts WPA Writers' project conceived the notion that it could make a contribution, not only to the Port of Boston, but to the city and the Commonwealth, perhaps even to the country in a time of national emergency, by telling the story of the Port from the time when the first shallop skimmed the harbor waters to the strenuous days when destroyers are building along the shores" (7). The volume structures the port's history in a cyclical pattern which implicitly inspires a larger confidence in the future, as "the vicissitudes of war and peace, of depression and recovery" roll around, punctuated perennially by the port's revival (69). The lively historical narrative, thick with anecdote and incident, places Boston at the center of international maritime relations (with South America, Europe, the Mediterranean, China, and India, among others) and of U.S. national development. Boston, we are told, "commenced the [American] Revolution" (65) while, in 1789, the city's merchants dictated the nation's financial and foreign policies (68). The Gold Rush of 1849 is told from the perspective of '49'ers who sailed west around Cape Horn; the Civil War gets short shrift because the port of Boston did not thrive during that conflict, its southern and transatlantic trade brought to a halt.

Stories of travel, trade, and war come vividly to life with excerpts from ships' log books, whalers' reports, chatty bills of lading, transatlantic travel diaries, and the like. A divinity student sailing out of Boston in 1760 records the accommodations below decks: "a dark and dismal region, where the fumes of pitch, bilge water, and other kinds of nastiness almost suffocated me in a minute" (56). The press reports the arrival of the *Columbia* in Boston Harbor on August 10, 1790, "the first American vessel to circumnavigate the globe" with a native "Ouyhee" on board: "Clad in feather cloak of golden suns set in flaming scarlet, that came halfway down his brown legs; crested with a gorgeous feather helmet shaped like a Greek warrior's, this young Hawaiian moved up State Street like a living flame" (77). An American prisoner on board a British sloop-of-war during the war of 1812 vividly details the "perfect hell" on deck after their loss to Boston's frigate *Constitution* (91). Here is the project's trademark archival thickness once more at work.

In the final chapters, the battleground shifts to interagency conflict and the commercial base of operations, and the roll call of heroic individuals, ships, and battles is supplanted by a paean to heroic organizations: the Maritime Association of the Boston Chamber of Commerce, the Foreign Commerce Club of Boston, the Propeller Club of the United States Port of Boston, Inc., and, above all, the Boston Port Authority. With this rhetorical shift, the appeal for community support becomes explicit: "Boston has had to fight incessantly to maintain its proper position as a port. . . . The awakening of the New England people to take a more active interest in the affairs of the Port, a revival of the proud spirit of the clipper-ship days, would be of the greatest importance in encouraging local manufacturers to use Boston as their import and export center" (265). In several senses, this publication brings the state office full circle. The impetus shaping three centuries of historical narrative is the effort to bring into cooperation government patronage, municipal organization, and community support—the combination which produced the pamphlet on Horace Mann onwards and on which the writers' project itself depended for its continuation.

LOCAL GUIDES

The pressures on the far-flung communities of Massachusetts during the 1930s were intense. Many were faced with economic extinction; those which could parlay their natural resources into recreational capital were faced with cultural extinction. WPA guides provided communities with economic and cultural lifelines, enabling them to tap into burgeoning tourism and business investment while preserving their past in the public record. These guides were primarily negotiated between local cultural organizations—anniversary committees, chambers of commerce, city governments—and district project offices. The state office gave final imprimatur; except in cases of extreme controversy, the national office kept its distance. This shift of scale, from the national to the local, changed the stakes in representation. While statewide and Boston guides aspired to the status and authority of historical texts (with their apparatus of academic and organizational consultants), local publications read more like cultural memory work which attempts to bind individual names, generational lineages, and local events into community remembrance (Nora, "Between" 8– 9). The pressures on this memory work were complex, however, since it had to satisfy both internal community dynamics and external economic opportunities.

Paul Connerton has theorized the body as the most powerful site of communal remembrance, because our bodies "sediment habit-memory" (72), which enables "acts of transfer that make remembering in common possible" (39). Michael Kammen has similarly analyzed commemorative rituals—local pageants and historical performances—as crucial props to community identity in the period, providing continuity and confidence in a time of crisis and loss. The form taken by local guides often seems to approximate embodied or performative memory. Some guides explicitly incorporate local pageantry, mimicking the ancestral lineages and iconic events which such performances privilege. *A Historical Sketch of Auburn Massachusetts* (1937), *A Brief History of the Towne of Sudbury in Massachusetts* (1939), and *The State Teachers College at Westfield* (1941) all include detailed programs for their anniversary pageants. The Westfield publication also prints the full texts of speeches delivered during the centennial celebration. Other guides draw readers bodily into the community by guiding them to walk in the footsteps of community members, educating them to a level of name recognition and pacing of events attuned to the local, and inviting them into group membership by the invocation of the "we." *Old Newbury Tales: An Historical Reader for Children* (1937) quotes Newburyport's famous son General Adolphus W. Greely on the "flood of immigrants" to the town: "We look to their children to make the Newburyport of the future the same city of standards and education that we hand down to them" (68). *Springfield, Massachusetts* (1941) opens with a direct exhortation to the reader: "we are so proud of our city, . . . and hope that you will become interested in Springfield as a place to live, as a place to work, and as a place in which to do business" (n.pag.). Connerton's description of the performative and formalized language of liturgical community reverberates here: "The community is initiated when pronouns of solidarity are repeatedly pronounced. In pronouncing the 'we' the participants meet not only in an externally definable space but in a kind of ideal space determined by their speech acts" (58–59).

Who was included in this normative "we" was, of course, a contested issue. These rhetorical strategies could have deeply conservative effects. The moving force behind local guides tended to be the cultural organizations with most social and political clout, and their exclusions and hierarchies were reproduced in guidebook copy. It is chilling, for example, given the young audience, that the Greely quotation carefully demarcates the "they" of the immigrants from the "we" of Newburyport. On the other hand, encroaching tourism and corporate takeover brought pressure to preserve varied lives—especially, in the 1930s, lives of labor—which brought visibility to some marginal groups. The dynamics of memory-making in two very different localities—Newburyport in the northeastern corner of coastal Massachusetts and the Berkshires in the far west of the state—suggest some of the strategies for cultural survival modeled by local guides.

Old Newbury Tales, one of the earliest project publications, achieves generational continuity by coming as close as the guidebook format allowed to pageantry enactment. Aiming "to bring to life in the minds and imagination of children of this industrial era a series of related pictures from three centuries of history" (Foreword), chapters run through romanticized moments—the Puritans landing in 1635 in what would become Newburyport, encounters with the friendly Pennacooks and "cruel Tarrantines" (18), sea-going adventures during the Revolution, the rise of the clipper ships in the nineteenth century—all crystallized in the adventures of local heroes and their children. The final chapter explicitly replays that roll call in the tercentenary parade of 1930. A procession of floats reenacts the historical scenes from the guide's narrative, featuring names and businesses still extant in the community—William Lloyd Garrison, Caleb Cushing, Major-General Greely, the Towle Company. The audience watching this scene, and framing the reader's access to it, reinforces the display of generational continuity. Grandmother Turner, daughter Anne, grandson Johnny ("his face scrubbed till it shone"), and granddaughter Jane ("pink ribbons fastened to each side of her golden head") share homilies about courage, perseverance, and respect suggested to them by the passing parade (58). The didacticism is determinedly localist—the guide's epigraph states: "Civic consciousness, beginning locally, should develop outwardly"—not in order to challenge or critique but simply to claim a place within the established national narrative. A modest, cyclostyled pamphlet, sponsored by the Historical Society of Old Newbury, this guide prefigures a technique broadly used—often to more complex ends—in local publications.

The guides to the Berkshires betray more of the double-edged dynamic which came with tourism, the economics of recreation at once promising to save the region economically and destroy it culturally. The earliest guides—*Winter Sports and Recreation in the Berkshire Hills* (1937), sponsored by the Berkshire County Commissioners, and *Motor Tours in the Berkshire Hills* (1938), sponsored by the Berkshire Hills Conference, Inc.—were pamphlets that contain this tension in muted form. Muriel Hawks's Foreword to the *Motor Tours*, for example, stresses the recreational delights of "the great Berkshire playground" (2), yet much of the ensuing, telegraphic information brings attention to the industry of the past and agricultural labor of the present which lie behind the recreational image. The book-length *Berkshire Hills* (1939), also sponsored by the Berkshire Hills Conference, flushes out this tension more fully. The extended narrative, a cross between a travel guide and a history, both acknowledges the decline of the area from its industrial past and contributes to its revival in particular ways. One community after another is dying: "industrial Lanesborough has now lapsed into oblivion" (57), Egremont is "drifting into shabby decline" (177), the prosperity of Otis, Becket, and Washington has "waned" (207), while New Marlborough, Monterey, Tyringham, and Sandisfield "drained backwoods Berkshire of its young blood" (187). The guide acknowledges that the counter to this decline has arrived in the economics of recreation, the Berkshires fast becoming the hiking and skiing playground of the northeast. However, from the introduction by Walter Prichard Eaton of Yale onwards, the guide exhorts visitors to appreciate "the Berkshire spirit" (xiii), to understand it not just as a recreational area distinctive for its natural properties but as a place of living history.

The volume organizes communities into thematic chapters which stress their distinctiveness, one vivid story after another linking natural features to the industrial past. Take, for example, Florida, at the edge of the mammoth Hoosac Tunnel, completed in 1875 after twenty years and $20 million. Its legacy is a split community: "the farming Mountaineers, who live on the summit, and the Tunnelites in Lower Town, most of them railroad and power plant employees" (10). The guide brings the Mountaineers and Tunnelites to life—the unremitting feuds over where to vote, where to hold town meetings, who holds the balance of power—a living, laboring community that the tourist would otherwise never know:

> Thousands of people drive over the Mohawk Trail through Florida every year, thousands more catch a glimpse of the settlement of Hoosac Tunnel before their trains disappear in the mountain, but few of these travelers know the name of the town through which they are passing. . . . Outsiders have discovered the State Forests, the picnic groves and the trout streams, and skiers have found that the snow on the Florida heights comes earlier and stays longer than on most Berkshire slopes. A new army may invade Florida, bent on pleasure rather than on a "job" as were their predecessors, the Tunnel workers. (13)

While the guide does pay fleeting attention to ancestral lineage, its interest in labor delivers a political analysis of these lines of influence. The mill owners in Hinsdale, for example, established their family lineage partly by cheating workers out of their savings, while the Cranes and Westons—the "paper kings"—of Dalton have run such profitable mills that they remain "paternal dynasts," the townspeople "still accepting the system of benevolent paternalism that has persisted from the early nineteenth century" (240, 234). In reviving industrial history, the guide notices an ethnically diverse population, some of whom have subsequently disappeared. There are, for example, the Chinese who were brought into North Adams by a factory owner in 1860 as unknowing strike breakers; "Of the hundred-odd who once lived in North Adams, not one is left today" (23).

The Italian marble cutters "imported from the old country" still form one-fifth of Lee's population (140). Sandisfield has pockets of Jewish settlers and Russian Cossacks (203). The Poles, French Canadians, Italians, and Germans outnumber the older Irish and Yankee groups in Adams (270). The description of the Great Barrington quarries includes a particularly resonant image of a racial group literally disappearing into the landscape: "The fine, almost snow-white powder films the nearby countryside, giving the small number of Negro quarrymen a curious, ghost-like appearance" (167).

The attempts to produce living histories in the guides to Old Newbury and the Berkshires suggest the fundamental challenges faced by all local guide-makers. The drive simultaneously to shore up community and to attract investment with the WPA guides, and the consequent pressure on who would be remembered and who forgotten in that process, became particularly intense in book-length guides focused on individual communities. Chapter 8 explores three local guides at length. Sudbury, Auburn, and Springfield all used project guides to create living histories, but to very different effect: one to protect its old-stock heritage against commercial takeover, one to protect individuality against suburbanization, and one to embrace capitalist modernity as its route to the future.

GUIDES TO MINORITY GROUPS

The stakes in achieving community remembrance became even higher when the group seeking such status was in an ethnic or racial minority. For many such groups, their appeal to the writers' project was part of a larger struggle for the basic tools of cultural citizenry—such as libraries, educational resources, and cultural organizations. Various proposals came forward to sponsor "racial surveys," from the Jamaican Associates, the Amportus Historical Society, the Associated Jewish Philanthropies, a committee of the Central Irish council, and representatives of the Chinese, Finns, Russians, Scots, and Italians in the state. There were plans to form a Massachusetts Swedish Historical Society with sponsorship in mind, and a group of Franco-Americans proposed a study of the state's French-language press. Few groups, however, had the economic resources or cultural power to move from proposal to implementation. At least in its early years, the state project seemed unable to break the vicious cycle whereby the least resourced communities were the least likely to be able to sponsor their own publications.

Two immigrant groups that did manage to secure sponsorship were the Armenian and Albanian communities, whose resources derived from the strong political pull to their homelands. The structure and emphasis of these guides differ both from the state and local guides and from each other. *The Armenians in Massachusetts* (1937) was produced in the early days of the project, under a somewhat assimilationist and preservationist vision, promoted by George Cronyn in Washington, and managed by Charles Goldenberg at the state level. The task, under this regime, was to record the "contributions" to American culture by individual Armenian immigrants as a way of preserving their past as they became assimilated into the dominant Anglo culture of the present. As a result, the volume is a static, nostalgic collection of names and achievements, followed by a melancholic paean to a vanishing people. *The Albanian Struggle in the Old World and New* (1939) paints a very different picture. It was produced under the model of cultural "participation" believed in by Morton Royse and Benjamin Botkin—both of whom Alsberg hired in 1938 as national editors of, respectively, social-ethnic studies and folklore. Royse encouraged the authors of the Albanian volume to treat cultural influence as a two-way street, a perspective which produced a considerably more challenging and uncomfortable account of the difficulties and possibilities of Albanian American existence. Chapter 7 explores these two volumes more thoroughly.

The project did encourage writers to record information from their own ethnic or racial communities. The dearth of African American and Native American employees limited the results on these fronts, but a great deal of material was gathered by employees who identified with Portuguese, Irish, Jewish, Italians, French Canadians, Syrians, Norwegians, Swedes, French, Greeks, Finns, Chinese, Japanese, Russian, Scots, and Estonians in the state. In the early days, these efforts tended to be swallowed into entries for the state guide. Josef Berger, on Cape Cod, managed to take the process further, as I discuss in chapter 6. One of the most established writers on the project, he had the clout to write his own guide and to treat Portuguese Americans, Cape Verdean Americans, and Native Americans with a detail and vivacity well beyond the rhetoric of the state guide. Berger did not belong, racially, to any of these groups, but he had lived and worked among them for several years, and he considered himself allied by labor and class lines. Taking an explicitly partisan position, he was able to advocate on behalf of marginalized groups and to write at eloquent length about the human absences and their causes in the state.

From 1938, the cultural recovery of marginalized peoples within the state took on a new level of priority. By this point, Berger had left the project on a Guggenheim fellowship. Alsberg wooed him back to advance the study of the region's Portuguese descendants. Other studies collected material into new combinations. "Working in New England" gathered interview material on workers according to ethnic and racial identification—including, prominently, African American red caps, Pullman porters, garment workers, domestic workers, and hotel employees. "The Social History of Massachusetts" charted slavery up to 1830. "Yankee Folk" included accounts of Irish, English, Scotch, German, and "Portuguese Pilgrims." When the project lost both Alsberg and its federal control in 1939, it lost the chance to publish these and many more volumes dedicated to minority communities. Only glimpses of what might have been ever made it into print. Ann Banks's *First-Person America* (1980) includes WPA-gathered stories from Azorean American fisherman Manuel Captiva on Cape Cod, African American presser and union organizer Mary Sweet in Boston, and Irish American domestic worker Marie Haggerty, also in Boston. A special issue of the journal *Spinner* (1988) on work from the Massachusetts Writers' Project features ethnic surveys of the Portuguese, Lebanese, Polish, Scots, and Irish of southeastern Massachusetts, as well as a powerful interview with Cape Verdean American seaman Captain Joe Antone.[2] These selections hint at the rich and productively uncomfortable accounts of the state's cultural diversity which the project was poised to produce.

Many of these publications have long since disappeared from print and public memory. Their sheer wealth of information—some dry, some passionate, some irreverent, all archivally rich—suggests how much has been lost from Massachusetts' knowledge of itself in the process. From the port of Boston to the backroads of the Berkshires, from the children of Newburyport to the Cape Verdeans of Cape Cod, storytellers, writers, audiences, and sponsors together produced richer, deeper, and broader accounts of the state than have existed before or since. The pressures on this production process fell into three main patterns: statewide and Boston guides came most closely under federal and state control, community guides reflect the agendas of local cultural organizations, and, at least in the project's early years, guides to minority ethnic and racial groups depended rather serendipitously on champions within or outside the project. The remainder of this book pursues the consequences of particular conditions on particular publications, revealing the depth of struggle involved for some individuals and constituencies working to put themselves on the "official" map of Massachusetts.

SECTION TWO

POLITICAL FALLOUT

3

"OUTSIDE THE PALE": THE SECRET SUPPRESSION OF SACCO AND VANZETTI

On August 23, 1927, Nicola Sacco and Bartolomeo Vanzetti were executed by the Commonwealth of Massachusetts to a storm of domestic and international protest. Since 1920, the incarceration of the shoemaker and the fish peddler—accused of murdering a paymaster and guard in South Braintree, Massachusetts—had violently polarized public opinion. The two men's supporters charged the state and federal judiciary with persecuting the Italian American immigrants for their anarchist beliefs, while the authorities closed ranks and refused to stay the execution.[1] A decade later, on August 19, 1937, another storm erupted, this time over the representation of Sacco and Vanzetti in *Massachusetts: A Guide to Its Places and People*. Although lives were not at stake this time round, echoes of the earlier controversy reverberated through the guide's tumultuous reception.

Supporters of Sacco and Vanzetti extolled the guide for including the two men in what was widely perceived as an "official history" of the state.

They understood the move as a form of government-sponsored reparation for executing the men and, more broadly, as recognition of political minorities as rightful citizens. Opponents—primarily state and local officials in Massachusetts and the conservative press—denounced the guidebook as a threat to state and national interests. They demanded that not only Sacco and Vanzetti but the guidebook writers themselves be expelled from the body politic. The guidebook's federal imprimatur, factual rhetoric, and grounding in the politics of place made it a powerful arbiter of cultural inclusion and exclusion, with the ability to define who and what was "American." A struggle developed over who would seize control of the guidebook to wield its cultural authority.

Contrary to received critical opinion, the guidebook's initial inclusiveness did not survive the controversy. Within a year of the guide's first publication, Henry Alsberg caved in to state political pressures. He instructed Massachusetts state editors secretly to excise the controversial Sacco-Vanzetti material and revise numerous other entries that had provoked local opposition. The results appeared in a silently revised edition, which had the lowest profile of any project publication and has been paid the least critical attention.

As a case study of the political limits on publicly funded expression, this story suggests three things. First, it shows how directly the political maneuvers sketched in chapter 1—the power struggles among federal, state, and local authorities over the shaping of cultural identities—affected the production, circulation, and reception of guidebook material. Second, it demonstrates the double-edged power of the informational genre. The guide could equally effectively challenge or reinforce assumptions about citizenry and social justice, depending on who controlled its low-key declarative form and authoritative truth claims. And, third, the story exposes how censorship works in public arts funding—not always as externally exerted pressure on principled dissidents, but by a governmental logic that enmeshes all parties in collusion and compromise, a process that in this case made project administrators and editors not only collude in the censorship but for sixty years deny that it ever happened.

SACCO AND VANZETTI IN THE GUIDE TO MASSACHUSETTS

The original guidebook's references to Sacco and Vanzetti were neither voluminous nor shrill. Indeed, they had been so thoroughly missed by State House aides in their prescreening of the contents that Governor Charles F. Hurley and Secretary of the Commonwealth F. W. Cook endorsed the work with an enthusiastic letter under the state seal that fronted the published book.

In the 675 pages of the guide, there are five references to Sacco and Vanzetti.

One paragraph in the city description of Boston describes the protests against the conviction and execution of "two obscure Italian laborers." The paragraph ends: "Sacco and Vanzetti had become, for a new generation to whom 'Haymarket' was scarcely more than a word, the classic example of the administering of justice to members of unpopular political minorities" (144). The entry on Dedham includes a paragraph on their 1921 trial in the Norfolk County Courthouse. As Tour 19 from Boston to Bourne passes through Braintree, it notes, "Here in 1920 occurred the hold-up and murder of a paymaster for which Sacco and Vanzetti were executed (*see DEDHAM*)" (587). And an entry on their execution appears in the State Chronology (636).

The longest entry appears in the essay titled "Labor" in the front half of the guide. This essay is a remarkable document which makes working people central to national and state mythologies. It declares, for example, that "the frontier of awakening labor" was just as important to nationhood as Frederick Jackson Turner's western frontier and that anonymous workers were the "pioneers of Massachusetts democracy" (65). The essay also recounts the history of Massachusetts as a long series of strikes and their violent suppression. One lengthy section details exploitative working conditions in the shoe and fishing industries, then turns to two particular workers in those fields. The sequence of information positions these two cases as the culmination of labor's systemic oppression:

> In 1920, a fish peddler, Bartolomeo Vanzetti, and a shoe-worker, Niccolà [*sic*] Sacco, both members of the Galleani group of anarchists, were arrested on the charge of murder and robbery in connection with the theft of a $15,000 payroll. Despite their alibis, the highly circumstantial nature of the evidence, and the recommendations of previous employers, they were ultimately both adjudged guilty. During the seven years that elapsed between the murder and the execution of the sentence, protest demonstrations were held throughout the world. President Lowell of Harvard, President Stratton of Massachusetts Institute of Technology, and Judge Robert Grant were invited by Governor [Alvan] Fuller to weigh the evidence and advise him. They upheld the finding of the court and Sacco and Vanzetti were executed on August 23, 1927. It was widely believed that, although legal forms were observed, the determining factor in the case from start to finish was the affiliation of the two men with an unpopular minority political group. (76)

The guide wrote Sacco and Vanzetti very literally back into the state's cultural landscape, in the process translating the polemics of the 1920s into factual, declarative prose. John Dos Passos's impassioned 1927 pamphlet, *Facing the Chair: The Story of the Americanization of Two Foreignborn Workmen*, argued that the politics of place deeply informed the Sacco-Vanzetti case. Presenting the evidence of their innocence, the author noted the political relevance of the area where the two men worked and where they were arrested: the "ring of industrial towns round Boston . . . one of the most intense industrial battlegrounds in the country" (52). Dos Passos argued that the labor relations of eastern Massachusetts not only nurtured Sacco and Vanzetti's anarchist alliances but also shaped the two men's public image. His argument amounted to a geopolitical class analysis: the arrest, conviction, and execution of Sacco and Vanzetti owed more to regional politics and patterns of labor exploitation within Massachusetts than to the actualities of the robbery at South Braintree.[2] The guidebook similarly reconnected Sacco and Vanzetti's struggle with a range of geographical locations within and beyond the "Hub" of Boston. Entries revivified the executed men's presence, encouraging readers to retrace their story by driving through Braintree, standing on the steps of the Dedham courthouse, or walking on Boston Common.[3] The controversy ignited by such entries suggests that the guidebook's factual invocation of place carried just as much political force as Dos Passos's more explicit polemics.

That force owed much to the terms in which the guidebook was introduced to the public. The promotional tag for the American Guide Series claimed that it was "Presenting America to Americans." Hurley and Cook repeated this trope in their prefatory letter to the guide: "Though designed to portray Massachusetts to visitors, it is also intended, as it were, to present Massachusetts to Massachusetts." In other words, the guide demarcated who belonged to nation and state, and who did not. Just a year earlier, Lewis Gannett, in his column in the *New York Herald Tribune*, had excoriatingly exposed how notions of citizenship worked to exclude minorities. Pointing out the contradiction in President Lowell of Harvard defending Harold J. Laski during the Boston police strike but not Sacco and Vanzetti, Gannett wrote: "But Laski was an educated gentleman who belonged. Sacco and Vanzetti were outside the pale. . . ."[4]

Gannett's vocabulary points us forward to the exclusions of race explored in chapter 4, to how tentatively European immigrant groups were being brought under the umbrella of "whiteness" in 1930s' America and how political affiliations could tip the balance of social acceptance. Other commentators confronted cultural exclusion as key to the assumption of Sacco's and Vanzetti's guilt. In their polemical essays and novelizations of the 1920s, Upton Sinclair, John Dos Passos, Katherine Anne Porter, and others challenged the widespread representation of Sacco and Vanzetti as alien, foreign, threateningly "other." Rocco Marinaccio has discussed these writers' attempts to "Americanize" the immigrants' radical politics by arguing in their polemical essays and novelizations that such beliefs were central to America's national identity and Massachusetts' founding mythologies (622). The guidebook could effect that maneuver much more powerfully (and, to some, more threateningly), inserting Sacco and Vanzetti into the consensual "we"—part of Massachusetts, part of America—simply by including them in the factual, chronological history of who "we" are.

THE GUIDE'S RECEPTION

Public controversy erupted within twenty-four hours of the guide's appearance. Detractors and proponents of the guidebook's vision raised their voices, state and municipal politicians went on the offensive, and the project began visibly to splinter. A journalist on the *Boston Traveler* began the outcry. In an article of August 19, 1937, he counted lines to report that Sacco and Vanzetti had been given four times as much space in the guidebook as the Boston Tea Party—considerably more, even, than the Boston Tea Party and the Boston Massacre combined. Hot on the heels of the *Traveler* came louder and louder denunciations. In the words of the *New York Post*: "Boston papers of Thursday exploded with black and blistering headlines usually reserved for world calamities." Front-page headlines in the local, state, and national press screamed throughout mid-August: "DEMAND U.S. PROBE 'SLURS' IN WPA BOOK"; "GOV. HURLEY HITS W.P.A. GUIDE BOOK"; "WPA GUIDE WAR ON 3 FRONTS"; "FIGHT ON WPA BOOK AROUSES BAY STATE" [5] Former Massachusetts governor Joseph B. Ely denounced the book as "propaganda," exclaiming that it should be burned on Boston Common—though he hurriedly explained that he was speaking "figuratively" when the obvious analogy with Nazi Germany was brought to his attention.[6]

One especially dismissive photograph appeared in the *Boston American*, captioned "WHERE HE THINKS IT BELONGS": "Right into his office wastebasket, Municipal Court Justice Leo P. Doherty tosses an offending page from the Works Progress Administration's newly published book, 'Massachusetts, A Guide to Its Places and People.' The volume's references to the state judiciary were characterized as 'grossly impertinent' by Judge Doherty."[7]

Some protesters targeted particular entries which threatened their self-interest. According to the *Boston Herald*, for example, "enraged financial and industrial leaders took violent exception to the guide's 14-page treatise on labor."[8] The Italian-American Club and the mayor of Marlboro protested one sentence on their town: "It has a large Italian population, who were encouraged to settle here as strike-breakers after a serious labor disturbance in 1899" (472). The mayor went so far as publicly to instruct his lawyer to look into banning the guidebook's sale and library use in the city.[9] Three words in a parenthetical phrase concerning the philanthropist George Peabody provoked another storm of protest from the town of Peabody: "He declined a baronetcy offered by Queen Victoria, accepting in-stead (a charming and perhaps not unstrategic gesture) the Queen's gift of a miniature of herself, now on exhibition in the auditorium" (422). The press reported that "Citizens of Peabody had John E. Murphy, Peabody representative, point out the alleged slur against the founder of their city to Governor Hurley. . . . Ex-Mayor S. Howard Darnell calls these words in parentheses 'the plain product of a distorted mind, intended to blacken the memory of our late benefactor.'"[10]

At the other end of the spectrum, supporters of Sacco and Vanzetti expressed delight at the guidebook's appearance. On August 20, 1937, Catharine Sargent Huntington, staunch supporter of the two men before and after their execution, wrote to Aldino Felicani, erstwhile treasurer of the Sacco-Vanzetti Defense Committee and close friend of Vanzetti: "Yesterday I . . . walked about the streets of Northampton . . . . Someone passed me carrying the Boston Daily Record with huge head-lines 'Pro-Sacco Blast in W.P.A. State Book' and as I hurried to buy a copy I thought, how like ten years ago—and that no time nor change can ever help those heroic names from staring the world in the face."[11]

Indeed the guide's controversial entries did aid the efforts of the Sacco-Vanzetti Memorial Committee by bringing public attention to their ongoing fight for justice. In August 1937, this group was hard at work organizing the annual vigil and struggling to get press attention for their attempts at reparation. The guide's publication several days prior to the anniversary of the execution put Sacco and Vanzetti back in the spotlight. Ernest L. Meyer, writing from Provincetown for the *New York Post*, applauded the guide's part in the fight for reparation while apprehending the threat of censorship presaged by the screaming headlines: "it is likely that the hubbub will add to the crowds expected at a memorial service for Sacco and Vanzetti to be held tomorrow . . . under the auspices of the International Labor Defense. Committees will later place wreaths on the graves of unionists killed for their cause. And, I hope, copies of the first (uncensored) edition of the Guide to Massachusetts."[12]

The guidebook controversy also brought attention to the Memorial Committee's attempts to have a monument to Sacco and Vanzetti "enshrined" on Boston Common. In 1927, the Sacco-Vanzetti Defense Committee commissioned Gutzon Borglum (of Mount Rushmore fame) to sculpt a bas-relief of the two men (Fig. 6). Periodically, the committee offered the bronze plaque to municipal and state administrations for public display only to be periodically (and publicly) reviled for their efforts.[13] An article in the *Boston Evening Transcript* of August 23, 1937—one among several—ends an update on official negotiations around the guidebook with the story of the Borglum plaque:

> It was ten years ago today that the two men were executed, and a committee chose this day to offer the State a memorial by Gutzon Borglum which they suggested be placed on the Common "as a symbol by which the people of our State may be constantly warned in the decades to come."
>
> Governor Hurley called it "a patently absurd gesture," and Mayor Mansfield said that if his were the final word the offer "has no possible chance of acceptance."

In the face of establishment obduracy, supporters' energies had been flagging in recent years. In 1935, for example, the Sacco-Vanzetti Memorial Committee had announced there would be no formal observance of the execution. Catharine Huntington's enthusiastic reception of the guide suggests the boost it provided to their cause.[14]

In response to the guidebook's inclusive inventories, Massachusetts politicians and the conservative press went on the offensive. They targeted particular project editors as un-American infiltrators of the guidebook project who, like Sacco and Vanzetti, should be excluded from citizenship in the state and nation. Leading the pack was Governor Charles F. Hurley. The day after the *Boston Traveler* exposé of the contentious entries, Hurley denounced the guidebook and its authors to the annual state convention of the American Legion in New Bedford:

> A blistering attack by Massachusetts' Legionnaire governor, Comrade Charles F. Hurley, on "the two or three men who are trying maliciously to besmirch the proud record of Massachusetts by adding prejudicial chapters to the WPA Massachusetts Guide Book," threw the American Legion convention session into an uproar of applause at noon today. . . .
>
> . . . Governor Hurley declared in no uncertain terms he would demand the removal of the offending [WPA guidebook] writers.

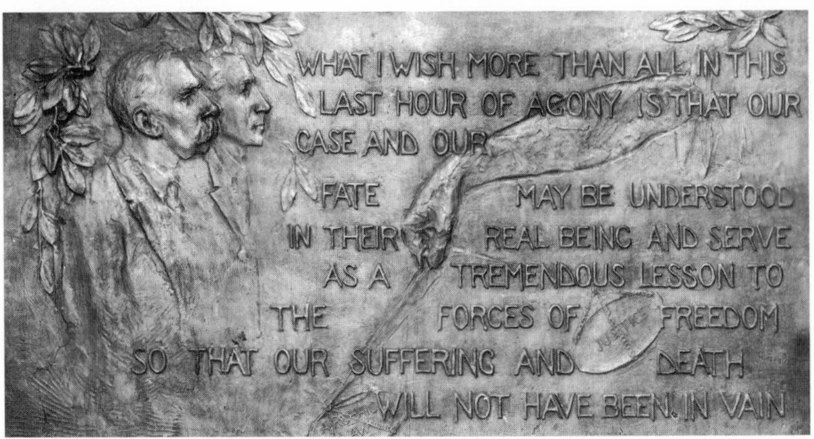

Fig. 6. Aluminum copy of bronze bas-relief of Sacco and Vanzetti by Gutzon Borglum. Boston Public Library/Rare Books Department. Courtesy of the Trustees.

> "If these men don't like Massachusetts and the United States, they can go—where they came from," cried Governor Hurley as the assembled gathering rose enmasse and cheered.[15]

Hurley recycled the Red Scare rhetoric that tarred the anarchists in the 1920s to smear those responsible for their representation in the 1930s. Communists were the primary focus of scaremongering in the 1930s. Anarchists—chief bogies of the 1920s and long-standing opponents of communism—had dwindled from view in America by that point (Avrich 211). When state authorities revived Sacco and Vanzetti as part of the contemporary "red menace," they conflated deep philosophical and political differences to manipulate an indiscriminate image of foreign threat for their own purposes. That image they then attached to project members, producing blaring headlines: "'PURGE WPA OF REDS,' GOV. HURLEY DEMANDS"; "GUIDE CHANGED BY REDS ON W.P.A"; "HURLEY HUNTS RED WRITERS OF GUIDEBOOK."[16] Claiming that state editors had inserted subversive material after Secretary Cook and he had approved the galleys, Hurley publicly demanded from the WPA administration the names and addresses of the guidebook authors. Without hesitation, he sought to identify "them as non-voters, non-residents, non-citizens and in some cases Communists" and to bar them from further public service.[17]

Hurley crafted his political career on this kind of rhetoric, and it garnered him widespread support across the state. "Hurleyism" incited Red Scare politics in Massachusetts and led to the first "little HUAC" (House

Un-American Activities Committee) in the country. "The Special Commission to Investigate the Activities within this Commonwealth of Communistic, Fascist, Nazi and Other Subversive Organizations," established early in 1937 (a year ahead of Martin Dies's House Committee on Un-American Activities), was stacked with Hurley appointees (Heale 150, 165). Despite the commission's broad title, its target was clear: eight pages reported on "Fascistic Activity" and eight more on "Nazi Activity," while the remaining 583 pages focused on the threatening "red menace."

Beginning in August 1937, denouncements of the guidebook's inclusion of Sacco and Vanzetti drew generally and specifically on the commission's rhetoric. As the *Boston Post* of August 23, 1937, reported, "Representative Edward D. Sirois of Lawrence, a member of a special Legislature commission investigating subversive propaganda, yesterday suggested to Governor Hurley that the State police seize all outstanding copies of the guide book." It was not long before other "supercharged patriots" scrambled to side publicly with Hurley and his supporters, as groups bolstered their own status as cultural insiders by calling for the exclusion of anyone linked with the representation of threatening difference (Heale 154). Down in New Bedford, where Hurley had first denounced the guidebook before American Legionnaires, a meeting of the Massachusetts branch of the Ancient Order of Hibernians made the headlines of the *Boston Post* on August 24, 1937, with a resolution "praising Governor Hurley's stand in urging deletion of portions of the new WPA Guide Book." The statement suggests how, as in the 1920s, ethnic solidarity crumbled before the demonization of Sacco and Vanzetti, fracturing communities internally and setting immigrant groups against each other in the scramble for political safety. Other critics demonized the project's Washington, D.C., office. Long-running tensions between Massachusetts Democrats and the Roosevelt administration fueled such accusations as that of Lawrence city councillor Robert Gardiner Wilson: " 'We find,' he said, 'a select circle of masquerading Democrats in Washington, belittling protests by our own Democratic Governor Hurley and former Governor Ely, because Red agitators and Parlor Pinks have at last found their "promised land" in the nation's capital.' "[18]

The rhetoric particularly targeted the academic editors in the Boston project office as anti-American aliens. Massachusetts Irish Democratic politicians of the period regularly paraded their animus against academics on the left. Hurley, as state treasurer (1931–1936) and then governor (1937–1938), repeatedly contributed the authority of his office to the political onslaught against the educational system. For example, he joined the attack against the appointment of Granville Hicks, a well-known Marxist literary critic, to the Harvard faculty, and he attempted to censor school textbooks. He also supported the teachers' loyalty oath crafted by Representative Thomas Dorgan and enacted into law in 1935 under Hurley's predecessor James Michael Curley. Huge controversy accompanied the introduction of the loyalty oath. It was opposed by every organized teachers' group in the state, the Massachusetts Federation of Labor, and many faculty members and presidents of Ivy League colleges, but enjoyed popular support. In 1937, Hurley kept the oath controversy alive by vetoing a repeal bill which had passed in both houses and delivering a number of speeches designed to exploit popular prejudice against intellectuals.

This context fueled politicians' and press attacks on the three state editors of the Massachusetts guide. Dorgan, "father of the Teachers' Oath Law," assailed Billington: "I can only say that it is indeed a fine example to the citizens of Massachusetts to find out that some professors, especially Dr. Ray A. Billington, who becomes assistant professor of history at Smith College, will stab in the back the very state that pays them. This example certainly justifies the stand I have taken against subversive, Communistic propaganda for the past three years."[19] The *Boston Globe* outed Merle Colby as the author of the "Labor" essay and as a suspected Communist. When Colby's wife denied his alleged party membership, the *Boston Post* continued the attack in more cautious terms, characterizing Colby as "another outsider who, while he may not be an enrolled member of the Communist party, has Communistic affiliations and is a contributor to the Communist magazine, the New Masses."[20] Opponents of the guide mounted the nastiest smear campaign against Bert Loewenberg, the Jewish academic about to leave for an instructor's position at the University of South Dakota. Although Loewenberg had been born and bred in Boston, the *Boston Post* used his connection with an out-of-state institution to construct him as an outsider and an alien: "As director of this guide to Massachusetts, a resident of South Dakota was imported here despite the wealth of competent Massachusetts historians. . . . It is impossible to escape the conclusion that certain radicals in the WPA, from outside Massachusetts, deliberately plotted to discredit the state."[21] Editorials by the *New Bedford Standard-Times* set "the North Dakota professor" against "all the people," who have paid for the guidebook with their taxes. "Considering that the people of Massachusetts were taxed to pay the writers who used the guidebook as a vehicle for running them down," the paper complained on August 22,

1937, "these writers would seem to be like the birds that foul their own nests."[22]

Under the pressure of public controversy, the project began to splinter internally. On the one hand, the American Writers' Union telegraphed Hopkins and Alsberg on behalf of its WPA members protesting Governor Hurley's demand for the guidebook authors' names: "ADVISE REQUEST BE REFUSED LESS PERSONNEL BECOME VICTIMS POLITICAL WITCH HUNT"; "LISTING OPENS WAY FOR DREADED POLITICAL PERSECUTION."[23] Other project employees outside Boston scrambled to disassociate themselves from the newspaper image of guidebook writers, disclaiming any responsibility for the controversial material. Fairhaven employees of the New Bedford district office—some of whom had links with the Legionnaires before whom Hurley made his inflammatory attack on the guide—apparently leaked stories to the local press about their disgruntlement with the state office. The *Fairhaven Star* published a story designed to distance local project employees from state editors and from the guidebook itself. The piece announced: "Blame for the present state of the guidebook in no way attaches to local writers on the project. Its misinformation is in despite of their best efforts to instill some degree of accuracy into the tome, which was written and edited by Boston writers, nee plumbers."

Without explicitly saying so, the newspaper implied that Boston editors inserted the controversial Sacco-Vanzetti material into the guide. The *Star* recounted the tale of a Boston editor mangling New Bedford copy with a rewrite which included "the forceful but entirely asinine invitation to 'visit the quaint old wharves in the vicinity of Pleasant and William Streets'"—a location that was off by about five blocks. On the face of it, the geographical error was innocuous enough—particularly as it was corrected before the guide went to publication—yet the journalist shrouded the story in political menace: "Incidentally, the author of the invitation is now an organizer for the C.I.O."[24] I assume that the anonymous target was Frank Manning, a Boston editor who, as we see in chapter 5, did some union organizing in New Bedford and was supervising the local historical records survey by the time the state guide went to press. He could not have been responsible for the Sacco-Vanzetti entries, but he provided a hostile press with the opportunity to heap up political innuendo. Still speaking in the name of patriotic local writers, the *Star* also targeted Loewenberg, playing on the caricature of the Jewish, academic, "effeminate" outsider: "Workers on the New Bedford District WPA Writers' Project hailed with poorly disguised relief invitations to a 'farewell dinner' for Bert James Lowenberg,

Ph.D., temporarily of Boston, upon whose rather narrow shoulders presumably rests responsibility for the compendium of inaccurate and misleading information known by courtesy as the Massachusetts Guide Book."

In fact, the guide's handling of Sacco and Vanzetti resulted from a more subtle interaction of national, state, and local perspectives than the sensationalist newspaper headlines claimed. The Boston editors did not smuggle the Sacco-Vanzetti material into the guide. They did not even generate it all. Merle Colby did largely write the "Labor" essay, though Washington editors approved it in galley form. Multiple state and national editors had a hand in the Boston entry, sending copy back and forth, tinkering with its proportions, ultimately reducing the coverage on the Boston police strike and increasing the material on Sacco and Vanzetti. A. R. Buckley, a local field worker with no record of radical activity, first wrote Sacco and Vanzetti into the Dedham entry. Buckley's earliest, handwritten field copy on Sacco and Vanzetti was considerably more voluminous than the published entry, with more detail about the trial and about protests from countries and individuals across the world. Much of the material he paraphrased from Samuel E. Klaus, *American Trials* (1931), a strongly narrative account which implied without stating sympathy with the accused. Buckley demonstrates his perspective in his selection of details; he added no overt editorializing of his own. Grace Kellogg and Melvin Peach maintained Buckley's focus when they edited his field copy in the Boston office, but in condensing his treatment to manageable proportions, they made the sympathetic perspective more explicit, and they added three words: "echoes still reverberate." National editors expanded that reference with examples from the 1930s: a Pulitzer Prize–winning play on Sacco and Vanzetti, a brochure protesting the Lowell Commission findings which was circulated at the Harvard tercentenary celebration, and Heywood Broun's famous comment, "Though the tomb is sealed, the dry bones still rattle."[25]

THE GUIDE'S REVISION

A very public game of chicken ensued, with Hurley on one side and upper-echelon project officials on the other. Hurley's administration attempted to seize direct editorial control over the guidebook, a role explicitly disallowed state politicians according to the constitution of the Federal Writers' Project. As soon as the controversy broke, on August 19, 1937, Hurley directed the state librarian, Dennis A. Cooley, to scour the guidebook for offensive references. A few days later, Hurley went public with a demand for the full expurgation of the guidebook. According to Ray Billington, Massachusetts officials demanded that "the publishers [not only] strike out every mention of the Sacco-Vanzetti case, but all references to strikes, unions, organized labor, welfare legislation, child labor laws and virtually every progressive act in the history of the state. They even proposed dropping Labor Day from the list of official holidays!"[26]

Project editors in Boston and Washington shrugged off the fuss, positioning themselves at an ironic distance from Hurley's overheated rhetoric. Ray Billington, deploying his credentials both as state director and as a historian, pronounced publicly that the Sacco-Vanzetti material was good, judicious, unbiased historical writing. The *Boston Globe* and the *Boston Herald* quoted Billington as saying that the references were "simply statements of fact" and "moderate statements," a judgment supported by Professor Arthur M. Schlesinger of Harvard University in those papers the next day: "Considering the references as a brief statement of a complex situation, they seem as fair as could be made."[27] Alsberg's opinion made headlines in the *Baltimore Evening Sun* and other out-of-state papers: "WPA Chief Insists Sacco-Vanzetti Story Is Necessary To Guidebook."[28] Harry Hopkins, WPA administrator in Washington and FDR confidant, went further, ridiculing the uproar as a "publicity stunt" designed to increase sales (which it did). As characterized by the press, Hopkins seemed almost glib about the challenge: "WPA officials, headed by Administrator Harry L. Hopkins, declared last night that no deletions will be made in the Massachusetts Guide Book put out by the WPA. . . . 'If we acted on every complaint we get down here,' Hopkins said, 'we would never get anything done.'"[29] Roosevelt exhibited a similar attitude: the next time he visited the central project office, he "mischievously jabbed his cane into a copy of the Massachusetts guidebook. 'I understand you had quite a bit of trouble over this book,' he drawled, then laughed uproariously" (Mangione, *Dream* 220). Washington officials felt confident of the hierarchies of government, demonstrating that, while the state might be bogged down in parochial interests and local pressure groups, the New Deal vision transcended petty politics. Hopkins sent an uncompromising message: this administration would not sacrifice scholarship to the endless political sparring between state and federal administrations or to the interests of local patronage; the guidebook was not available for revision.

Behind the scenes, however, Washington officials were feeling considerably more beleaguered than their public statements allowed, and frenzied negotiations were underway. Henry Alsberg spent several months attempting to square New Deal mandates, his own ideological commitments, and Massachusetts' political realities. In September 1937 he wrote with evident consternation to his regional field supervisor Joseph Gaer about another New England project. Arguing that the title of the planned book should change from "The Condition of the Working Classes in New England" to "How New England People Live," Alsberg cautioned Gaer: "we must be very careful that we do not give the impression that we are doing a class-angle study. . . . We have had so much criticism already for alleged bias that we must be most careful."[30] By October 1937, Alsberg was retreating by inches, desperately holding to the principle that if state officials were demanding changes, they had to do so formally, in writing. Otherwise, Hurley "could easily say that we ourselves thought we had done a poor job as we volunteered to make changes without any formal request from officials." Alsberg feared that the project would be "accused of censoring our own book," a point he made repeatedly: "We would be willing to add the material, but we hesitate to write a new Labor essay since in that case, we might be accused of volunteering to censor our own work."[31] A triumvirate from Boston—representing political, project, and publishing interests—arranged a secret meeting to thrash out possible compromises: "Unofficially, after a period of jockeying, Mr. Cook agreed to drop into a restaurant where Professor Billington and Mr. Linscott of Houghton-Mifflin were taking lunch. The matter was informally discussed under pledge, however, that as far as the public was concerned, Mr. Cook had never met or talked to either of these gentlemen."[32] As a result of this meeting, the pressure on Alsberg escalated. Billington offered to rewrite the "Labor" essay, and Linscott urged Alsberg not only to accept that offer but to make additional changes suggested by Cook. Houghton Mifflin found itself boxed in after the rapid sell-out of the guidebook's first run of 10,000 copies. Hurley's administration was threatening not only to block the second printing on which the publishers depended to recover some of the scarce resources they had gambled on the guidebook, but to exclude all Houghton Mifflin textbooks from Massachusetts schools, a loss of income that the publisher could not have survived. Clearly, the pressure exerted by the Massachusetts administration was considerably more effective and more precisely calculated than the New Dealers' jokes acknowledged.

By January 1938, Hopkins had passed the buck to Alsberg, putting the final decision about textual changes in his hands. Billington had written a version of "Industry and Labor," then resigned to take up his assistant professorship at Smith College.[33] Alsberg was still dithering. He was caught between the gritty politicians who controlled Massachusetts patronage and the good opinion of leading liberals whom he respected. Citing Lewis Mumford, Robert Morse Lovett, Malcolm Cowley, and Bruce Bliven specifically, he averred privately that "a large number of leading educators, critics and others have commented very favorably on the book as it stands now."[34] As late as April 1938, the publisher Linscott was still pleading the case for revision: "As far as the policy changes are concerned, please bear in mind that these were made, not at our request, but at the request of the State, transmitted through us, with the explicit threat the State would withdraw its sponsorship if they were not made." A few days later, Linscott wrote a second letter in the face of Alsberg's reluctance to fund such changes, citing pressure from local groups as well as the state administration: "It will, of course, be necessary for us to explain to the State, and to the various communities and organizations, why the errors which they have called to our attention will go uncorrected."[35]

Eventually, Alsberg passed the task of thoroughgoing revision down to the state office. By this time, all three state editors had gone. Billington went to his new position at Smith College, Loewenberg took up teaching duties at the University of South Dakota, and Colby was spirited out of Massachusetts by Alsberg, who felt he would be less of a political liability working on the guide to Alaska. These three escaped the situation with their feisty image as "WPA lads" intact. Harry Hansen labeled them thus, championing the Massachusetts writers in his *New York City World-Telegram* column: "They called the Plymouth Rock landing a myth and made Sacco and Vanzetti pop up in unexpected places. . . . Here is no whitewashing of the powerful, no obeisance to the ruling factions."[36]

The nitty gritty of the revision process fell to Muriel E. Hawks, who found herself in a transitional position during these harried months, as her status shifted from assistant state director to acting state director to state director in Massachusetts. As described in chapter 1, Hawks came to the Boston office from the position of district supervisor in Essex County. Her focus seems to have been more administrative, more attuned to public relations, and less Boston-centric than the academic editors'. The record suggests that she fine-tuned the "Industry and Labor" essay and directed her workforce in the state office in the painstaking job of trawling through the many objections, calculating the political risks and doctoring the guide material accordingly.[37]

In July 1938, Houghton Mifflin announced a "second printing" of the guidebook, with no public acknowledgment that the new volume amounted to a revised edition. The 1937 and 1938 volumes appeared identical in binding, length, and appearance. Editors had systematically expurgated the contents with such care that the pagination remained undisturbed, the table of contents and index needed almost no revision, and few paragraphs visibly changed length. The most noticeable alteration is the simple deletion of the date "1937" from the title page. Within this carefully sustained framework, the revisions are myriad and detailed. Some changes correct previous errors in dates or figures, but many more revisions amount to rhetorical shifts, large and small, which reorient the political implications of many entries. Large changes included the rewriting of the entire fourteen-page "Labor" essay. The essay entitled "Labor" became "Industry and Labor" in the new version, a startlingly different account that lost its militant edge, paid far less attention to the organization and conditions of the working classes, and focused on the technological and manufacturing triumphs of the state. Editors also rewrote the sentence which the Italian-American Club and the mayor of Marlboro had protested: from "It has a large Italian population, who were encouraged to settle here as strike-breakers after a serious labor disturbance in 1899" to "Marlborough's several racial groups have been attracted to the town by the opportunities offered in various trades" (472). And the parenthetical words which had enraged the town of Peabody were changed from "(a charming and perhaps not unstrategic gesture)" to "(a charming and typically democratic gesture)" (422).

The most stunning changes concern the guide's representation of Sacco and Vanzetti. The 1920 robbery and murder of which they were accused vanished from the description of Braintree; the 1927 execution disappeared from the list of events in the State Chronology; and the paragraphs in the Dedham and Boston descriptions shrank to one sentence each, the latter not referenced in the new index. The revised "Labor" essay severed the paragraph on Sacco and Vanzetti from labor history, thereby reorienting the case's political associations. Because the intervening paragraphs on oppressive work conditions have been cut, the text now moves directly from the Boston police strike to Sacco and Vanzetti—that is, from one political disturbance to another rather than from a story of labor to particular laborers (Fig. 7). Moreover, the men are now figured primarily as anarchists:

> The Sacco-Vanzetti case hinged about two members of an anarchist group, Bartolomeo Vanzetti, a fish peddler, and Niccola [*sic*] Sacco, a shoe worker, who were arrested in 1920 on the charge of murder and robbery in connection with the theft of a $15,000 payroll. (76)

The final sentence of the paragraph also underwent revision. The original version read: "It was widely believed that, although legal forms were observed, the determining factor in the case from start to finish was the affiliation of the two men with an unpopular minority political group" (76). The revision reads: "It was contended by liberals and radicals that, although legal forms were observed, the determining factor in the case was the affiliation of the two men with an unpopular minority political group" (76). The substituted language minimizes public sympathy and distances any assertion of their innocence from majority opinion. Through such tiny, cumulative changes, the space for metonymic figures of social justice—on the cultural landscape and in the official narrative of the state—had shrunk considerably, as the revised text pushed dissenting voices to the margins.

CONTINUING SECRECY

Then and later, project insiders kept the revision process secret. Up to a point, the motivation for this secrecy seems strategic and local to the exigencies of 1930s Massachusetts politics. But the denial of the guidebook revisions continued for decades beyond the closing of the writers' project in 1943. A larger dynamic was at work. Cultural insiders—in this case, former project officials—wielded information as a means of cultural inclusion and exclusion, participating in a broadly governmental management of public knowledge which continues to shape popular perception and scholarly study of the guidebook's making.[38]

When the silently revised guidebook appeared in mid-July 1938, project officials and the publisher kept a close watch on its reception. Frank Manuel, regional editor for New England, contacted Alsberg on August 16, 1938: "The new edition of the Massachusetts Guide has been on the stands for the past month. Nobody has apparently noticed the revisions and changes."[39] A month later, Linscott wrote to Alsberg with relief: "The second printing of the Massachusetts Guide is selling slowly and steadily and so far no one has even spotted the fact that a new printing is out or that changes have been made—which is perhaps just as well."[40] No one publicly acknowledged the political compromises that led to these revisions. Alsberg even managed to persuade Merle Colby to let his name stand in the preface to the revised volume.[41] This desire to sustain the invisibility of the revisions points to the larger complicities and political accommodations that informed the act of censorship.

76 Massachusetts: The General Background

price, even after the deal is closed. Should a number of vessels bring in full loads of fish immediately following such a sale, thus increasing supply and driving the price lower, the buyer may refuse to accept such fish as have not been taken out of the hold. Usually he offers a lower price; and as he has taken the freshest fish — those on top, hence caught last — the skipper generally makes a concession. The chief burden of this sort of dealing falls, of course, upon the crew — the 'partners' in the voyage. The only chance such men have to make an unusually large 'stock' is to tie up at a wharf with a full hold when no other vessel has one. And the chances against this are large. For these reasons, mainly, the fisherman is almost invariably poor. On account of the share system, fishermen have remained largely unorganized.

In 1920, a fish peddler, Bartolomeo Vanzetti, and a shoe-worker, Nicolà Sacco, both members of the Galleani group of anarchists, were arrested on the charge of murder and robbery in connection with the theft of a $15,000 payroll. Despite their alibis, the highly circumstantial nature of the evidence, and the commendations of previous employers, they were ultimately both adjudged guilty. During the seven years that elapsed between the murder and the execution of the sentence, protest demonstrations were held throughout the world. President Lowell of Harvard, President Stratton of Massachusetts Institute of Technology, and Judge Robert Grant were invited by Governor Fuller to weigh the evidence and advise him. They upheld the finding of the court and Sacco and Vanzetti were executed on August 23, 1927. It was widely believed that, although legal forms were observed, the determining factor in the case from start to finish was the affiliation of the two men with an unpopular minority political group.

The Women's Trade Union League secured, in 1921, an extension of the fifty-eight hour law for women to further industries. Employers of woman labor in the textile industry were given power under the National Industrial Recovery Act of 1933 to make codes of fair competition, and in that year they secured the suspension of section 59 of chapter 149 of the General Laws of Massachusetts which prohibited the employment of women in textile mills after 6 P.M. This suspension was continued from year to year after the collapse of the National Industrial Recovery Act.

Of the 122,389 workers in the textile mills of the State in 1937, forty per cent were women. In the textile industry, women are a permanent labor force. Most of them enter the mills at a very early age and remain there for the greater part of their lives. Even marriage does not always take the textile working girl out of the mill, for the earnings of her husband seldom

76 Massachusetts: The General Background

opposed to the 'public safety again being placed in the hands of these same policemen.' A new force was on duty November 10, and the defeated strikers sought jobs elsewhere. The reputation gained by Calvin Coolidge in the Boston police strike has always been considered a decisive factor in his career.

The Sacco-Vanzetti case hinged about two members of an anarchist group, Bartolomeo Vanzetti, a fish peddler, and Niccola Sacco, a shoe worker, who were arrested in 1920 on the charge of murder and robbery in connection with the theft of a $15,000 payroll. Many were convinced that the evidence used against the defendants was circumstantial and inadequate, that their alibis were truthful, and that they were being condemned to the chair more because of their radical views than because of their guilt. During the seven years that elapsed between the murder and execution of the sentence, protest demonstrations were held throughout the world. The case was twice passed upon by the Supreme Court of Massachusetts, and applications for a new trial denied. President Lowell of Harvard, President Stratton of the Massachusetts Institute of Technology, and Judge Robert Grant were invited by Governor Fuller to weigh the evidence and advise him. They upheld the finding of the court and Sacco and Vanzetti were executed on August 23, 1927. It was contended by liberals and radicals that, although legal forms were observed, the determining factor in the case was the affiliation of the two men with an unpopular minority political group.

Recent developments in the Massachusetts labor situation have indicated some of the difficulties that both industry and the workers face in the Bay State. Textile employees, entrenched in the United Textile Workers since the beginning of the century, staged a series of spectacular strikes in 1934, but secured no great concessions from an industry sadly crippled by the depression. The union was weakened by this loss of prestige, and in 1936–37 deserted the American Federation of Labor to cast its lot with the Committe for Industrial Organization.

Recent attempts to organize the shoe industry have led to serious internal disputes within labor organizations and to the migration of many shoe factories to other States. One bitter struggle occurred in 1929 when the shoe workers of Lynn, Boston, Chelsea, and Salem struck, with the major demand for recognition of their union, the United Shoe Workers of America, as opposed to the Boot and Shoe Workers' Union, an A.F. of L. affiliate. The strike lasted six months and strike-breakers were imported from neighboring States, but it was finally broken by a court injunction based upon findings that the strike was illegal. During this strike many

Fig. 7. Page 76 from *Massachusetts: A Guide to Its Places and People*, 1937 and 1938.

In the immediate context, we can speculate that it suited the interests of both federal and state politicians to cut a quiet deal that basically gave Hurley his way without embarrassing New Dealers in Washington. Above all, the writers' project and its backers in Roosevelt's administration did not want further controversy, especially with the Dies Committee beginning to investigate alleged communists in the Federal Arts Projects and amid accusations of subversive activity on the New York Writers' Project and the Federal Theatre Project.[42] Hurley may also have been keen to avoid a further public relations row with Roosevelt's administration in 1938, since that was a year of primaries for Congress and state governor. Hurley did have his image to protect. The Massachusetts press had portrayed him as defender of the state's reputation. A throng of guidebook opponents—including Representative Edward D. Sirois of Lawrence, the library trustees of Peabody, the mayors of Leominster and Marlboro, and a Fall River councillor—had demanded action of Hurley. His nemesis, Georgia governor E. D. Rivers, had trumpeted the guidebook controversy as Hurley's personal embarrassment.[43] The compromise position—achieving the requested revisions without publicizing the victory—allowed Hurley to prove his political clout to those constituents with continuing interest in the guidebook while restoring relations with the Washington office. In any case, in late 1938, he lost the governorship nomination contest to James Michael Curley and went on his way to a new career in real estate.

Project editors and administrators long continued to collude in the act of censorship by suppressing the fact of the guidebook's revision, denying the capitulation of New Deal administrators to Governor Hurley, and insisting that Boston and Washington officials stood by their stated resolve to protect the guidebook's integrity. Ray Billington's 1961 retrospective of his time as state director suggested that no changes were made: "Fortunately Harry Hopkins and the other WPA administrators treated the whole episode as the teapot tempest that it was, while the publishers went ahead with a second printing, and a third" (478). In 1972 Jerre Mangione, who was national coordinating editor on the project, minimized the changes and misdated them as occurring in 1939: "No changes were made in the Massachusetts Guide while Alsberg was national director. After his departure, its publishers deleted a statement by Heywood Broun on the Sacco-Vanzetti case" (220n). Billington certainly knew of the changes and indeed contributed some of them. Mangione would not have been directly involved in crafting the revisions but very likely knew of their existence. These highly interested versions of the Massachusetts controversy erased the account of Hurley's influence from the public record. They worked to exclude Hurley and his administration from the arena of cultural authority just as thoroughly as Hurley had worked to exclude Sacco and Vanzetti and the guidebook authors from the Massachusetts scene.

The expurgated version of the guidebook's making became received wisdom. When Houghton Mifflin commissioned Ray Bearse to produce a "second edition" (really, a wholesale revamping) of the guidebook in 1971, his introduction followed Billington's published version of the controversy: "Fortunately WPA administrator Harry Hopkins and the publishers did not knuckle under to the emotional pressures of the era." Jane Holtz Kay's introduction to the 1983 reprinting of the original guide (and it *is* the original text) assumes that there was only one version of the guide.[44] Scholars have unearthed some consequences of the Massachusetts controversy, including the addition of a euphemistically labeled "policy editor" (actually, an internal censor) to the project's Washington office in 1938. This employee, Louise Lazell, subsequently gave damaging evidence to the Dies Committee. No one has addressed (or exposed) the censorship involved in a systematic rewriting that was officially denied.[45]

The bleakest reading of this suppressed story would make it complicit in the fate of Sacco and Vanzetti. The two men profoundly challenged the structures of governance not only with their anarchist beliefs in communitarian values but by the example of their treatment. Upton Sinclair's massive novelization *Boston* (1928) powerfully presented their case as an indictment from beginning to end of U.S. government at every level—federal, state, municipal, judiciary, executive, and legislative—and of multiple sites which extend governmental control—the universities, the churches, the media. Sinclair represented all these arenas as refuges for the corrupt, the racist, the self-interested, the cowardly. The writers' project depended on those governmental systems for its existence, and they shaped both the logic of the guidebook genre and the conditions of its making. Despite the initial challenge mounted by the volume's architects, ultimately the genre revealed its capacity to function as the perfect carrier of governmental control, silently disappearing Sacco and Vanzetti one more time.

POSTSCRIPT

There is another reading of this story, one that returns us to the guidemakers' initial achievement in making Sacco and Vanzetti part of Massachusetts' official memory. This reading follows Michael Denning's approach to John Dos Passos's *U.S.A* trilogy (191-99). Throughout the 1920s, Dos Passos protested zealously on behalf of Sacco and Vanzetti, and their execution motivated his novel. Yet the two men were finally so foreign to him, in ethnicity and politics, that he could not bring himself to embrace them as fully realized characters in his book. Instead he represented them indirectly through recurring figures of Italian American anarchism, the Anglo-Americans who witness and protest their victimization, and the Camera Eye consciousness of their "passion." The trilogy feels saturated by characters who never solidify: "The men in the death house remain the necessary absence that produces *U.S.A.*" (Denning 192). If we read the Massachusetts guide in the context of the controversy, suppression, and accommodation reconstructed here, its landscape feels similarly haunted by Sacco and Vanzetti. Conscious of their erasure, we look for their traces in the essay on Brockton (where Vanzetti was arrested), in Plymouth (where Vanzetti was blacklisted and in whose jail both he and Sacco were imprisoned), in the tours through Bridgewater (where they were both incarcerated in the insane asylum and where an earlier robbery, of which Vanzetti was also accused, took place), through Stoughton (where Sacco lived and worked at the time of his arrest), through Charlestown (in whose death chambers they languished for a considerable time and where they were ultimately electrocuted), as well as finding them more solidly present in Braintree, Dedham, and Boston.

Guidebook writers, heavily dependent on government sponsorship as they were, showed considerable courage in forcing an official remembering of an event that many in power preferred to forget. They stand in a distinguished line of Sacco-Vanzetti supporters in Massachusetts who have weathered public opprobrium in the cause of justice and cultural entitlement. Well beyond 1937, Sacco-Vanzetti supporters continued to offer the Borglum plaque to state officials, only to be repeatedly rebuffed. Arthur Schlesinger reports: "Twenty years after the electrocution, in 1947, a group of distinguished citizens, including Mrs. Franklin D. Roosevelt, Albert Einstein, Herbert H. Lehman, Dean Wesley A. Sturges of the Yale Law School, and Provost Paul H. Buck of Harvard University, offered to the Commonwealth of Massachusetts a bas-relief plaque of the two Italians—the work of Gutzon Borglum—for erection on Boston Common, but the Governor to whom fell the decision considered that public opinion in the state was still too divided to justify acceptance" (xii). Not until 1977 did government authority publicly remember Sacco and Vanzetti: speaking on the fiftieth anniversary of their execution, "in the crowded Senate Chamber at State House," Governor Michael Dukakis proclaimed "Tuesday, August 23, 1977, 'NICOLA SACCO AND BARTOLOMEO VANZETTI MEMORIAL DAY'" and stated that "whether or not Sacco and Vanzetti were jointly or severally innocent or guilty, there was little doubt that by today's standards they had not received a fair trial. The Proclamation was publicly accepted by Spencer Sacco, Nicola's unseen grandchild who then travelled to Italy to give a copy to Bartolomeo Vanzetti's surviving sister" (Jackson 89, 88). Even at that late date, the press had a field day reporting outrage in and beyond government circles: a motion from Republican senators that the Proclamation "violated all legal, ethical and constitutional precedents" (Jackson 95); objections by Democratic representatives to Dukakis's act; the anger of Governor Fuller's sons. "The case still split party ranks and loyalties and fractured what are now euphemistically called the ethnic groups: Beacon Hill Anglo-American Boston, South Side Irish Boston, and North End Italian. But it didn't fracture them externally. . . . It split them on the inside" (Jackson 98). Finally, twenty years on again, in 1997, Boston's first mayor of Italian descent—Mayor Thomas Menino—officially accepted the Borglum bas-relief, at the Boston Public Library. Even now, its display is a long way from Boston Common, set unobtrusively into a wall in the hushed and low-lit entrance to the Rare Books and Manuscripts Division, deep in the labyrinthine corridors of the building.

The Massachusetts guide stood at the beginning of this lineage of struggle, an early demonstration of the stakes involved in forcing an official remembering of Sacco and Vanzetti. The guide's low-key factual, declarative form insistently wrote Sacco and Vanzetti back into the state's official narrative, making them visible on the Massachusetts scene once more, endowing them with full citizenship in the Commonwealth and nation. Press, politicians, and public officials responded to this attempt with a maelstrom of questions about cultural citizenship—who belonged to the state and the nation and who got to decide—trained not just on Sacco and Vanzetti but also on the project employees responsible for these entries. When the project's leaders capitulated to this political pressure, the same governmental structures that enabled the guidebook's production kicked in to fetter its reach and silence its story. The revised volume camouflaged its systemic exclusions, continuing to present its information as commonsensical and beyond challenge. This suppression and its denial, echoing down the years, quietly withdrew the guide from the struggle mounted by Catharine Huntington and others toward public reparation, collective taking of responsibility, and an overhauling of the assumptions underpinning the national "we."

4

MAPPING "RACE" IN MASSACHUSETTS

The same editors who stuck their necks out—indeed, risked their livelihood—to take a stand on class politics and minority rights in the state guide could not commit to equitable representation of racial difference. *Massachusetts* gives almost no sense of a Black presence in the state: the guide fleetingly names half-a-dozen African Americans within a largely Euro-American narrative of history and identifies no contemporary Blacks, individually or collectively. Years later, Jerre Mangione acknowledged "the gross neglect of the American Negro in the six New England state guidebooks" (*Dream* 259). The omission is the more striking because Massachusetts state editors repeatedly assured Sterling Brown, national Negro Affairs editor, that the guide would give comprehensive coverage to Black people in their state.[1] The guide affords more recognition to Native Americans, although as vanished figures, sketched with full-blown "nostalgic remorse," not as contemporary, politically relevant presences in the state (Eco 10).

Whereas Ray Billington publicly defended the guidebook's inclusion of the Sacco-Vanzetti controversy—"Its mention was necessary for interpreting contemporary Massachusetts"—he and his assistant editors apparently did not find the inclusion of African and Native Americans equally necessary.[2] How could this be?

This chapter addresses that conundrum, first asking how, why, and to what effect the Massachusetts guide so thoroughly overlooks African Americans. The answer concerns both large- and small-scale conditions: the climate of thinking about race during the period, and the position of Blacks within the New Deal generally and the writers' project specifically, combined with the details of how project writers gathered, organized, and edited guidebook copy. In this scheme, the publication of the state guide in August 1937 serves as a dividing line: the generation of African American material, so hesitant and inadequate from 1935 to 1937, took off in 1938. Through the lens of the African American case, I then explore, more briefly, the guide's limited treatment of Native peoples. Again, the inquiry looks at dominant understandings of Aboriginal cultures in the discourse at large, reinforced by processes of production on the project itself.

There is no "smoking gun," no specific story of censorship (as with Sacco and Vanzetti) to explain the suppression of African American material and the limited treatment of Native Americans in Massachusetts publications. The answer to the conundrum comes down to the relationship between the two meanings of representation—employment and textual coverage—on the project. Those cultural groups enjoying highest rates of employment on the project also appeared most visibly in its publications. Recognition as workers—the very category on which the project was built—brought voice and agency in the contemporary scene drawn by the writers' project.

AFRICAN AMERICANS

When we think about the race politics surrounding and infusing the writers' project, the issue of classification comes and stays to the fore. First, there was the larger discursive climate in which the project operated. In the 1930s, public discourse was moving away from "race-consciousness" toward "color-consciousness" (Guterl 6), and the resulting redrawing of race lines hardened the binary between "white" Americans and African Americans in particular. European immigrant groups began to be classified under the collective designation "Caucasian": this "consolidation of a unified whiteness" (Jacobson 93) cast African Americans into an equally indistinguishable and complete blackness. Fifty years later, Ishmael Reed talked about living with the racism of this categorical division: "I guess in the United States, ethnicity is interchangeable with being black. In other words, 'blacks' are the only ethnic group in the United States. . . . Blacks have difficulties claiming the multi-ethnicity of their heritage because such a claim renders millions of people less 'white.' We threaten people" (226–27).

Various social and political conditions had fed this change. Public hysteria over immigrant groups, which had been rising since the 1840s—with the influx of Irish, Italian, East European, and Asian groups—was calmed by the National Origins Act of 1924 which established quotas by ethnic group, to limit drastically the numbers eligible to settle in the United States. Where it had seemed crucial to classify myriad racial groups according to language, nationality, and religion, there was now an increasing move to fold immigrants within a unifying "whiteness." The new racial threat from the southern states propelled that tendency further. The "Great Migration" northward and westward of African Americans brought nearly one-and-a-half-million Blacks north between 1915 and 1929 (Sullivan 15) and close to another half-million in the 1930s (Jacobson 38). Northeastern city dwellers came into much closer proximity with multiplying numbers of Black Americans, with attendant suspicions and hatreds fueled by the grim economic conditions and job scarcity of the Great Depression.

This profound hardening of the color line made its mark even on engaged intellectuals who were arguing against biological determinism. It had taken until this period for Franz Boas's ideas about environment and culture, rather than nature, shaping racial identity to percolate through anthropological and social science scholarship more broadly. In the 1930s, Ruth Benedict and Aldous Huxley, among others, produced influential studies of the effects of culture on the formation of race and on race relations, demonstrating the constructedness of classifications—such as Anglo-Saxon, Celt, Slav, Hebrew, Iberic, Saracen—which had previously held sway. A new tolerance emerged from this thinking, particularly in opposition to the Nazi rhetoric of Aryan superiority, which Huxley denounced as "pseudo-science." In the words of Harvard Sitkoff, "Nazism had given racism a bad name" (195). Yet for all the new inclusiveness in notions of "whiteness," the belief that people of color were biologically and actually different remained in place. Benedict was typical in challenging "micro" divisions of racial difference while holding to the "major" divisions of "Caucasian," "Mongoloid," and "Negroid." In the words of Matthew Jacobson, "Much of the antiracist work of the period was founded upon the very epistemology of race that it sought to dismantle" (103).

In this categorical thinking about racial identity, governmental classification operated as a powerful tool that could be turned in progressive or conservative directions, depending on which interests dominated at a given moment. Those engaged in the hard work of "becoming Caucasian" (Jacobson 8) relied on government definitions of race—from the first U.S. law of naturalization in 1790 onwards—as a crucial court of appeal. Groups now entering under the umbrella of whiteness could even use the segregation statutes of southern states to their advantage, because those laws clearly distinguished "white" from "colored." The periodic U.S. censuses also provided a politically potent baseline of racial and ethnic identities. The quota system instituted by the restrictive immigration legislation of 1924, for example, rested on the categories established by the 1890 census. From 1920, the census contained no "mulatto" category, a shift which influenced "the politics of skin color" within and beyond African American communities (Guterl 132). Cape Verdean Americans—the "Black Portuguese" clustered in southeastern Massachusetts—remained officially invisible until the census of 1980 (Halter 152). Pushing in a more inclusive direction, the industrial codes of fair practice under Roosevelt's National Industrial Recovery Act of 1933 strongly supported the struggle to recognize "Negro laborers" as "American laborers" (Sullivan 52). The writers' project was poised to intervene meaningfully in this terrain of categorization and classification. By virtue of their federal and state sponsorship, project guides translated governmental classification into a recreational key—into a taken-for-granted set of categories through which readers viewed the American scene. The project was nicely positioned to challenge—as it did in the case of Sacco and Vanzetti—assumptions about who did and did not belong to the category "American."

AFRICAN AMERICAN REPRESENTATION ON THE FEDERAL WRITERS' PROJECT

The writers' project, however, shared some of the New Deal's larger ambivalence about Blacks. Mainly because of the Democratic administration's dependence on the dominant southern wing of the party, Roosevelt, Hopkins, and others at first soft-pedaled Black rights within the new social safety net of "alphabet agencies." According to Matthew Guterl, "reform always came at a glacial pace and was inevitably conceived and implemented with the color line—the adamantine hardness of the line between whiteness and blackness and between whites and blacks—firmly in place" (148). Harold Ickes, head of the Public Works Administration, stood virtually alone among white federal bureaucrats by taking a strong public stand against racial discrimination from the beginning. He insisted on employment percentages at least proportionate to the racial composition of the 1930 census, and he coached Black New Dealers in devising "an affirmative policy to ensure the full participation of black labor in federally funded projects."[3] By 1936, twenty-nine cities had implemented this policy. Generally, from the Second New Deal in 1935, Black voters increasingly influenced the administration's decisions, and statistics suggest the impact on employment patterns. In 1930, only one percent of employed Americans were African Americans "in trade, the professions, or public service."[4] By 1939 the Black journal *Opportunity* could celebrate the effect of New Deal agencies: "in the northern communities, particularly the urban centers, the Negro has been afforded his first real opportunity for employment in white-collar occupation" (qtd. in Sitkoff 72).

Within the writers' project, racial representation—in terms of both employment and textual coverage—developed unevenly. On the one hand, the project has been justly celebrated for generating a large and rich volume of ex-slave narratives, which have proved invaluable sources for scholarship and writings about Black experiences in the United States, and for keeping alive public memory of the horrors of slavery. Lawrence D. Reddick, an African American revisionist historian at Kentucky State College, proposed this activity even before the writers' project was approved, and over the years it profited from widespread support by project administrators and workers—including Alsberg, John Lomax, Sterling Brown, and Benjamin A. Botkin (Botkin 198; Penkower 17). On the other hand, there arose considerable resistance to hiring Blacks to do the work, with southern staff refusing to accept local Blacks as qualified interviewers (K. McKinzie 152). Also, the ex-slave narrative project was limited to the eighteen southern and border states, in effect keeping Black history at arm's length from Massachusetts. Jerre Mangione has also written about his consternation, as an Italian American most recently from Manhattan, at "the preponderance of white government employees who were well clothed, well sheltered, and well fed" in the Washington, D.C., office (*Ethnic* 227). The NAACP brought pressure on the project's administrators to employ more Black writers and to research the role of Blacks in the history and contemporary life of New York, and Mangione reports the "black cabinet" in Washington lobbying for Black employment on the WPA (*Dream* 255). Yet, according to Katherine McKinzie, "the question of deliberate inclusion of qualified Negro writers on state projects and research in Negro history drifted unresolved into 1936" (136). In that year, only about 3 percent of writers' project employees, around two hundred writers, were Black (K. McKinzie 137; Sitkoff 71–72).

That climate of thinking directly impinged on the project's production methods. When the central office issued its first version of the American Guide Manual in October 1935, it included "race" as a category for writers' attention, but it did not specify African Americans anywhere in the document—with what textual results we will see later in this chapter. Earl Conrad's judgment of the cultural climate in general—that "the Negro issue was trailing the labor question by a few years. . . . until 1943, the Negro-white situation was to remain a dubious or undesirable theme to most publishers and editors" (51)—seems applicable to the upper echelons of the writers' project. Editors in Washington and Boston would go to great lengths to represent labor conditions in the guides, not only constantly pressing writers for more copy on the subject, but—in the case of Katharine Kellock—smuggling controversial stories of labor disputes into tours and—in the case of Merle Colby—devoting an entire essay to Massachusetts' tumultuous labor history. Certainly in their dealings with northern states, no project administrator outside the tiny office of Negro Affairs afforded African American subjects anything like this level of priority.

A commitment to more equable Black representation began when Alsberg and Cronyn dined at Howard University with "15 prominent blacks of Washington" in fall 1935 (K. McKinzie 135). Under this group's urging, the Washington editors recognized that the project needed Black leadership if its employment patterns were to become more racially inclusive and if its guides were to chart "Negro culture in America" adequately.[5] Alsberg created the position of national Negro Affairs editor and offered it to Sterling Brown, an academic at Howard University with a rising reputation as a literary critic, author, and champion of Black culture. As a full-time teacher, Brown was reluctant to take on an additional task, but prominent Black activists were eager that an African American scholar should accept an influential position on the writers' project. Strong encouragement came from John P. Davis, "National Negro Congress leader and articulate New Deal critic," Ralph

Bunche, a rising leader in the NAACP, and Alfred E. Smith, chief assistant to Harry Hopkins for Negro Affairs in the WPA (K. McKinzie 136). In the face of this persuasion, Brown joined the project in April 1936, at $15 per day for a maximum of twelve days per month, heading up an office on Negro Affairs which initially had 2.5 employees through whose hands all relevant state and city copy passed.

Brown was a "Harvard man" of a different order from his white fellows. Graduating with an A.B. from Williams College in 1922, then with an A.M. from Harvard in 1923, with further study at that university in 1931–1932, he was currently an associate professor of English at the historically Black Howard University. He was also a published poet, critic, and scholar with a distinctive commitment to African American folklife.[6] During his tenure on the project, he continued to publish literary and scholarly work that won him a Guggenheim fellowship. In all his roles—as teacher, writer, and political spokesperson—he held an unequivocal position on Black culture. He not only challenged stereotypes of African Americans in a wide range of literary works, but, in the face of considerable established opinion to the contrary, claimed the entitlement of Black authors to represent their own people: "the exploration of Negro life and character rather than its exploitation must come from Negro authors themselves. This, of course, runs counter to the American conviction that the Southern white man knows the Negro best, and can best interpret him" (203). When Benjamin Botkin and Morton W. Royse signed onto the project in 1938, as national folklore editor and national editor in charge of social-ethnic studies respectively, Brown joined forces with them to generate Black first-person life histories and folklore. From the day he joined the writers' project in 1936 to the day he resigned in 1940, Brown consistently pushed for the employment of more Black writers and for the generation of reliable, informed material on African American culture, historically and actually, throughout the country.

AFRICAN AMERICAN REPRESENTATION ON THE MASSACHUSETTS WRITERS' PROJECT

The Massachusetts project seemed immediately responsive on both fronts. Although employment figures are unstable, the contrast before and after Brown's intercession is clear. Whereas, under Alsberg's prompting, Clifford Shipton had been able to come up with somewhere between two and four Black employees by early 1936, pressure from Brown plus Billington's accession to state director raised that number to somewhere between fifteen and forty by the end of 1936.[7] Simultaneously, Brown's request that all states submit their material on African American culture produced a document from Bert Loewenberg on December 10, 1936, that promised an "almost exhaustive" coverage of Blacks—more complete than that of any other state.[8] Having bigger worries on his mind—blatant discrimination against Black employees in the South, racist representations of Black people and culture in southern guidebook copy, material on Blacks in Washington to produce in a hurry for the capital's guide—Brown relaxed his surveillance of Massachusetts.[9] He exempted Billington's office from his memorandum, sent out under Alsberg's name, chastising other state directors for state copy in which "the Negro is either left unmentioned or inadequately treated."[10] As Brown wrote in early 1937, "the extensive list of subjects is likely to be covered fully and well as Massachusetts has a good staff of Negroes employed, and sympathetic directors."[11] In short, he trusted the editors in Massachusetts.

Only gradually did it become clear that the promises from Massachusetts were empty. Throughout 1936, the Massachusetts office alluded to its wealth of African American research. Loewenberg wrote to Brown: "We have a great deal of material which has been collected and which can be sent to you in a short space of time if you so desire it."[12] The state office gave the Black press the impression that guide essays "will contain the history of the Negro in Massachusetts, giving facts concerning his distribution over the state, his economic conditions, occupations, professions, and his political affiliations. Also there are essays on the Negro's social condition, his cultural activities, his achievements in literature, art, the theatre, music and sports."[13] It was well into 1937 before Brown noticed that the only material submitted to his office was one-half page on Blacks in Boston and two pieces of field copy on Black education and Black religion.

Moreover, the Black employees responsible for this coverage were having to fight for their retention. First, Brown alerted Alsberg to the case of William E. Harrison, a Black non-relief worker who was pursuing a Ph.D. at Harvard, had recently received a grant from the Rosenwald Fund, and was dismissed because he put the project over its non-relief quota.[14] Billington had, of course, retained several white non-relief workers. Then, in July 1937, many Black WPA workers in Massachusetts received pink slips, a development which the *Boston Chronicle* regarded as clearly discriminatory: "The Negro worker particularly is in an unenviable position. In most cases there is no private industry to absorb him because he has to wait until all the white workers are taken care of—and he can't live on that long. . . . Daily we read high sounding and hopeful utterances by Administrator Hopkins in Washington, but his underlings here practise a different creed" (July 10, 1937). One of those workers was Edythe Mae Gordon, a figure in the Harlem Renaissance who had completed an innovative master's thesis, "The Status of the Negro Woman in the United States from 1619 to 1865," at Boston University in 1935. Having separated from her husband, Gordon was clinging to subsistence by her fingernails.[15] She made a particularly heartfelt plea directly to Alsberg, laying out her educational and writerly achievements before and during the project—graduating with a B.Sc. and M.A. from Boston University, publishing poems and short stories, organizing a Literary Workshop Group, gathering and writing project material on Massachusetts Blacks and on the history of Boston. Her letter ends: "I am wholly dependent on this job for means of support. I have no relatives at all. I have no friends to whom I can go for aid." With the intercession of Brown, Alsberg, Lula M. Scott (regional director of Women's and Professional Projects in Boston) and Ellen S. Woodward (assistant WPA administrator), the Massachusetts office cancelled Gordon's dismissal.[16] It is on record that all four arts projects in Boston consistently underemployed African Americans (Trout 190–93). For all the promises and protestations, it appears that the writers' project made the least visible contribution of them all to African American culture.[17]

The structures of production on the writers' project at least partly explain the gap between promise and result. The American Guide Manual from the central office did not name African Americans as a category. Working with those guidelines, and preoccupied with class and labor politics, the state editors failed to dedicate an essay to African Americans, or even to race. Moreover, in developing a template for field workers documenting their local communities, state editors inadvertently further exacerbated Black invisibility. A trawl through the details of copy production—from field editorial copy to state editorial copy to final copy—demonstrates the structural elision of Black histories and cultures in the Massachusetts guide-making process.

From October 1935, field workers across the state documented their local communities within the categories established by the American Guide Manual. The manual divided every community, large or small, into thirty-three categories that covered the contemporary and the historical, the natural, social, political, and cultural. Attention to race came under the category

"Ethnography," which directed workers to record "different racial groups," naming only Irish and Italian as examples.[18] State editors further schematized these categories for district employees, subdividing them into sixty-nine topic assignments. They renamed Ethnography "Racial Elements" and attached to it four topics (none of which specified any particular race): "Racial Groups," "Racial Cultural Heritage," "Relationship of Racial Groups to Community Development," and "Contemporary Racial Groups Retaining Ethnic Identity."

How writers understood these categories differed wildly depending on their own racial identity, their sources, and the politics of the district in which they were employed. The most striking pattern is that, throughout the cities and towns of Massachusetts, few writers saw the Blacks in their communities. For many writers, the term "race" evoked European immigrant groups—those whom Guterl and Jacobson analyze as "becoming Caucasian" in this period. The assignment "Racial Groups" flushed out acknowledgment of Irish, Portuguese, Italians, Jewish peoples from various countries, Poles, Greeks, Lithuanians, Scots, French, Latvians, Finns, Estonians, Ukrainians, Germans, Armenians, and Japanese, as well as that group variously dubbed English, Anglo-Saxon, "native American," or Yankee—but rarely African Americans. Black invisibility did not relate directly to population size—some of the European American groups were tiny—so much as to category conventions.

For many field writers—Black and white—Black Americans did not constitute a "race." Winnie C. Matthew's field copy on Abington, for example, explicitly sets Blacks apart:

> The greater part of Abington's foreign-born population is Polish and Lithuanian. Other races in order of numerical strength are: Canadians, Finns, Swedes, Irish, English, Russian, Italian, Greek, Scotch and Chinese.
>
> In 1930, the white population numbered 5863, and Negro 5.[19]

Even those writers who did note African Americans as a racial group rarely remembered their presence in the recording of cultural and community impact. Roger T. Balloch was typical in his treatment of Mattapoisett. Under "Racial Groups" he reported, "According to Government reports the population of Mattapoisett in 1930 was 1,501, including 65 negroes," and he divided Portuguese residents into "white Portuguese" and those "from the

Brava Islands" (i.e., Cape Verdeans). When he turned to the three subsequent categories dealing with race—cultural heritage, community development, and contemporary ethnic identity—however, the Cape Verdeans and the "negroes" simply disappeared.[20] Similarly, James F. McKenna listed 3,631 "negro" and 1,509 Cape Verdean residents in New Bedford under "Racial Groups," but none at all under the next three topics.[21] So it was with Mary Wiatt Chace's portrait of Plymouth, Louis McBay's of Carver, and numerous other Massachusetts communities across the state on which, according to project writers, Black residents made no cultural impact at all. Quite a number of writers found the categories of "race" and "culture" fundamentally incompatible, tersely noting of their communities:

Racial Cultural heritage	Not applicable
Relationship of racial groups to community development	Not applicable
Contemporary racial groups retaining ethnic identity	Not applicable

Sources exacerbated the tendency toward cultural invisibility. The 1930 census, on which most writers depended, did not recognize certain racial identities, such as Cape Verdean American, thus mutely encouraging writers to fold those people into the (implicitly "white") Portuguese. Local histories from the nineteenth and early twentieth centuries were often racist even in the context of 1930s thinking and adhered to elitist definitions of culture which seem at odds with the American Guide Manual's ethnographic bent. Local officials, a prime source of authority, had their own agendas. It comes as little surprise, for example, that Sara Tyler notes of Wareham, "There is no racial cultural heritage to be found amongst the Cape Verdeans in this town," when her single "consultant" is "Mr. Medina, pastor of the Methodist Church."[22] Various workers used members of the police force as their sources and were likely to get judgments about races as upstanding citizens (or not) when asked about their cultural or community characteristics.[23] The final source on which writers relied was "personal observation," a highly situated quantifier, but the one they were least likely to question given that they were documenting communities with which they felt intimately familiar.

There were two exceptions to this dominant pattern of perception and documentation. Black writers tended to point to Black presences, because their experience of the community and their choice of sources differed from their white colleagues'. Ernest E. Ormsby was typical in faithfully recording Black populations, however small the numbers, as well as demonstrating a more consistent respect for "other" minorities, who were more likely to be glossed over by writers belonging to the community's dominant racial group. Documenting "Racial Groups" in Barnstable, for example, Ormsby wrote: "According to the 1930 census the native white population of the town of Barnstable was 5,615, of which 4,097 were of native parentage, and 1,719 of foreign or mixed parentage, and 944 were foreign born. There were at that time 484 Negroes and 27 others." Catherine M. Vanni, a white worker reporting on the same town, chose the Barnstable chamber of commerce and the town clerk as her sources, showed none of Ormsby's numerical precision, and disappeared the town's Cape Verdeans under the designation "Portuguese."[24]

Ormsby also consistently worked to humanize the Black presence, individualizing, for example, the "2 Negroes" living in Burlington in 1800: "one African male belonging to the family of Abigail Jones and one African female, belonging to the family of James Reed." He went on, with a quiet sense of irony, to narrate that the male slave Cuff was forced to sit in the gallery of the meeting-house "but as he had to care for the grand-daughter of Madam Jones, he took the child with him."[25] White writers rarely paused over such details about nonwhite residents. George Gloss, for example, speedily dispensed with the Blacks of Holbrook: "There are very few negroes living in the town."[26] Harry O. Bowles, another African American writer, notes "Negroes" among the population of Charlestown (along with Irish, Italians, Greeks, French, Swedes, Poles, Japanese, Chinese, Filipinos, "as well as Americans") under "Racial Groups" and continues that recognition under "Contemporary Racial Groups retaining ethnic identity" even though he acknowledges that there are only about fifteen Black families. This last piece of information he gleaned not from his native informants—the librarian of the Charlestown public library and Sergeant Herbert E. Schultz of the Charlestown Police Station—but from a published source, *A Century of Town Life* by James F. Nunnewell (1888).

The other exception was the occasional writer who questioned the given categories. Otto Abrahamsen in Harwich defined "race" so that it applied across color and social location: from "the colored race . . . represented by the descendants of the Africans from the Cape Verde Islands, which in this generation, are a mixture of the African and the Mashpee Indian" to "the white race" and the "race" of summer visitors. Having established this schema, Abrahamsen could sustain inclusive representation in his assignments on community development and contemporary ethnic identity.[27] The most aggressively interrogative writer was Josef Berger in Provincetown. In complete contrast to the "not applicable" school, Berger named, queried, and hypothesized the causes of race-based absences. His paper on racial groups in Provincetown is a six-page rant on the lack of "any traceable heritage from the aboriginal race, the Pamets of the tribe of Wamphanoag," which explains their absence by detailing the grasping depredations of white settlers and apologias by white historians. He handled "Racial Cultural Heritage" by arguing that the same dominant society which robbed minority groups of their indigenous culture then plundered it for their own artistic glory. And he demonstrated that the retention of ethnic identity by contemporary groups had become almost impossible under the social, political, and economic pressures of American assimilation.[28]

These interrogations of guidebook categories could not, however, survive the editing process. When district supervisors passed field editorial copy up to the state office, state editors—most often Grace Kellogg, whose progressivism focused on gender more than race—condensed it into state editorial copy under five standard headings: History, Noted Citizens, Points of Interest, Cultural Agencies, and Recreational Facilities. Any material which did not fit those headings disappeared. Because race in and of itself was not recognized as a category, those "racial groups" deemed by local writers to produce neither "Cultural Heritage" nor "Community Development" also did not feed the history, noted citizens, or cultural agencies sought by state editors. Thus Carver, which in Louis McBay's field copy had "200 Cape De Verdeans" [*sic*] who made no impact on cultural heritage, community development, or contemporary ethnic identity, appears in the guide without racial markings, simply "a peaceful farming community" with a seventeenth-century battle site and an eighteenth-century house (535). The counter-history offered by Berger was too unconventional to fit the template, while Abrahamsen's racial scheme was thwarted when guidebook editors deleted the Cape Verdean Americans from Harwich but retained the information on summer visitors (592).

State editorial copy became, in turn, the raw material out of which Boston and Washington editors negotiated final copy for city and tour descriptions. By this stage, there was little material on Black Americans left to work with, plus which national editors (mainly Katharine Kellock) discovered that they needed to reduce the copy by more than half to meet the publishers' specifications.[29] Further cuts to Black details—among others—ensued. For example, Ermin Markella's specification of a Black Underground Railroad operator —"An educated Negro named Easton"—running a foundry in North Bridgewater was folded into a general statement about the community supporting abolition, which was assumed to be a dominantly white movement.[30] Roxbury, a Boston neighborhood, had appeared in Frank L. Gallagher's field copy as heavily Black, with thirty-four different kinds of African American religious expression, several Black churches, a memorial, and a settlement house, and Blacks as one of two races (the other, the Jews) which have "most thoroughly retained their ethnic identity."[31] In the final copy, state and national editors agreed to combine Roxbury with West Roxbury, Jamaica Plain, and Dorchester, defining the resulting area by class, not race: "a combined population of approximately 450,000, a large majority of them Boston's less well-paid workers" (137). The motor tour of South Boston, Roxbury, and Dorchester includes none of the Black sites listed by Gallagher.

In this production process, with its established categories and priorities, left-liberal editors further up the project hierarchy failed to value field specificity. Sometimes, at the eleventh hour, a state or national editor would add a generalization about race. For example, one editor added to the final copy on Boston two statements explicitly eschewing racial prejudice: "As for the legend of ethnic homogeneity [in Massachusetts' population], that is so much pernicious twaddle" (136), and "Boston is still the Boston of the Lowells, the Lodges, the Cabots, but it is from newer stocks that it derives much of its color, its hope, and its unquenchable vitality" (145). With the reduction in specific examples of "color," however, such statements read like token gestures, possibly the result of Sterling Brown's belated prompting.[32] They are also the mark of a double blindness in the project's perception of Black Massachusetts. Many field workers failed to see and bring alive the Black presence in their communities. State editors failed to recognize and encourage the contributions of those few who did.

AFRICAN AMERICANS IN THE GUIDE TO MASSACHUSETTS

In terms of attention to African Americans, then, the published guide to Massachusetts reads like so many of the state office announcements of 1936 and 1937—a promise deferred. Tantalizing glimpses of foundational Black activity come to nothing. For example, the first section of the guide—124 pages of essays—includes a single Black name: "Phillis Wheatley was one of a long line of Negro women of Massachusetts who contributed to the State's literature, art, and social movements" (6). Yet no Black women (or Black men) appear in "Literature," "Literary Groups and Movements," "Art," "Music and the Theater," or in any essay that touches on social conditions. There is, for example, no mention of Pauline Hopkins, the successful novelist and editor of *The Colored American Magazine* (1900–1904), who played a key role in the Black Boston renaissance, "a sustained attempt to develop an Afro-American popular fiction" (Carby xxix). Hopkins lived most of her life in Boston and died there in 1930. Nor is there attention to Maria Louise Baldwin, a native of Cambridge and "the first black principal in Massachusetts in 1889" (Richard Brown 219). According to the guide's essays, despite the token comment about "a long line of Negro women," the state had no African American writers or artists or social activists, historical or contemporary, worth mentioning.

The "High Roads and Low Roads" of the tour section contains two, equally embryonic, mentions in the smallest of print. Tucked into Tour 6, at Westport Mills, stands a memorial to Captain Paul Cuffee (1759–1817), "son of a freed Negro slave; Captain Cuffee, a Friend, amassed a fortune at sea and won important civil rights for his race when he successfully refused to pay the personal property tax, basing his refusal on his lack of citizenship rights; he was the first Negro to be granted all privileges enjoyed by white men in Massachusetts" (501). And Tour 25 stops in Somerset: "Henry Bowers, son of the founder of Somerset, purchased and brought home as a slave the son of an African chief. All efforts to tame his free wild spirit failed and he was shipped to sea. He made his escape at the island of Haiti and participated in the slave uprising then in progress there. The revolt was successful and he became emperor under the name of *Toussaint L'Ouverture*. In 1802, Napoleon's army overthrew his empire and he died in 1803 after a term of imprisonment in an Alpine dungeon" (618). Because the guide does not bring these founding moments of Black history to fruition, however, they remain historical curiosities without relevance to the present, their originary potential inert.

The few additional African Americans named in the guide provide "color" to critical moments in the white American narrative of history. We see glimpses of "a West Indian slave named Tituba" during the Salem witch-hunt hysteria (344) and "Peter Salem, the Negro slave" at the Battle of Bunker Hill (520). "Crispus Attucks, a mulatto" at the Boston Massacre is glimpsed both in the written text (435) and, perhaps, lying in the middle

Fig. 8. Print of Boston Massacre, courtesy of Goodspeed's Book Shop, Boston, in *Massachusetts: A Guide to Its Places and People*. Crispus Attucks may be the prone figure lying in the middle ground.

ground of an early print of the massacre included in the guide (Fig. 8). Not only are isolated Black figures slotted into a white historical narrative, Black history is told in overwhelmingly white terms. Although antislavery references and Underground Railroad stops appear frequently in the guide, they consistently mark white abolitionist activity. Frederick Douglass appears as an isolated Black abolitionist, cited in passing in the New Bedford and Springfield entries. There is neither Harriet Tubman nor William Wells Brown (nor, of course, the "educated Negro named Easton" recovered by Ermin Markella). No mention is made of the legal and constitutional educational struggles of Blacks in nineteenth-century Boston, nothing of nineteenth-century civil rights activists such as W. C. Nell or of twentieth-century politicians such as Julian D. Rainey.[33]

The lack of Blacks in the present era is even more complete. Only twice does the guide acknowledge a contemporary African American presence in

Fig. 9. "Seeding Clams," Commonwealth of Massachusetts, in *Massachusetts: A Guide to Its Places and People.*

the state. The Boston essay reports, "There are also in Boston 20,574 Negroes" (136), but then it does not document any of them. Among the "cosmopolitan" (393) population of Worcester, "the Negroes also form a definite group" (394). Again, however, we are told nothing of their occupations, neighborhoods or cultural activities. Instead, the Worcester entry reverts to the Black as historical curiosity, in this case a freak: "here the amazing P. T. Barnum gravely produced an ancient colored woman who he declared was George Washington's nurse—161 years old!" (393). Again, the guide's illustrations include one image of what may be Black workers in the present, with a photograph of clam-seeders whose ethnicity goes unnoted (Fig. 9). The Massachusetts guide provides eruptions of Blackness which, often disjunct from the main trajectory of the narrative, may give the current inquiring reader food for thought but offered little continuous information or commentary for the guidebook audience at the time.

There are hints of the suppressed awareness at work in this forgetting of the state's Black citizens—compensatory gestures in editorial statements, textual details, and moments of reception. First, there were the repeated protestations by state editors that Massachusetts would treat its Black citizenry more comprehensively than any other state. Then there are textual discordancies. Take, for example, the handling of Great Barrington, in the Berkshire Hills, the birthplace (and, in 1963, the chosen burial place) of W. E. B. Du Bois. Du Bois was a towering figure on the American scene with direct connections to the writers' project: prominent civil rights leader, author, editor, scholar, and cultural innovator, a hero to many New Dealers, his works cited as sources in Massachusetts project writings, his achievements honored many times in the WPA volume *New York Panorama*, an authority consulted by writers' project administrators, and proposer to them of an encyclopedia of African Americans. In *The Souls of Black Folk* (1903)—already a classic by the 1930s—Du Bois wrote of his coming of age as a Black boy in Great Barrington: "I remember well when the shadow swept across me. I was a little thing, away up in the hills between Hoosac and Taghkanic to the sea," and proceeded to tell the story of his social rejection "in a wee wooden schoolhouse" (2).[34] Yet Du Bois appears nowhere in the state guide or in any of the project's guides to the Berkshires. What does appear in the Great Barrington entry in *The Berkshire Hills* (1939) is a series of oddly toned references to Blacks disappearing into the past: the ghostly quarry workers, a minstrel performer from the 1840s,[35] and an 1857 foot race at Housatonic Fair. The last event is treated at some length. The race had three competitors, "two of them Negro boys"; "The committee 'experienced some embarrassment in regard to the first two prizes in view of the Dred Scott decision, the prizes having been taken by a couple of gentlemen who are not legally recognized as citizens, but another consideration overcame this scruple, that it was our duty to encourage the habit of running among a class who earn their freedom only by the best exercise of this power'" (163). The emphasis here is at odds with the main thrust of *The Berkshire Hills*, which usually eschewed stories of entertainment and display to detail the laboring lives obscured by tourism. The account also has the oddest echo of Du Bois's response to the color line in Great Barrington, as he articulated his attitude to his white classmates in *Souls of Black Folk*: "That sky was bluest when I could beat my mates at examination-time, or beat them at a foot-race, or even beat their stringy heads" (2).

A final sense of unease emerges in the guide's reception. When Bernard De Voto, another voice of cultural authority in the 1930s, published his highly eulogistic review of all six New England guides in the *Saturday Review of Literature*, he did not explicitly acknowledge the exclusion of Black figures and subjects. His comments on the Massachusetts guide, however, seem driven by the need to compensate for those omissions. De Voto managed to light on the only Massachusetts tour containing two references to African Americans in close conjunction. He emphasized the randomness of his act: "I thrust a finger into 'Massachusetts' and turn up page 433, part way along Tour 1C, 'From Beverly to Uxbridge.'" Here he encountered both Captain Kidd's treasure "guarded by the ghost of a murdered Negro" and Crispus Attucks. Protesting too much, De Voto reiterated: "That is a fair sample, an ordinary, unimportant tour" (14).

AFRICAN AMERICANS IN MASSACHUSETTS—BEYOND THE GUIDE

We can measure the depth of the guidebook's omissions by contrasting them with developments from 1938 onwards. By this time, the barrage of requests and reminders issuing from Sterling Brown's office had become a steady pressure, and they were not letting states with smaller Black populations off the hook: "it is our opinion that any contribution of the Negro in such a state, because of his scarcity, is all the more important."[36] As well as overseeing guide copy on African Americans, Brown was coordinating three national studies: "The Portrait of The Negro as American," "Go Down Moses: The Struggle Against Slavery"—a study of the Underground Railroad, which grew into a larger exploration of Black abolition activities—and "A Selective Bibliography on The Negro." The tiny team of African American employees—Glaucia B. Roberts plus, at different times, Ulysses Lee, Eugene Holmes, and Frank Sutch—collated material from the states, produced their own research, and wrote up drafts to varying degrees, while Brown remained the final author and editor. In 1940, Brown described "Portrait": "The Negro in America has been greatly written about, but most frequently as a separate entity, as a problem, not as a participant. . . . the Negro has too seldom been revealed as an integral part of American life."[37]

The "Portrait," in particular, produced a considerably different picture of Massachusetts from the guide. Names not significant enough to appear in the state essays achieved new prominence in the national context. For example, chapter 2, "The Struggle for Freedom," devotes several pages to Anthony Burns, a fugitive slave whose arrest in Boston in 1854 brought together Black demonstrators and white abolitionists, revitalizing attacks upon the Fugitive Slave Law. Other names that appear as passing curiosities in the guide appear here as crucial agents in the history of race and nation. Paul Cuffee becomes a major force in the antislavery struggle, the "first actual colonizer, who in 1815 transported and established 38 Negroes on the west coast of Africa." For the state guide, state and national editors had endlessly tinkered with the brief entry on Crispus Attucks—should they say he led protestors in the Boston Massacre, should they not?—finally producing the rather pallid phrasing, "Crispus Attucks, a mulatto resident of the town [Framingham], was a member—some historians say a leader —of the mob that attacked the King's soldiers in Boston on March 5, 1770" (435). In chapter 14 of "Portrait"—"At War"—Attucks cuts a much more unqualifiedly heroic figure: "leader of the attack made by Boston citizens upon British soldiers in the Boston Massacre (Mar. 5, 1770) and first American to die in behalf of American liberty." Most thought-provoking of all is the treatment of Phillis Wheatley in the draft chapter "Black Abolitionists." In itself, this focus was progressive, the dominant representation of abolitionism at that time (as in the guide) treating the movement as the achievement of white philanthropists.[38] The analysis in "Portrait" transforms Wheatley from the guide's token literary figure into a political catalyst whose poetry makes a crucial contribution to Black abolitionism: her "intensely race conscious" writings and her very existence were "a deadly blow" to the theory that "Negroes were not human beings at all, but only an especially useful type of beast of burden."[39] As part of this enriched representation of Black abolitionism, in 1938 Warren E. Thomson in the New Bedford office also wrote up the local Underground Railroad, including stories of Harriet Tubman, William Henry Johnson, and Henry Box Brown.

Alongside this activity in the Negro Affairs office, another major turning point came in 1938 with the appointment of Botkin and Royse. At times these editors explicitly collaborated with Brown—Brown and Botkin worked together on the ex-slave narratives, for example—but their influence was also more general. These men represented a new attitude to cultural diversity. They were interested in groups' social and cultural "participation," a less hierarchical, less closed, more dynamic and continuing measure than the traditional emphasis on groups' social and cultural "contribution."[40] Thirty years later, Royse described "the approach I tried to instill into some of our work—acculturation rather than the traditional melting-pot notion—a two-way street in terms of action and reaction."[41] The manuals for social-ethnic studies and for folklore studies, both issued in August 1938 and designed to complement each other, articulated paramount principles for the collection of material. It must involve "a staff of field workers drawn from the group or community being studied," and interviewers must maintain an attitude "of sympathy and respect" in working through the items in the very detailed and carefully measured questionnaires.[42]

A very significant dimension of the Botkin-Royse approach was their valuing of labor *as* culture. Their presence revitalized a cluster of labor-based projects, some of which had begun early in 1937 but had been scared off—at least in Massachusetts—by the Sacco-Vanzetti controversy. Using interviews and life histories as "a bridge between individual and group or community history," these projects were quintessentially interested in manual labor (Botkin 198). The project which began under Joseph Gaer as "The Condition of the Working Classes in New England" became variously retitled "How New England People Live" (Alsberg's reaction to the bruising fallout from the Sacco-Vanzetti debacle),[43] "Living in New England," "Working in New England," and "We Work in New England." At different times it was directed by Gaer, Frank Manuel, Horace B. Davis (a Marxist economist who, years later, was blacklisted by Joseph McCarthy's committee), and Merle Colby. Harold Rosenberg put together a book manuscript of interviews entitled "Men at Work." Royse spearheaded "We Work on the WPA." Botkin and Manuel planned "Living Lore in New England," designed to give voice to twenty ethnically different workers (McDonald 716); "This sharp break from the traditional approach to old Yankee stock would have revealed ethnic and racial interrelationships which, until then, had gone unnoticed" (Penkower 153).

It was in this context that the long-promised study "Negroes in Massachusetts" finally began to appear. The bulk of the extant papers were produced under the "Working in New England" project, and they consist of interviews with a range of Boston workers—Pullman porters, red caps, dining room waiters, elevator and utility men, women in the garment industry and in domestic service, WPA workers. In these materials, the city feels thick with contemporary Black presences. Interviews take place in stations, hotel lobbies, union halls, on the steps of Boston Public Library, on Boston Common. The careful documentation of numbers—350 to 400 Blacks in the garment industry in Boston, 350 red caps in Massachusetts—opens individual life histories into more general social patterns. Because interviews begin with work situations, there is much felt detail on union activity, on racial discrimination and paternalism, and on the complex tensions between gender and race solidarity and between ethnic groups within and across the color line. Some excoriating social criticism results: one West Indian immigrant comments: "the big joke to me is—calling the States, 'The Land of the Free and the Home of the Brave.' I'll take off my hat to anybody who can show me that burning and lynching people is free and brave."[44] Despite violent discrimination, there is a rich Black social scene, in the working heart of the city and in south end neighborhoods, especially Roxbury, which emerges as vibrant with Black cultural and political energy—clubs, politics, sports, intimate social and family relations.

The "Foreign Press in Massachusetts" project—headed up by Charles Goldenberg in the state office—also enabled workers to take note of Black cultural activity. In 1939 Zylpha Mapp—an African American worker who had been on the Massachusetts project since 1936—produced three papers on the late-nineteenth-century Black press: the *Boston Courant, Boston Republican,* and *Cambridge Advocate*. The archival research clearly affected Mapp in terms similar to Ralph Ellison's project experience in New York City. Ellison said that researching Black folklore "threw me into my own history" (qtd. in Banks xix). Mapp moved from documenting historical evidence of achievement and resistance, as well as differences within Black communities and between Blacks and others in Massachusetts society, to making her own political commentary about the present. For example, about the 1899 article "Color Line Can't Be Drawn in Public Houses of Our City," she comments: "It shows the feelings in the hearts of the Negro people against this bugaboo of prejudice, the battle they have been fighting unsuccessfully ever since the emancipation and one which will continue until the system of education is changed in this country."[45] Moreover, writings by non–African American project employees of this period suggest that the "integration" sought by Sterling Brown, the recognition of Black lives and culture within the American scene, was in process: evident, for example, in Otto Abrahamsen's paper "Slavery to 1830" and Myriam Sieve's "Servant, Negro, Indian regulations and conditions in provincial Massachusetts," both part of the "Social History of Massachusetts."[46]

None of the material on Blacks in Massachusetts produced from 1938 saw publication. When Alsberg was ousted in August 1939, Black cultural projects lost an important ally. John D. Newsom, the new national director, did not have his predecessor's appetite for innovative and potentially controversial undertakings, especially given the dependence of the reorganized writers' program on the goodwill of state administrations. Despite Manuel's prompting, the New England life histories gradually faded as a priority, revived only as a source of information for the War Division in 1943. Brown himself became unhappy in the reorganized project, suspecting discrimination against himself and his remaining assistant, Glaucia Roberts, and anxious that he was about to lose authorial control over the national African American studies.[47] In mid-1940, Brown resigned.

NATIVE AMERICANS

I could have titled this section "Identity in Mashpee: An Addendum from the Thirties" in homage to James Clifford's brilliant study of the landmark case in 1977 when Mashpee Wampanoag of Cape Cod went to court to establish their tribal identity (a fight that, at least for the moment, they have lost). Clifford's account demonstrates the numerous cultural conventions which feed the construction of collective identity—censuses, government structures, academic disciplines, public images—the power interests which inform those conventions, and the material consequences which, sooner or later, follow from those constructions. The American Guide Series participated in that process of identity-making—in some respects challenging, in other respects reinforcing assumptions about cultural identities such as "American," "Yankee," "Indian," "Negro." The Massachusetts Writers' Project's representation of the state's Native peoples was very different from its treatment of African Americans, though that difference often amounted to absence of a different order. The number of Native Americans employed on the writers' project nationwide was tiny—I have not been able to identify any Native employees in Massachusetts—and they never had the kind of visible lobbying afforded African Americans by Sterling Brown. In the early days of the project, D'Arcy McNickle, a Cree/Salish and Kootenai writer from Montana, served as editor of Indian Affairs in Washington. However, he left the project in 1936 for a position he had long sought in John Collier's Bureau of Indian Affairs, the New Deal agency of choice for many Native Americans. On the recommendation of Franz Boas, leadership then passed to Edward Kennard, a non-Native liberal anthropologist from Columbia University who specialized in Hopi culture. The title of the national position changed to editor of Indians and Archaeology.[48]

That shift made its mark on the American Guide Manual governing the collection and writing up of guidebook data. From the beginning, the central office mandated at least one essay in each state guide dedicated to the Native peoples. The first version of the manual classified the topic as "Indian Tribes and Reservations," and supplementary instructions carried the title "Indians and Indian Life." Six months later, however, a new supplement yoked Indians to archaeology. The requisite guide essay, titled "First Americans," was subtitled "Archeology and Indians" and occupied a separate category from the essay titled "History," whose first subsection focused on culture contact from the European perspective: "Explorers, traders, trappers, missionaries, early settlement." Meanwhile, Shipton's state office schematized assignments for district supervisors and field workers according to the same antiquarian logic. Under the title "Archeology and Ethnology," assignments required writers to document "Earliest human remains," "Indian remains," and "Names of Indian Origin," while the only assignment to acknowledge Natives as living presences tucked them into a catch-all topic as "remnants": "Indians: History and anthropology, reservations, tribal remnants not on reservations."[49] Although subsequent guidelines addressed the present—"Archeology and the history of the Indians should be woven into a continuous story brought down to the present day where there exist distinct Indian groups"—the classificatory system had already irretrievably assigned Indians to the past.[50]

The effects on collection and composition were predictable. Field workers conscientiously detailed known information about the seven tribes of the area—the Massachusetts, Wampanoags, Nausets, Pennacooks, Nipmucks, Pocumtucs, and Mohicans—and most of them avoided the racist language against which Washington editors had warned them: "In speaking of conflicts between Indians and white men, do not call every Indian victory a 'cruel massacre of whites,' and every white aggression 'a courageous and noble defense of homes.'"[51] But the sites, events, names, legends, and known figures all belong to long-dead peoples. There is no sense of writers grappling with difference in the present.

The published guide shows the density of Native marks on the Massachusetts landscape: traces of Indian habitation and legends abound in city descriptions, motor tours, and foot tours; innumerable place names derive from Native words; and tales of white settlement consistently acknowledge the aggression of the invaders. Conrad Aiken's description of Deerfield—a piece whose experimental voice was championed by state editors but scathingly critiqued by the central office—is suffused with the memory of genocide: the town "is, and will probably always remain, the perfect and beautiful statement of the tragic and creative moment when one civilization is destroyed by another. . . . 'I dared to be beautiful, even in the shadow of the wilderness'; but it is also saying, 'And the wilderness haunts me, the ghosts of a slain race are in my doorways and clapboards, like a kind of death'" (223). Indeed, the liberal acknowledgment of culpability is one of the guide's most consistent notes: "One of the blacker pages in the history of the relations of the colonists and the Indians is the chronicle of English treatment of the Christianized Naticks" (25–26).

At the same time, however, the guidebook text puts writers and readers into a paternalistic relationship with Native peoples, one that infantilizes them by removing the possibility of agency. The essay "First Americans"—on which the consultant was a Harvard professor of anthropology, B. A. Hooten—repeatedly puts the reader in the position of knowing more than Native actors. The highly detailed account is framed as "almost the last act of a tragic drama" (20), filled with proleptically tragic figures: Samoset "had learned a few words of English . . . and he spoke them with unconscious drama, unaware that they spelled the doom of his race" (22); "Massasoit, chief of the Wampanoags, whose favorite residence was at Pokanoket (Mount Hope, Bristol, Rhode Island), a spot which was to witness the death not only of his son Philip but of the hopes of his race" (22). The impression that editors were veering toward what Umberto Eco calls "nostalgic remorse"—the method by which American culture repeatedly comforts itself for its subjugation of minorities—is exacerbated by the opening of the following essay, "Enough of Its History to Explain Its People," which asserts that the state's history begins with Martin Luther and his legacy to the Pilgrims. It could not be clearer that the Native peoples are the history which is to be left behind. Hard as these liberal accounts work to respect the Native peoples' presence, they also become complicit in their erasure.

Within the frames of reference set by the guidebook of 1937—as in those set by the federal courtroom of 1977—the Mashpee Indians lost their identity. All sources—published authorities, local historians, field writers' "personal observation," project editors—agreed that the distinctive population of Mashpee, widely recognized as an "Indian town," was of a mixed ethnicity deriving predominantly from the Wampanoag, Cape Verde Islanders, Portuguese, and African Americans. The problem was that the guide's classificatory system provided no easy way of writing about hybridity. For decades, "Mashpee's unabashedly mixed population" had defied governmental categories (Hutchins 141). Francis Hutchins describes the efforts of federal enumerators:

> In 1840, when the choices were only "colored" or "white," it had been fairly easy to describe everyone in Mashpee as one or the other. . . . Then, in 1860, Mashpee's "colored" became predominantly "Indian"; in 1870, Mashpee's "Indians" became predominantly "black"; in 1880, Mashpee's "blacks" became predominantly "mulatto." . . . in 1900, Mashpee's "mulattoes" once again became "Indian." Mashpee residents may have found it amusing to be told every ten years that they belonged to some new category, but for whites

> determining racial classifications was a deadly serious business. . . . If Mashpee residents were "really" black or mulatto, this would tend to lump them with southern slaves; if they were "really" Indian, they could be supposed to resemble the "wild" Indians of the west. (141–43)

For the guidebook, Emma A. Paulding was assigned the topic of racial elements in Mashpee. Her field copy on "Racial Groups" visibly struggles to shape the material to the narrative of tragically vanished Natives: "The last pure-blooded Indian departed about 1800, and the racial group in Mashpee at the present time is an infusion of the African negro, the Cape Verdean, and the Portuguese. Few of these now retain any particular ethnic identity." In a clearly class-inflected understanding of "culture," she distances them from that quantity. Under "Relationship of Racial Groups to Community Development," she writes that, because of interracial intermarriage, "the inhabitants of Mashpee at the present time show little cultural tendency. They are unskilled laborers and earn their living as carpenters, painters, or as 'hands' on the cranberry bogs and the shell-fish beds, farm hands, and berry pickers." Cultural heritage and the retention of ethnic identity she deems "Not applicable." Finally, writing up the town history, she allows herself the judgmental commentary that the guide manual had asked writers to avoid: "The Mashpee Indians were a poor, lazy and improvident lot"; "At the present time, there are about 380 inhabitants, a mixture by intermarriage of the Indian, Cape Verdean, and African negro, a shiftless and ambitionless lot."[52] These comments came at the very time that the Mashpees were working toward increased visibility for their distinctiveness, with the founding of the Wampanoag Nation in 1928, tribal meetings and "Indian Day" services reported in 1930s' newspapers, and the controversial public induction of Governor Michael Curley into the "Mashpee Tribe" in 1936 (Clifford 291; Hutchins 151).

State and national editors deleted the negative comments, but did no better a job of accepting these hybrid people in their own terms as complex contemporary presences. In addressing the "only two places in Massachusetts where the Indians have been able to preserve a semblance of their ethnic identity: Mashpee and Gay Head," the guide treats both as remnants of a more authentic purity. The Native people of Gay Head, on Martha's Vineyard, "have kept their racial stock more nearly pure here than elsewhere," yet their commerce in pottery shows only how far they have fallen: "The sale of these souvenirs by silent Indian children waiting by the roadside for the hordes of summer tourists is the last reminder of a primitive culture that could not survive the rape of its free forests and wide lands" (27). In developing the Mashpee copy, Grace Kellogg dropped the individual Native names supplied by Paulding. Kellogg apparently considered Simon Popmonet, Ebenezer Attaquin, Daniel B. Amos, Rev. William Apes, Eben Attaquin, and Reuben Cognehew ineligible to sit with Richard Bourne, the seventeenth-century missionary to the Mashpee people, within the category "Noted Citizens." Then the authors of the guidebook essay "First Americans" attempted to connect these hybrid people to the present by mounting their familiar class analysis. The result reduced the Mashpee to a diminished people who embody the stages toward extinction: "the real sight in Mashpee is the cranberry bogs, the principal support of the town, which belong mostly to the white non-residents who employ the Indians as pickers. In the season, bending their backs over the bog, can be seen the half-breed descendants of the proud and friendly savages who once roamed the windswept dunes of Cape Cod" (26).

Black writers and scholars, in the 1930s and since, have acknowledged the importance of the Federal Writers' Project to Black cultural communities. Thadious Davis, for example, has argued that "a generation of Black writers became professional writers largely due to their work experiences with the federal writers' project and their social experiences with writers involved in that project." She cites Richard Wright and Ralph Ellison on the crucial impact of Sterling Brown's program of Black research. Despite the fact that only one of Brown's planned volumes (*The Negro in Virginia*) saw publication, involvement in his vast research program "allowed many Negroes to achieve their identities as artists."[53] Arna Bontemps has talked of the project supporting the development of "the social consciousness of the 'WPA black writers' school'" (Penkower 147). Norman R. Yetman judges that the ex-slave narrative collection "today stands as one of the most enduring and noteworthy achievements of the WPA." Sterling Brown himself "later argued that states took blacks more seriously because of the guides and the 'collateral' publications which followed" (Penkower 143).

At least in its early years, the Massachusetts project was not one of the high points in WPA support for Black culture. The state office promised more than it produced, and it failed to prioritize Black projects. The case of Massachusetts does, however, graphically demonstrate—and may well have helped to bring home to Black writers—what it took to change Eurocentric priorities. The editorial processes detailed in this chapter, when read in the context of dominant attitudes to race in the 1930s, show, first, that change depended on writers questioning established categories of identity—as did Josef Berger and Otto Abrahamsen in one way, the little-known African Americans Ernest E. Ormsby and Harry O. Bowles in another. Second, members of the underrepresented community needed to occupy positions of authority if their voices were to make a difference. Sterling Brown had that authority as national Negro Affairs editor, though the underresourcing of his office undercut his efforts to a degree. The Black interviewers and interviewees who recorded working lives of Massachusetts in the project's later years gained authority of voice in a different sense. Once those two conditions were in place, by 1938, a much richer version of Black culture in Massachusetts began to emerge.

That two-part change never did happen with respect to the Native peoples of the state. Fewer writers, even, questioned classifications and cultural assumptions in their field copy on Native peoples than on African Americans. Josef Berger went furthest in parlaying resistance to given categories into a more inclusive representation of Aboriginal and mixed-race peoples in his unconventional guide *Cape Cod Pilot*. But the project did not endow members of the Native American community with leadership positions, and Berger's initiative was not pursued statewide. Without counter-authority from within the minority group, there was no challenge to the Massachusetts state editors' priorities, and the relationship to Native subjects remained paternalistic and partial.

Ultimately, the details of the editorial process suggest to me a deeply buried process of suppression, a resistance to surrendering cultural authority, operating at the level of editors' classificatory and organizational practices in ways which were at odds with their conscious, articulated ideologies. It was one thing to speak out on behalf of murdered Italian American workers; it was quite another to hand over voice and agency to those who still existed, in the present, beyond the color line.

5

"WORKER-WRITERS" ON THE WPA: NEW BEDFORD TO PROVINCETOWN

> Writers have been out of work; they have been on relief and on the W.P.A.; they have gone on strike for their own demands; they have picketed not only in sympathy with workers in other fields but for themselves; they have organized mass demonstrations, been arrested and beaten; they have sent delegations to Washington and negotiated with their employers. Their experience at work, out of work, and in their trade unions has been the experience of other American workers.
>
> Joseph Freeman, "Toward the Forties" (1937)

Being a writer on the WPA wasn't always the heroic experience that Joseph Freeman celebrates here. In response to the Second American Writers' Congress, in 1937, Freeman evoked the standard 1930s' version of "worker-writers," a term coined by Jack Conroy at the Congress two years earlier.[1] This vision assumed that the Works Progress Administration empowered writers by aligning them with laborers, folding them into the celebration of physical labor promoted by the New Deal, an assumption which reverberated widely both at that political moment and in more recent discussions. A unique cache of papers from the New Bedford district office of the Massachusetts Writers' Project makes it possible to test that assumption by reconstructing the experience of the largest but least examined group of writers on the project—the lowly field workers. Their stories suggest that bringing together the categories of worker and writer under New Deal sponsorship was a much less seamless, less heroic, and less masculinist operation than Freeman and others assumed. For many of these writers-in-the-making, WPA classification provoked contradictory class allegiances, tensions between local loyalties and federal directives, and challenges to their community identities. The most powerful local writing resulted from those who most fully embraced their status as workers, but that position was not easily or most commonly achieved.

Both the rhetoric and the employment conditions of the writers' project stressed its blue-collar orientation. When critics challenged Harry Hopkins, WPA administrator, to justify the inclusion of writers in a relief agency primarily aimed at manual labor, he delivered the famously throwaway remark: "Hell, artists got to eat, just like other people" (qtd. in Mangione, *Dream* 4). He also headed up a system whereby writers were paid hourly wages, their output was measured in terms of quantitative "productivity," they did not own the fruits of their labor, and they came to have the right to unionize.[2] Some highly politicized units—New York City is the most obvious example—and ideologically schooled writers—such as Richard Wright and Jack Conroy—did succeed in using the WPA as a launching pad for the kinds of resistant activity listed by Freeman and for the forging of a proletarian style, thereby cementing solidarity with the working classes. Michael Denning and Michael Szalay have analyzed how inclusion in the category of wage-earning worker enabled these writers' political engagements. Denning has explored how the introduction of plebian artistry into a state apparatus contributed to the wholesale "laboring of American culture." Szalay has shown how the project organized radical writers into a professionalized collective which participated in and to some degree shaped "the reinvention of modern governance."[3]

But the writers who were most literally enmeshed in the apparatus of the New Deal welfare state—that is, the vast majority of writers funded by the WPA—were not proletarian authors with their political commitments and literary styles forged on the barricades, and they did not have the ideological agency and metaphorical facility of the more famous cases studied by Denning and Szalay. The writers' project reached more broadly across greater numbers of employees than any U.S. arts program before or since and more deeply into the population, using a capacious definition of "writer" in its criteria for eligibility. Very many project employees were white- or pink-collar workers who had not previously been classified as writers, did not have strongly articulated ideologies of authorship, and hence came to forge public identities as writers under the impress of government sponsorship. That was certainly true of the assortment of employees—the white-collar destitute, widows, impoverished gentility—in New Bedford and vicinity. Here, I reconstruct the project experiences and writings of five employees from in and around New Bedford: Leroy Bradford, James McKenna, Julia Keane, Elsie Moeller, and Nellie Coombs. Their conflicted experiences become starker in comparison with three atypical employees attached to the New Bedford district office whom I more briefly characterize: Josef Berger, George Willison, and Carl Malmberg, who had developed authorial personas prior to joining the project and worked out of Provincetown. These reconstructions suggest that WPA employment was more often in tension than in solidarity with working-class practices. The dynamics of government bureaucracy most often left these employees stranded between the categories of worker and writer, attempting (with limited success) to negotiate a resolution in both their social and their narrative positions.

NEW BEDFORD

New Bedford, in southeastern Massachusetts, was a town twice depressed before the Depression, with the failure first of its whaling industry in the nineteenth century and then of its cotton textile mills in the early twentieth. Seymour Louis Wolfbein has labeled it "a typical example of a depressed one-industry city" (12). More recently, and more colorfully, Sebastian Junger wrote: "If Gloucester [Massachusetts] is the delinquent kid who's had a few scrapes with the law, New Bedford is the truly mean older brother who's going to kill someone one day" (77–78). Certainly, the dominant industries engendered tough public rhetorics of labor: first the hellish working conditions of whaling converted into individualistic bravado—"A Dead Whale Or A Stove Boat" declares the bronze sculpture still dominating City Hall square—then the rise of the cotton textile mills with their images of collective labor, turned militant in the textile strike of 1928. The strike split apart New Bedford's workers—and their allies—along the division between "skilled" and "unskilled," terms that also coded differences of ethnicity, religion, class, and gender. That polarization echoed down the years. It came to bear directly on the social positioning of the writers' project in New Bedford because out of the conflict came the most visible and available public images of collective labor .

Two unions organized strikers. The Textile Council was the locally established craft union of mainly Anglo and Celtic skilled workers (spinners, weavers, loomfixers) who had good press relations and time-honored ways of negotiating with mill owners (themselves from the same ethnic group). During the 1928 strike, the Textile Mill Committees came to New Bedford: CIO organizers from New York City and Boston, to support the unskilled workers—mainly Portuguese, Cape Verdean, Polish, many female and child laborers—who were previously without union voice or strike relief.[4] The Textile Mill Committees met strong opposition from the Textile Council and the local press, denounced (in terms familiar from the Red Scare years) as "outside agitators," "bloody foreigners," and "radicals."[5] Ultimately, the strike collapsed. In Wolfbein's judgment: "Although New Bedford had a long history of labor organization behind it, the disastrous strike of 1928 and the unemployment which followed it had broken the militant labor spirit in the city" (115).

When the WPA came to New Bedford in 1935, its employment figures made it tantamount to New Bedford's third dominant industry.[6] However, it also represented another incursion into the local organization of labor, now at the hands of federal government, and the agency did not sit easily within the established codes of work. Although elsewhere WPA work was celebrated in the conventional terms of productivity (especially by Washington officials seeking renewed appropriations from Congress), that rhetoric never took hold in New Bedford where, as relief, WPA employment was always socially stigmatized, the sign of failure and dependency on public handouts. Yet it also lacked the tools to promote radical or oppositional solidarities: at least in the early days, employees were denied the rights of collective bargaining and withdrawal of labor, on pain of being struck off the dole.[7] The New Bedford WPA came to be publically celebrated as the linking of the local and the federal, not along the axis of workers' rights or the dignity of labor but along a chain of governmentality, one agency echoing and celebrating another. On New Bedford WPA Day, September 23, 1936, the WPA state administrator came down from Boston to eulogize the display of labor: "Here one can see the results of careful municipal planning and close Federal cooperation. . . . Let me remind you that it was no Federal official who laid out and initiated the projects we have seen today. It was Mayor Ashley and his department heads representing the City of New Bedford."[8]

The WPA Writers' Project was even less assimilable to local images of labor and community. New Bedford contained the office for district 4 of the writers' project which, from 1935 to 1939, had responsibility for Bristol, Plymouth, Barnstable, and Dukes and Nantucket Counties. When the project began, the local press lampooned the initiative with a nationally syndicated cartoon by Herblock: "When the Job Relief Plan for Writers

Goes Through" (Fig. 10). More local mockery took the form of bad rhyming couplets: "Landing Jobs Not Hard If You're an A-1 Bard":

> Can you build verse? As bad or slightly worse than average rhyme? You can? That's fine. You're [*sic*] living's fixed; depression's jinxed! For Uncle Sam, Santa Claus man, has found a novel way to make the world more gay; a brand new scheme to spend his jack, keeping a shirt on each poet's back.
>
> He plans to hire word rhyming smiths, clever, long haired meterists. For poets must live from sun to sun as well as curbing setters, masons or anyone.[9]

These jokes trade on the rhetoric of labor which leads directly to the policing of norms—of class, race, sexuality, gender—and has long held sway in national debates about arts funding. Lewis Hyde has traced the history of U.S. public funding discourse, showing how conceits of both productivity and dependency feed normative binaries: "productivity and utility are heterosexual virtues, and any argument in favor of art turns out to be an argument against heterosexual love and its social embodiment, the family. This is nuts, of course, but that doesn't mean it carries no political weight" (268). By these assumptions, work which is not productive in utilitarian terms (that is to say, not "virile," not normative) is associated with gays (or "effeminates"), Blacks, feminists, members of political minorities. At the same time, dependency is always gendered female, and all of this links up with an image of literary production as an effeminate aesthetic, so to have writers drawing on the public purse is triply outrageous. There is also a classed separation of these categories: effeminate, unproductive, unskilled writers don't belong in the same classification as virile, skilled, blue-collar laborers. Both the form and the content of the newspaper mockery demonstrate the absurdity in any scheme which shortcircuits those normative divisions to bring the two together. Positioned within the WPA, particularly in a community that closely linked productivity and manual labor, stranded somewhere beyond the recognized categories of labor, the work of the New Bedford Writers' Project largely sank into invisibility both in the press and in the agency's local publicity, not even on display during WPA Day.[10]

By September 1936, however, New Bedford had a bustling office, with a district supervisor, G. Leroy Bradford, and a workforce of fifty-six: forty-three on the writers' project and thirteen on the historical records survey. Just over twenty employees were residents of New Bedford and its near-

Fig. 10. Cartoon, copyright 1935, by Herblock in the *NEA*. *New Bedford Standard-Times* August 14, 1935.

suburb Fairhaven, across the Acushnet Inlet. Their public invisibility partly resulted from their own unease with their situation. Most employees refused the label "WPA writer" in the public record—not surprising, perhaps, given how uncomfortably the category sat within local rhetorics of labor and how enmeshed it was within long-standing community tensions and suspicion of "outsiders." Only two workers in the local office listed themselves as writers in the biannual municipal enumeration, and only one of them explicitly attached her role to the writers' project, while the rest self-identified via their organizational roles—"supervisor," "secretary," "clerk"—without office designation.

The marks made by WPA employment on the public spaces of these employees' lives are graphic. The disposition of living space—then and to some extent now—in New Bedford is fairly stark. The north and south ends of the town are crammed with mill housing, clustered around the mills—now decayed—that employed the inhabitants of these multiple-family dwellings (Fig. 11). Many of the employees in the New Bedford Writers' Project were born and bred locally and had started life in that mill housing, rising socioeconomically via newspaper employment, teaching, or office work, to rent their own individual family dwellings, oftentimes across the river in Fairhaven, a smaller, less industrialized town with larger lots, wider streets, more green spaces, and a less dense population (Fig. 12). At least one inhabitant remembers Fairhaven as something of a refuge. Jack Custodio was a Cape Verdean American, the doubly displaced Afro-Portuguese whose defining experience in America, according to Marilyn Halter's analysis, was the "discomfort of not belonging, the invisibility of residing between race and ethnicity" (xiv). Custodio, who had a long history on the receiving end of racism in New Bedford and elsewhere, said: "I loved Fairhaven. At that time, Fairhaven was tolerant of particularly Cape Verdeans in the context of Portuguese" (qtd. in Halter 167).

When the writers' project office was established, it was initially put in the Mary B. White School in north end New Bedford, alongside other blue- and white-collar WPA projects. The school—no longer extant—was pressed in on all sides by mill housing. Going to work for some project employees meant, quite literally, crossing back over to their earlier class and race environment, a rather graphic symbol of their precarious financial condition in the midst of the Depression. These were, after all, people who had been existing on local relief provisions and were now on a program that was constantly experiencing job cuts.[11] At one point, when the state office chivvied Bradford for turning in tour copy too slowly, he tried to give Boston editors a sense of local economic conditions: "The truth of the matter is that no one has received any transportation expense in two months and as a result, few if any of our decrepit cars are available at the present time. The need of new tires, batteries, etc. can be met as soon as one or two checks are received."[12] In weekly field reports, pencil-written scrawls indicated that local writers had run out of writing materials, index cards, even paper clips, and neither they nor the district office had funds for refurbishment. In this precarious con-

Fig. 11. The South End of New Bedford, Massachusetts, 1985. Photograph by Joseph B. Thomas, courtesy of Spinner Publications.

Fig. 12. Center Street, Fairhaven. From the Collection of the Millicent Library, Fairhaven.

text, employees' self-identification as petty bureaucrats can be read as their bulwark against not only the stigma of WPA employment but also the long slide back to blue-collar labor.

The threat of reduced status certainly affected Bradford who, as district supervisor, was the most immersed of all the local employees in the writers' project work and culture. Before the Depression, Bradford was something of a local dignitary, first as a newspaperman on the *New Bedford Times* and the *Morning Mercury*, during the period when the *Times* had claimed to broker the 1928 strike, throwing its weight behind the Textile Council and against the Textile Mill Committees. He himself had won a little local fame for organizing a group of New Bedford men on a fishing trip whose catch was distributed to the families of mill strikers.[13] His public profile continued to rise as he chaired the New Bedford reception committee for visiting notables, stood twice as Republican candidate for state representative from the 7th Bristol District, and the like. Meanwhile, his material circumstances seemed also to improve, as he moved from mill housing in south New Bedford in the early 1920s to a series of increasingly substantial houses and somewhat wealthier neighborhoods in Fairhaven, where he lived with his family until his death in 1959.[14]

On the writers' project, however, Leroy Bradford's public role slipped from representing the local community to brokering its relations with government at various levels, a middleman hemmed in administratively and editorially by a host of bureaucratic directives.[15] He oversaw the implementation of directives handed down by the state office, judged when work was ready to pass back up to that level, mediated conflict among field workers, and sought the advice of local consultants—part of the bigger job of trying to win public sympathy for the project, and one which involved a great deal of diplomacy and conciliation. Competing imperatives came at him from all sides. For example, urged by national and state editors to highlight labor organization and industrial action, Bradford approved the write-up of New Bedford by James McKenna, a local writer with inside experience of the textile unions.[16] The field editorial copy allotted several pages to the textile strike of 1928, not only empathizing with the workers but asserting "the solidarity of the entire community with the strikers' cause."[17] When Bradford sent this material out to the voluntary consultant, William H. Tripp, curator of the Old Dartmouth Historical Society, however, the response had a different cast: "I think altogether too much prominence and too much space has been given to the textile strike of 1928. It would be a pity to advertise New Bedford in that way. There is now far too much unrest and trouble between capital and labor to stir up more strife."[18]

Although, at the federal level, the project boasted of its adventure in cooperation and collectivity, the vertical relations of bureaucracy distanced Bradford from clear alliances with any group. He corresponded with colleagues and community members in an estranged, contained voice, repeatedly speaking in the name of federal authority, "the directors of the project," and "the government," enforcing bureaucratic imperatives and the government's ownership of all project writing. Although he championed the writers in his district, he also internalized protocols and procedures to such a degree that he bore down more draconianly than the state editor required on writers' tendencies to "editorialize."[19] His rare recourse to the personal voice was primarily to protest his impotence, for example in denying reemployment to veteran newspaperman Clarence W. Ryder of Wellfleet. Ryder, by then over eighty, found himself usurped as recorder of his local community by Carl Malmberg, the much younger writer without residence, roots, or what Ryder called "local knowledge" in Wellfleet.[20] Bradford explained to Ryder that, personally, especially given his own career history, he would prefer to assign a resident and ex-newspaperman. However, "There are as you can imagine restrictions and regulations which made it impossible for me to name you when a certified WPA worker was available for your community."[21] Behind the scenes, Bradford was speaking up for Ryder, whom Muriel Hawks eventually reinstated.[22] The telling point is that the only public persona available to a project manager was one of personal impotence in the face of government regulations.

James McKenna, who wrote the field copy on New Bedford, also became contained by government pressures, but in a different sense. He came to the project with more experience of labor organization than any other employee. In 1928, he had served as secretary to the United Textile Workers Union, which had joined with the Textile Council with the support of the American Federation of Labor. On the project, he initially sustained the persona of union man, inflecting his field copy with union sympathies and playing a significant role in attempts to unionize project writers. Yet his class allegiances began to shift when he was appointed supervisor of the local historical records survey. He distanced himself from the union and produced "Narrative Reports" which documented the local accomplishments of the WPA in terms so praising of both municipal and federal management that the state administrator used them in his eulogy on WPA Day. Less than a year later, he parlayed his position into a different kind of political opportunity: he left the project in 1937 to become secretary to Mayor Carney of New Bedford, soon adding WPA coordinator to his duties.[23] McKenna's residential pattern traces his rise. He moved with his wife from cramped conditions in the west end of New Bedford in 1928, to occupy a small wooden bungalow in Fairhaven, then to return to a new, custom-built apartment building close to City Hall in New Bedford with his new position in 1937. Soon, however, he found himself embroiled—with the mayor and the rest of his entourage—in scandal. Indicted by the Bristol County grand jury for larceny, bribes, and kickbacks, he was finally acquitted eighteen months later, only soon to die of a heart attack at age forty-one.[24]

When we match the lived complexities of gender as well as class against Freeman's heroic vision of the WPA worker-writer, the gap increases. The case of Mrs. Julia Keane, another Fairhaven neighbor who joined the project in 1936, is paradigmatic in its evasions and contradictions. From 1932 Julia Keane makes frequent appearances in the local press, in her various public duties as American Legion Auxiliary clubwoman: serving as president of Fairhaven Post 166, then of the Bristol County Council unit, being installed at the state convention, fulfilling public speaking engagements, traveling as delegate to local and national meetings. Keane was a self-supporting widow with one son, and her strong identification with the legion can be understood to solidify the class position signaled by her move (apparently around the time she joined the project) from a rooming house in New Bedford to a one-and-a-half story duplex in Fairhaven.[25] According to William Pencak, "Most Legionnaires were middle-class—self-employed businessmen or clerical, skilled, and professional workers" (16). The women's auxiliary functioned as the good works arm of the American Legion and lacked its quasi-militaristic structures. Nevertheless, to progress through committee ranks as Julia Keane did was necessarily to function within a climate which fiercely policed the limits of "Americanism," with particular virulence directed at any kind of leftist affiliation. Given the project's local image, it is not surprising that Keane kept her employment out of her public biography. During her three years on the project, she not only consistently entered herself as "stenographer" in the *New Bedford and Fairhaven Directory*, she managed to keep her considerable press coverage completely silent on her WPA employment. Her initial project classification was "writing assistant," a position involving mainly administrative duties. It took some time for her to find her voice on the project and when she did, it came directly out of the tension between her two identities, as clubwoman and WPA writer.

The one New Bedford employee who identified as a project writer in the public record from the beginning was Elsie S. Moeller. Like Julia Keane,

Elsie Moeller was a single parent, but in very different circumstances. After accompanying her husband—an artillery captain—for three years on military service in the Canal Zone, Panama, she was left destitute when he disappeared in Oregon in 1925, deserting her and their young son. Moeller's experience sounds traumatic. First hounded by the local newspapers about her husband's disappearance, then suing to divorce a man whom she wasn't sure still lived, she then discovered, on applying for WPA work in 1936, that she had lost her citizenship. Lacking proof that her husband was a U.S. citizen, she had to repatriate in order to qualify for welfare. In all of this she managed to cling to her social standing. She returned to New Bedford in 1925 to live in genteel shabbiness with her maiden aunts, the Snows, one of the city's oldest families with well-respected abolitionist credentials, whose spacious property is tucked just west of the millionaires' mansions on "the hill" in central New Bedford.[26] Moeller was initially employed by the historical records survey, then, again like Keane, joined the writers' project as a "writer's assistant." In 1938, producing social-ethnic copy under Morton Royse's guidelines, she graduated to professional status. Having thought of herself as a writer from the outset, she was understandably delighted by the endorsement.[27] In later life, by dint of enrolling with a vanity press, she became one of the few from the New Bedford office to publish her own book. By the time she died in 1958—snugly lodged in Mattapoisett, a summer resort east of New Bedford, "in a tiny cottage on the edge of a golf course overlooking Buzzards Bay"—she was established as a local writer and artist (Moeller, Jacket Note).

PROVINCETOWN

Meanwhile, down in Provincetown a very different group was assembling, with a different attitude to the project, to their own identities as writers, and to their locale. Provincetown was a smaller community with a population just over 4,000, compared to more than 120,000 in New Bedford and Fairhaven. Its generous harbor accounted for its long history as a fishing village, dominated first by English, then by Portuguese (and a few Cape Verdean) immigrants. Since the late nineteenth century, the town had also housed a distinct artists' colony. First visual artists, then writers and theater people had been attracted to its cheapness, its relative isolation, and its sheer beauty, perched on the edge of a tiny spur of land pointing out into the Atlantic. By the 1930s, Provincetown was famous for fostering such names as Eugene

O'Neill, Sinclair Lewis, John Dos Passos, Susan Glaspell, and Mary Heaton Vorse and for enabling the creation in 1915 of the Provincetown Players. This experimental theater group subsequently moved to New York City where, in the 1920s, Henry Alsberg worked with them as producer and member of their advisory board. After the First World War, with the advent of automobiles and state highways, Provincetown also became massively popular as a summer tourist destination. At the same time, "the boom days of fishing had stopped with the war," so the tourist trade increasingly became the main source of income for townspeople (Vorse 283).

The distinct groups within the community experienced both a degree of interdependency and felt tensions. Mary Heaton Vorse, who became a long-time resident of Provincetown but never did "belong," humorously exposes some of the friction between local laborers and artists. She tells of the Provincetowner who cordially equates the "leper colony down to Pasque" with the art colony "down to Provincetown." And she quotes Mrs. Enos, wife of the fisherman who fell from his roof and took to painting clamshells for tourists: "'Go'dammit,' said Mrs. Enos, ''s lucky he fell down the right side of the roof. If he'da fell down the left side he mighta been a writer instead,' so voicing in one pregnant sentence a section of public opinion in Provincetown concerning writers and painters" (210–11).

In the 1930s, Josef Berger, George Willison, and Carl Malmberg moved to Provincetown, the first two from the Rocky Mountain states and all three via New York City.[28] All had published fiction, nonfictional prose, and journalism, and each had decided to withdraw to a location where the standard of living and the artistic climate might enable him to focus on his writing. Berger in particular became committed to documenting the skills, culture, and living conditions of the fishing community around him. By 1935, all three were finding it difficult to support their families, and they rejoiced at the creation of a visionary writers' project. When they approached Clifford Shipton for employment, however, he deemed them ineligible. The national ruling that WPA employees had to be registered for relief as of November 1935 had been backdated in Massachusetts to May 1935. Because at that date there had been no project for writers, none of the three men—despite their desperate circumstances—had registered as certified paupers. When, a few months later, Hopkins adapted the regulations to allow for a 10 per cent non-relief capacity, they applied again. This time Shipton informed them that the Massachusetts quota was full. When Berger approached the New Bedford district supervisor, however, Bradford told him that, although the quota was full, "not one-tenth of the territory in Massachusetts has been covered by assigned writers," no employees lived in Cape Cod, and much of the quota had been filled with "literate 'non-writers.'"[29]

Willison and Berger swung into action, galvanizing their culturally influential contacts, including New Deal insiders George Biddle and Ellen Kennan, and Mary Heaton Vorse, resident of Provincetown and a friend of Alsberg's. They also wrote to Elizabeth Shoemaker, director of the Cape Cod Advancement Plan, and to Reed Harris and Henry Alsberg in the national office. Their letters addressed not just their own qualifications as writers, but the vision promoted by the American Guide Manual and its betrayal in the apathy and indifference displayed by project officials. Berger felt particularly incensed at the failure to respect authorial skills. To Vorse, he complained: "The book apparently is to be written, at least in Massachusetts, by unemployed plumbers or men of any other qualification." And to Alsberg: "multiply myself by hundreds, and substitute these hundreds with the same number of plumbers and men trained along other lines, and there may be a danger to the book worthy of your attention."[30]

Several attitudes distinguish the Provincetown writers from the New Bedford employees. First, they had confidence in authorship as skilled labor, allied to but distinct from other skills. Second, as artists who had worked to perfect their craft, they considered government support a right. And, third, they saw that support as enabling their attempts to cross the divide between artists and workers in Provincetown—not to escape from but to grapple more closely with the labor conditions of their environment. Alsberg reacted with a speed and decisiveness that often came upon him when he recognized artistic talent, particularly in promising young men. He reached past all the protocols and procedures, directing Clifford Shipton not only to add Berger, Willison, and Malmberg to his workforce but to pay them at "the highest security rate for professionals in Boston," $23 per week (as opposed to the Provincetown rate of $17).[31] Shipton made his irritation known to both Alsberg and Bradford, but complied with the orders.

The three writers followed the rules of their jobs conscientiously, filling out and sending to Bradford their weekly field reports and covering their assigned communities: Berger wrote up Provincetown, Malmberg covered Wellfleet, and Willison, Truro. Yet their attitude to the work differed palpably from the dominant climate in the New Bedford office. All three submitted unusually eloquent and thoughtful copy with Berger, as we have seen in chapter 4, taking a particularly interrogative approach. None tried to hide his project affiliation. George Willison, for example, was still announcing his credentials on the Federal Writers Project, 1936–1941, in the jacket note to his best-selling book *Saints and Strangers* in 1945. These writers' relationship to the institutional space of the project also differed from those in New Bedford and vicinity, since they did not work in the project office. These men stayed in their communities, interviewing fellow residents, scouring local libraries, writing up copy in their homes, and mailing it in every week.

JOINING THE UNION

The effort to organize WPA writers' labor brought the two groups, from New Bedford and Provincetown, together. In 1934, the American Writers' Union grew out of the John Reed Clubs to provide a broader vision of writing and social change than did the more professionalized League of American Authors (Denning 87). Lobbying for government funding was also central to the union's platform. They insisted that WPA writers were employees, not relief clients, in an attempt to shift public discourse away from the language of dependency to a recognition of workers' rights.[32] The Writers' Union envisaged strong links with blue-collar labor. In Massachusetts, the union allied itself with the CIO Textile Mill Committees, not the more established and more conservative Textile Council.

The Writers' Union came to New Bedford in May 1936, via a network forged during the 1928 textile strike. Frank Manning and Donald Thompson had come from New York City and Boston in 1928 ("outside agitators" in local press parlance, no doubt) to inject some militancy into the Textile Council, and had become acquainted with James McKenna. Frustrated by the established hierarchies of that group, they eventually decamped to the Textile Mill Committees. Now all three men were employed on the writers' project: Thompson in New York City, Manning in the Boston office, and McKenna in New Bedford. Manning came to New Bedford in his project capacity in 1936, signaling the continuity of his class affiliations by returning to the same kind of mill housing that he'd left eight years earlier. With some pinch-hitting from Thompson in New York City and McKenna as the local liaison, Manning began an organization drive. Fifty years later, Eunice Turgeon, one of the New Bedford writers, still remembered the latter two men as a charismatic pair: McKenna was "tall and gangly, witty and helpful"; Manning "had such fluency, such a vocabulary" (Donaghy and McCabe 24).

The reaction of project employees to the unionization of their labor speaks volumes about the conflictedness of their self-identification as government-sponsored writers. On the one hand, New Bedford District Local No. 15 of the American Writers' Union became the largest group in Massachusetts outside Boston, with thirty-nine members in October 1936. It met regularly, built a committee structure of governance, developed bylaws, sent representation to the state council of the Writers' Union, and participated in face-to-face lobbying of congressmen and WPA administrators at the state and national levels. The local showed solidarity with the union's opposition to job cuts, differential wage scales, government classification of writers (demanding eradication of the unskilled "intermediate" category), and supported the drive for a permanent bureau of letters. It also participated—a little—in what Michael Denning calls "proletarian forms of resistance" (101). The group's most militant act came on June 28, 1937, when it conducted a one-hour work stoppage, part of a coordinated statewide demonstration to protest the dismissal of 129 Massachusetts writers in the forthcoming "quota cuts."

On the other hand, there were definite limits to the New Bedford writers' commitment to unionist ideology and action. Clearly, scaremongering was happening locally. From the beginning, Frank Manning had to cajole people into membership by insisting: "We are not organized behind any theory but are rather held together by a very definite program of enlightened self-interest."[33] The majority of members in local 15 were prepared to pursue the principle of self-interest to protect their jobs with something they called "Trade Unionism (non-Political)," but they were leery in the extreme of strike action, the dominant symbol of worker solidarity in the period.[34]

We can see this conflictedness in individual reactions. James McKenna, the member who most clearly self-identified as a union man, served as first president of local 15.[35] Initially, McKenna nudged the group toward a minimum of militancy. For example, in response to the motion that "Strikes are not in accord with the opinions of this local," he persuaded the group to accept his more judiciously phrased statement that "The New Bedford District Local is in favor of stoppages, strikes, etc., only when convinced that all constructive and positive measures for bringing about continuance and expansion of projects are exhausted."[36] After three months, McKenna resigned his presidency, hinting at conflict of interest with his new role as supervisor of the local historical records survey. Behind the scenes, bigger things were afoot, and by early 1937 he had left the project to work with Mayor Carney. Leroy Bradford's position in the union was always ambiguous. He refused nomination as president of the local, then as representative to the state council, in both cases on conflict-of-interest grounds. He remained a dues-paying member, attending meetings regularly, yet his voice was strongest in denying the politics of their position, arguing consistently that "we are a non-partisan organization."[37] Moeller was very quiet. She did join the Writers' Union; whether she attended meetings is unclear. Later in life she openly voiced her suspicions of labor organization, criticizing the teachers' union in the local newspaper and the shipworkers' unions in her 1955 travel book, *Pack a Bag*.

The most pronounced voice was Julia Keane's. In many ways, her public profile as legionnaire auxiliary makes her least likely as a union member. Yet she not only joined but became corresponding secretary for the local in 1937. The sense that she was simultaneously occupying mutually exclusive public roles is suggested by two photographs from the period. The first is the picture accompanying a *New Bedford Standard-Times* report of her trip to the Los Angeles National Convention of the American Legion Auxiliary, as Massachusetts State Department delegate. Here, she emanates the groomed, competent leadership of the clubwoman extraordinaire (Fig. 13). The second, from about a year earlier, records an outing of local 15 of the Writers' Union to Cape Cod, designed to consolidate a collective identity out of an assorted group of unemployed teachers, office workers, newspapermen, and recent high school graduates, a move very much in line with the CIO "culture of unity," fostered through participation in collective recreational activities (Cohen 333; Fig. 14). Here, Keane's aspect and body language bespeak a very different role, as she performs the camaraderie and solidarity of the worker-writer.

In June 1937, a series of protest letters went out over her signature, to Ray Billington, Harry Hopkins, John McDonough (Massachusetts WPA administrator), Representative Charles Gifford, Senator Henry Cabot Lodge, and President Franklin D. Roosevelt. She also wrote in individual protest to McDonough and Hopkins. This correspondence never invokes workers' rights, the bedrock of union alliance. Representing their district as "the Cradle of American History," the members speak as grateful, hard-working dependents of a government agency. They also demonstrate a profound suspicion of radicalism and centrism, the local suspicion of "outsiders" and the interests fueling their actions (familiar, again, from the press treatment of "foreigners" and "outside agitators" in 1928) triumphing over the search for workers' solidarity. Suspecting the Boston local of arguing for the retention of its members at the expense of others across the state, the group addressed McDonough:

Fairhaven Resident Deplores Missing September Hurricane

"I SAW Los Angeles. I saw the Grand Canyon. I saw the Garden of the Gods and I saw Mt. Rainier . . . but I didn't see the Sept. 21 hurricane," laments Mrs. Julia L. Keane of 114 Pleasant Street, Fairhaven, who was attending the National Convention of American Legion Auxiliary in California when the big storm struck.

"Upon my return I was prepared to sing praises about the Garden of the Gods and the Colorado Grand Canyon, natural wonders that have been in existence for thousands of years and will remain for thousands more," continues Mrs. Keane, past president of Auxiliary to Post 166, American Legion, of Fairhaven, and past president of Bristol County Council, who attended the convention as a Massachusetts State Department delegate.

"And I came home to find the great hurricane of Sept. 21, the catastrophe of a lifetime, the talk of the town."

MRS. JULIA L. KEANE

Mrs. Keane said the first word of the disaster was received by telegram when a New England city official was recalled to his home city. Little detail was given. The following day every newspaper carried headlines concerning the hurricane and floods.

"When I read that New Bedford was under water and that Fairhaven virtually was wiped out, I was frantic. Others in the party were terribly upset and tried to communicate with their relatives here but telegraph and telephone companies were making no contact with the area.

"We left that morning and I believe I lost five pounds on the trip from worry. Our train was the first to cross Western Massachusetts on the Boston and Albany line. When I saw whole orchards flattened as if by Army tanks I shuddered to think of what had happened to this vicinity. Progress by rail was at snail's pace for there had been numerous washouts.

"When we arrived in Boston at 10:30 p. m. other members of our party registered at a hotel, since there was no train service to New Bedford until the next morning. However, there was a bus to Providence and I came directly through to find that my home had been high and dry throughout the storm, although flood waters from Harbor View had surrounded the neighborhood, making it a veritable island."

Fig. 13. Story about Julia Keane, *New Bedford Standard-Times* November 3, 1938.

Fig. 14. New Bedford WPA writers and friends on an outing on Cape Cod. Julia Keane is seated in the front row. Bradford stands far right. Photograph by James F. McKenna, courtesy of Spinner Publications.

> The New Bedford local of the American Writers' Union . . . is apparently in the ill graces of the Boston local because it has declined to picket or "sit down" for petty grievances. . . . We haven't been "sitting down"—we've been working—we haven't sought publicity, but we can—we're thankful for the opportunity which the Works Progress Administration has given us to work. But we do resent any attempt on the part of a Boston organization to say that they and they only, should be continued at work.[38]

Keane's language was blunter in her individual letter to McDonough: because the New Bedford local "has not been as radical as the Boston Local, and has not occasioned as much publicity unfavorable to the W.P.A., it appears now that it will be made to suffer."[39]

New Bedford union members were also suspicious of the Provincetown writers. At about the same time as the formation of the New Bedford local, Berger, Willison, and Malmberg (among others) founded the Artists and Writers Union of Provincetown, with first George Willison, then Carl Malmberg as corresponding secretary. They were also keen to participate in local 15 of the Writers' Union. Immediately the New Bedford union officers threw up a series of bureaucratic impediments and wrote to Boston to verify that Berger, Willison, and Malmberg really were "actual and bona-fide members" of the Writers' Union.[40] The Provincetown writers showed a considerably more militant understanding of unionism than their New Bedford colleagues. They pushed for demonstrations and statements of solidarity, which never won majority votes in the local. One particularly sharp exchange developed when Berger proposed that members write to the *New Bedford Standard-Times*, protesting the union bashing in the column "He That Runs." McKenna forcibly rejected the notion, suggesting that Berger keep his ideas to himself. The details of the ensuing exchange were struck from the minutes.[41]

By the second half of 1937, the Writers' Union at the national level began to fold, many of its locals allying themselves with the Workers' Alliance as a more broadly based representative of WPA employees. A speaker came down to New Bedford to persuade local 15 to do likewise, but members feared the radicalism of the Workers' Alliance, especially its reputation for Communist affiliations. Local 15 took a vote on the future. Of the twenty-four ballots cast, none voted to "disband and maintain no organization whatsoever," one voted to "enter the Boston unit of the Workers' Alliance," eight voted to "procure a charter from Workers' Alliance headquarters and form our own Workers' Alliance unit," and fifteen voted to "continue without affiliation with any national organization, as an independent organization." Then, in August 1937 came the controversy surrounding the state guide. Some Fairhaven writers leaked their unhappiness with the Boston office to the local press, generally attempting to distance the local office from the larger organization. By the time that the American Writers' Union officially disbanded, in October 1937, all visible union activity on the New Bedford project had ended.

WRITING

In 1937, Meridel Le Sueur offered another paradigm for worker-writers when she published a pamphlet demonstrating how WPA writers could reshape conventional notions of authorship and writing methods. An out-of-work writer at the time, Le Sueur was employed by the Minnesota WPA to run writing classes for manual laborers in Minneapolis. She encouraged her students to surrender notions of possessive individualism and reconceptualize authorship "as a collaborative reworking of shared cultural resources," a fundamental step in changing "the economic and political structures that disempowered many working-class women and men" (Greer 608, 610). Le Sueur taught them that workers were the well-spring of literary creativity: "Who has kept language alive, freshened it out of his own experience? Who put the new words in the dictionary? It's the man on the street, the worker who has the new experiences first, who makes up a word, adds a word, creates new tools as he needs them in his work" (6). *Worker Writers*, her WPA pamphlet, shows the results of these teachings, as women students and teacher together produce a series of communal pieces which sew writers', readers', and workers' identities inextricably together. Le Sueur's exhortations in many ways encapsulate the challenge facing the New Bedford writers—how to surrender individual authority and make common cause with their fellow workers in their writing practices. Without a teacher such as her to codify the process for them in quite these terms, they stumbled toward that goal in different ways and with different degrees of success.

The material conditions described above directly fed workers' attitudes to themselves as writers, which in turn shaped their production of material. Those employees who seemed most vulnerable in their social positions as WPAers—and most nervous about crossing categories between writer and wage-earning worker—developed narrative positions that gave them compensatory authority and kept their subjects at arm's length. In contrast, those project employees who vigorously pursued their allegiances to the working people around them forged out of common political ground a common narrative voice. Some of this writing issued in publications which hit the national press; more of it issued in manuscripts which hit district and state office reject piles. In all cases, however, the nitty-gritty details of the writing demonstrate how interconnections among worker, writer, and community—the links between literature and society which the project was so keen to inculcate—played out in practice.

The insecurity of the New Bedford writers marked their distinctly checkered output, and very little of their writing reached publication. Leroy Bradford found himself pulled, as ever, in contrary directions—one way as a community member, another as a project official—and his attempts to write from this conflicted position ultimately paralyzed his creative faculties. In 1937, Bradford complied with a request by the New Bedford post of the American Legion to put together a city history for distribution at the state organization's annual convention—the very one at which Hurley denounced the guidebook's treatment of Sacco and Vanzetti. The booklet, "Yesterday, Today and Tomorrow in New Bedford, Massachusetts," amounts to a thoroughgoing whitewash, with no acknowledgment of the city's labor troubles, union organization, or working conditions, and a brief, dismissive mention of the "mythical

Underground Railroad" as the single gesture to New Bedford's role in abolitionism.[42] The booklet was never published. A year later, in response to Sterling Brown's initiative to recover the histories of Black abolitionists, Bradford produced work of a very different cast. He dug up little-known material on the local station of the Underground Railroad and, drawing on information from Elsie Moeller's aunt, wrote up the story of Isabella White, who escaped from slavery in a barrel of sweet potatoes bound for New Bedford (a story which saw publication thirty years later, in *Spinner* magazine).

Bradford also successfully oversaw the publication of *Whaling Masters*—"an annotated directory to the thousands of nearly forgotten men who made the word Yankee famous on the Seven Seas in the days of 'iron men and wooden ships'"—in 1938, and *Fairhaven*, a local guide to his own city, in 1939.[43] The latter work required him to play his familiar middleman role, mediating the competing priorities of Fairhaven selectmen who wanted to pay homage to local benefactor Henry Huttleston Rogers and state editors who insisted on "a more objective attitude."[44] Bradford's breaking point came when Muriel Hawks urged him to enliven the guide by injecting some of his own memories of the 1938 hurricane that had devastated Fairhaven. The attempt to write from a personal viewpoint (rather than as collator or editor) for the first time on the project did not empower Bradford. Unable to sustain his twin identities as government writer and local resident, he first wrote his project identity out of the account, then found his material excised from the final copy by editors above him in the project hierarchy. Three weeks after the appearance of *Fairhaven*, on July 27, 1939, he resigned from the project, backing away from the authorial role to take up a position with the Acushnet Process Co., which he served first as carpenter, then as safety manager until his retirement.

James McKenna also wrote a limited amount, because his tenure on the writers' project was brief, but his emphasis on New Bedford's labor history did survive in the published guide. When Frank Manning—working at that point in the Boston office—edited McKenna's field copy, he increased the emphasis on labor. Among other additions, Manning wrote in his own role in the 1928 strike, and Grace Kellogg accepted that version, although ultimately it was cut back in the published guide. McKenna was more conservative in his handling of race. While he did enumerate Cape Verde Islanders among New Bedford's racial groups, he omitted them in his coverage of cultural and community impact. We can measure the depth of this omission from Mary Heaton Vorse's contemporaneous account of New Bedford. Vorse paints a vivid picture of the decrepit houses—formerly whaling captains' homes—on the New Bedford waterfront: "They were inhabited by Bravas, Portuguese Negroes. With the soft, guttural, honeyed syllables of Portuguese dripping from their tongues, the Bravas form a town as alien as anything you might find in the mysterious islands" (*Time and the Town* 142).

In 1938, Morton Royse's appointment as national social-ethnic studies editor created the breakthrough for some New Bedford writers. Royse had predicted that his project would flush out new talent. Writing to Alsberg from his field travels, he described retraining field workers in their fundamental attitudes to writing: "The workers are so bogged down with guide ways, compiling stuff that no one can make much use of . . . that it takes repeated sessions getting them to look at the world around them and write in a natural way." Royse recommended that Benjamin Botkin, national folklore editor, also get out on the road with his guidelines: "He will discover talent unsuspected from the remote Washington, and in no other way will he uncover it."[45] Under the broad social-ethnic rubric, New Bedford writers set about gathering textile workers' slang for "A Lexicon of Trade Jargon"; conducting research and interviews for studies of Portuguese, Jews, Syrians, Lebanese, Irish, and other local ethnic groups; and interviewing fellow WPA workers for a study titled "We Work on the W.P.A." Also in 1938, the New Bedford writers became heavily involved in the composition of *New England Hurricane*.

During this period both Julia Keane and Elsie Moeller received promotion to the professional classification and began to produce their own writing. Their fundamental orientation to work, however, seems to have remained unchanged. Keane's commitment to established class hierarchies is visible in her approach to the "Lexicon of Trade Jargon." For her contribution, on silk weaving and rope manufacturing, she approached only members of the managerial class: the office manager of the National Silk Spinning Company, the manager of the Lambeth Rope Company, and the superintendent of the New Bedford Cordage Company ("A Lexicon of Trade Jargon" 134–35). Her commitment to membership in patriotic organizations was confirmed and extended during the war years, when she joined the Women's Air Corps Service.

Elsie Moeller produced a great deal more writing than Keane, and she recorded a wider range of social types, but, as author, she never quite comes down from the hill. Her write-ups of New Bedford and Cape Cod for the social-ethnic study "The Portuguese in New England," for example, are heavily inflected by her own normative position. Her narrative voice adopts the dominant "American" (that is to say Anglo-American) "we," while she maps "the foreign elements" as racially stereotyped "aliens" in the most benevolent of tones. We can read these narrative strategies as the voice of doubly threatened privilege at both the personal and social levels. Not only had Moeller's own citizenship status been directly challenged, but she lived in a city in which, by 1905, less than one-fifth was of Yankee ancestry, with the Portuguese the largest immigrant group (Halter 131). Moeller's defense lay in playing what Paula Rabinowitz calls the "ethnographic imperialist," invading the privacy of her subjects while protecting her own. In her invasion of Portuguese domestic space, for example, there is no sense that Moeller's brush with destitution might ever have threatened her own intimate living arrangements: "The Latin immigrant's conception of the sacredness and exclusiveness of the homes is not what it is in the Anglo-Saxon mind. They are not fastidious as to crowding. The man and wife occupy one bed and all the children, and maybe a boarder, a bed in the other corners of the same room. This may be abominable to our point of view, but it does not necessarily imply immorality on the part of the immigrant, to whom it is all a regular part of existence" (Rabinowitz 202; Moeller, "Living Conditions" 103). This lack of felt self-positioning stayed with Moeller in her later writings. Her 1955 travel book, *Pack a Bag*—dubbed a "laughalogue" by its publisher—uses humor to deflect characterization from the autobiographical narrator. The emphasis falls on the exotic "natives" in Panama, the stereotypically "ethnic" shipyard workers in California, with coy and coded references to "My brand-new army husband," "A.C.," who disappears without comment halfway through the book.

District 4 also produced two versions of a more integrated worker-writer style, one closer to the masculinist emphasis of Freeman and Conroy, the other to the collectivity envisaged by Le Sueur. The masculinist version came from the Provincetown contingent, whose strong sense of writerly entitlement fed their productivity. Josef Berger, George Willison, and Carl Malmberg produced a steady stream of copy on Cape Cod towns for the state guide, and they developed several book projects: Berger published *Cape Cod Pilot* and completed a series of tall tales about "Bowhead Pete, the Sea-Going Cowboy"; all three collaborated on pilgrim and Native histories with volumes provisionally titled "Myles Standish Country" and "Mashpee Kingdom." Although only Berger's work survives in finished form, the field copy from all three writers consistently carves out topics and values historical and contemporary actors through the lens of labor, making visible a much richer racial diversity than in many other Massachusetts guides. They consistently acknowledge their writing as a collaboration with local workers: Berger, for example, described his tall tales of Bowhead Pete as an amalgam of his own inventiveness and "details and color such as I have gathered at first hand from old-timers."[46] Ultimately, however, they insisted on the individuality of their authorial voices. At some point late in 1937, they negotiated to split their collaborative projects into individual undertakings, Willison arguing that they would be "happier working alone."[47] While all three were left-wing writers with strong commitments to working-class culture, they also insisted on a level of individual recognition counter to the WPA's collective practices (and to the kind of collaborative community advocated by Le Sueur). Berger, in particular, mounted and won an exhausting battle against project administrators to be credited as individual author of *Cape Cod Pilot* and the Bowhead Pete series. Their work was cut short when the national office transferred Malmberg to the interim directorship of the New York City project and Willison to the central office in Washington, while Berger left the project in 1938 to take up a prestigious Guggenheim fellowship.[48] Only *Cape Cod Pilot* stands as published evidence of the valuable inclusivity produced by the worker-writer perspective.

Another, very differently situated, district 4 employee also crossed the gap between writers and "other American workers," using her status as a WPAer to develop a narrative voice that speaks of and for the common ground shared by the dispossessed. This was Nellie Coombs, who joined the project late, in 1938. Coombs worked out of North Dartmouth, a community on the western edge of New Bedford which was even more precariously positioned, clinging to the larger city for economic sustenance. At under 10,000, Dartmouth was less than one-tenth the size of New Bedford. Over the years it had depended on whaling, then tourism, though during the Depression it seemed to revert to a more agricultural base. Coombs lived there with her mother, supporting them both on her WPA wage, and she was keenly alive to the class and race disparities which ordered life in her community.[49]

As project interviewer, Coombs made direct approaches to local working people, inadvertently showing up some of the faultlines and suspicions that continued to cluster around the WPA. The instructions for "Lexicon of Trade Jargon" stipulated: "We want living slang, not technical terms. . . . The worker should obtain these terms in conversation with employees of the mills and especially with persons in the offices of the unions."[50] Pen in hand, Coombs approached local Portuguese mill employees and union officers at their workplaces, thereby causing considerable consternation on the part of William Batty, president of the New Bedford Textile Council. He accused her of being a spy from the CIO and threatened to expose her in the newspapers. Eventually, Bradford calmed him down, while Hawks quietly suggested that it might be more politic if Coombs visited unionized workers in their homes.[51]

Coombs's most powerful production was an interview with Captain Joe Antone, Cape Verdean American seaman now on the WPA, for the planned collection "We Work on the WPA." In terms of dominant practice on the Massachusetts project, Coombs was unconventional both in her choice of interviewee and in her self-positioning as interviewer. New Bedford was known as "the Cape Verdean capital of the New World," and yet its community was triply disadvantaged. Colonized by the Portuguese, the islanders had come to America via the hellish conditions of whalers, and on shore were virtually shut out of skilled labor opportunities, crushed into the south end, three Cape Verdean families to each single-family residence (when they housed Anglo-Americans) and 50 percent of them unemployed during the Depression (Halter 131–61). As far as I can tell, there was no Cape Verdean American in the state or district offices, and so no direct access to a project voice. Coombs's interview was the closest approximation to self-representation. Whatever techniques, shaping structures, and silent elisions the interviewer may have employed, Coombs did present Joe Antone with the opportunity to individualize his experience and to train his gaze and representation on "the Americans" from the "other" side.

Antone's stories speak entirely to power and exclusion: instances of racism on and off shore, the complex social positioning of the "black Portuguese," and the dishonesties of high society he has encountered during his long life. Rather poignantly, given the dominant role played by Harvard graduates on the Massachusetts project, one of the targets of Antone's criticism is a "Harvard man" who crews for him on a scientific voyage. The man refuses his assignment (to clean the toilets), then jumps ship when Antone confronts him with the power which is his at sea: "Because I'm a Cape Verde you do not want to obey me. What you or I am on shore does not matter here. As long as I am the captain, the crew has to do what I say. If you refuse to do so, then I shall have to turn you over to the consul to be placed in jail for breaking the maritime law."[52] Antone also alludes to shady practices and hostile dealings among the WPA, the mayor's office, and the American Legion locally. Clearly he feels his employment on the WPA is a further slide down the social hierarchy, trapping him in other men's machinations. From the late nineteenth century to the mid-twentieth, he tracks discrimination: "I arrived in New Bedford, June 27, 1894, and that ended my slavery on the American whalers. That's what it was—slavery. How do you think those ship owners built their fine mansions on the hill?"; "In this country they say we're a democracy, but nobody gets anything here unless he belongs to the sixty families. I don't call that democracy" ("We Work on the WPA" 127, 131).

Coombs positions herself in the interview scene very briefly, but her method decisively aligns her with Antone's critique. She moves from presenting herself as the vehicle of his stories to blurring the boundary between self and other with her final shift into free indirect discourse:

> You don't need to wind up Captain Joe Antone to make him talk. You don't need to put a nickel in him either. All you do is shove him in your car, drive him out to the wilds of North Dartmouth, ease him into a comfortable chair beneath a pear tree and then take the plugs out of both your ears. He'll talk all right, and you need a dictaphone to take it all in because he thinks nothing of setting you down in Buenos Aires and just as you're becoming accustomed to the climate, he's yelling at you from 'way over in Lisbon. Or else he's in Bermuda and the next minute he's over in New Orleans, berating the white man there because they class him as a negro and he isn't a negro. He's a Cape Verdean and why do people have to be so stupid. ("We Work on the WPA" 130)

If the series was indeed planned "to illustrate how the WPA served as a salvation for America's proud workers," Coombs's copy hardly conformed to government directives. As with so many worker-oriented studies, publication of "We Work on the WPA" was prevented by the project's reorganization in 1939. Fifty years later, *Spinner* magazine resurrected the interview as a powerful lens on the underbelly of life on the sea, on land, and in the local politics which enmeshed WPA workers at all levels. The interview also gives a glimpse of the rhetorical power of the voice of solidarity when worker and writer came together—across boundaries of race, gender, class—on common ground.

Filling in some details of WPA writers' lives and writings demonstrates that the alignment of literature with labor, particularly under the conditions of public funding, presented a considerably more complex challenge than envisioned in the heroic rhetoric of the period. Because project assignments focused field workers on their own localities, in mapping their communities these writers-in-the-making were also mapping their own professional identities, within structures and guidelines handed down from the central office in Washington. The four writers living in New Bedford and Fairhaven ultimately seem trapped in a fissure or a binary, forced to choose between the governmental and the writerly. As worker and public figure, Keane remained more committed to the American Legion than the writers' project or the Writers' Union and McKenna to achieving a municipal position—understandably enough, given that the one provided social and the other financial security. Moeller seemed intent on maintaining her class and race position by floating a public and narrative persona untouched by public funding. Meanwhile Bradford visibly struggled to bring together his role as state representative with his commitment as a local writer, and that struggle ultimately was not productive of voice or visibility.

The writers who most closely embraced their subjects were those with the strongest identity as workers. The Provincetown writers—Berger, Willison, and Malmberg—came to this position from their commitments as published, politically organized authors and an environment in which artists had long identified as members of a working community. Coombs's route to solidarity with the working class was more direct. Writing was the work currently available to her, and she understood her position as a precariously employed worker clinging, like her neighbors in North Dartmouth, to a temporary living. Out of this solidarity with the socially marginalized and the attempt to give voice to the unheard came the closest thing to a "proletarian poetics" (Rabinowitz 190) to emerge from the Massachusetts project.

SECTION

THREE

LOCAL FORAYS

6

CAPE COD PILOT

Josef Berger produced the Massachusetts project's proudest publication by breaking all its rules. Having fought for special dispensation to gain a berth on the project, he then insisted that he be exempt from the WPA rule regarding collective authorship. His guide *Cape Cod Pilot* (1937) also broke all Washington's rules about style and organization: it had a pronounced personal voice, a polemical edge, and tour directions which go up one coast of the peninsula and down the other. The author's explicit self-positioning also led to the most inclusive representation of race in any of the Massachusetts project's published guides. The key to Berger's achievement and its enthusiastic reception lay in his privileging the worker as his defining category. Insisting on his own rights as a worker, he also insisted on recognizing and respecting fellowworkers, of various races and ethnicities, around him on Cape Cod.

AUTHORSHIP

Through Alsberg's intercession, Berger (along with his fellow Provincetown writers) won privileged conditions on the project, working only four days a week out of his home. This arrangement enabled him, in the first few months of employment, to complete a guide to Cape Cod for which he had been gathering material for some time and which Paul Smith had contracted to publish as the first book from the Modern Pilgrim Press. Jerre Mangione tells the story of how this work came to be taken under the WPA umbrella:

> One Sunday, while Berger was correcting galley proofs, he had two unexpected callers from Boston: the industrious Joseph Gaer [New England field supervisor] . . . and Merle Colby [assistant state director in Massachusetts]. . . . the sight of the galley proofs spread all over the Berger living room immediately engaged their attention. . . . Immersed in the material, they paid no attention to Berger's explanation that the book was one he had written on his own time. Finally, Gaer looked up from the galleys and said to Colby, "Just what we want. This is just what we want." (*Dream* 212)

Project administrators were looking for published results to set against congressional and press derision of a "boondoggling" project that was wasting public money. Gaer and Colby exerted maximum pressure on Berger, appealing to his conscience and his self-interest: given that he had been living off government money, the book really was not his private property, they argued; identifying the guide as a WPA publication would also bring it additional attention. With misgivings, Berger capitulated.

But Berger, with his pride in himself as a skilled worker, had expectations which project administrators, for all their rhetoric about literature as labor, clearly had not thought through. The guide copy so desired by Boston administrators is deeply imbued with the author's sense of himself and his subjects—contemporary and historical—as workers worthy of recognition and respect. When Berger translated this sense of authorial entitlement into material expectations, the project's bureaucracy balked. Project policy forbade the naming of guidebook authors, instead crediting each project as a collective under the direction of a few identified officials. Berger, writing under the pseudonym Jeremiah Digges, wanted more individualized credit than this. Several writers—especially Nathan Halper—did contribute their research, but the composition, voice, narrative perspective, and stylistic flair were all Berger's. He provided an acknowledgment page, written in the first person and signed "J.D.," which stresses the bonds of labor between writer and subject: "I am deeply indebted to my friends and neighbors on Cape Cod, especially to the crew of the schooner *Mary P. Goulart*, with whom I have gone Banks fishing."[1] The Massachusetts state office would not accept this draft. After considerable negotiation and some compromise on both sides, Berger and Gaer agreed to a title page crediting Jeremiah Digges as author "With Editorial and Research Assistance of the Members of the Federal Writers' Project" and a preface opening somewhat tortuously:

> This book deviates from the form used in others in the American Guide Series, for it attempts to present guide material as a personal experience. Though it is a collective task, the editors felt that the folklore and yarns that constitute the major part of the book would be enriched in presentation by the use of the personal pronoun. Jeremiah Digges is one of the Federal Writers' Project workers, and he is rightly credited with the major writing, rewriting and editing of this book.

National and state officials, however, continued to downplay the book's individual authorship. A memorandum to all state directors, apparently authorized by Alsberg, accompanied the publication of *Cape Cod Pilot*: "The 'Jeremiah Digges' who is listed as the author is a fictitious character and actually represents several workers of the Massachusetts Federal Writers' Project."[2] When the *Boston Globe* reviewed the guide three weeks later, it stated: "The work is the result of research by a large number of relief workers and is ostensibly written by Jeremiah Digges, representing the W.P.A. writers. . . . Merle Colby, director of the guide series in Massachusetts, directed the writing and publication of the volume." Berger suspected, with some justification, that the Boston office was so desperate to prove results that it had appropriated his work. He immediately protested to the press, Gaer, and Colby. He couched his appeal to Colby entirely in terms of a worker-writer standing by his collectively bargained rights: "I know that you, as a writer, are aware of the legitimacy and the value of a by-line. And as a trade unionist, certainly you must see that I am within my rights in expecting a by-line, once agreed upon, to stand without being sniped at from the sidelines."[3] Soon another memorandum appeared over Alsberg's name, professing to "correct a statement" in the previous one, though in fact still refusing individual authorship to Berger: "while we were correct in stating that several writers of the Massachusetts project wrote this book, we were not correct in assigning the name of Jeremiah Digges to more than one person." The national office was not about to surrender its control over writers' labor. But it also wanted to avoid confrontation with an author of rising reputation. The filed carbon copy of the memo includes a note, initialed by Cronyn: "This letter sent to all states except Massachusetts."[4]

BERGER'S CAPE COD

Berger balked at the project's racial categories just as vigorously as he did at the authorial policies. As a resident of Provincetown, he was set the task of documenting the town's racial demographics for the state guide according to the template set by Washington, D.C., and Boston. As we have seen in chapter 4, he—along with a small number of fellow workers—tended to question the limits of this classificatory system. His response under "Racial Groups" is a rant of considerable length, exposing how the procedures for gathering field copy simply reinforce the colonial erasures and genocide practiced on Native peoples:

> Neither in pure descent nor in admixture of blood does there survive in Provincetown or the lower Cape area any traceable heritage from the aboriginal race, the Pamets of the tribe of Wampanoag.
>
> While in many other localities the same phenomenon might scarcely deserve comment, on Cape Cod, where adherence to the land has been such an outstanding trait, manifesting itself in the perpetuation of family names in many towns through three centuries, the complete disappearance of a whole people does not fit in naturally as a chapter of the land's history. Indeed, considering that the native population of this relatively small area was between two and three thousand, (Charles F. Swift, *Cape Cod, the Right Arm of Massachusetts*, Yarmouth, 1897, based on estimate of Governor Hinckley, Ch. XIX, p. 330) this complete disappearance puts a cast upon the community's history which proud descendants of the early comers should not be eager to play up prominently.
>
> In other words the despoliation that took place here, under the grasping aegis of the early proprietors, the downright cheating and the wilful undermining of moral stamina were fully as harsh and cruel as anything that went on during the conquest of the West. It was less violent only because the Indians, being of a more compliant nature here than in the West,

> offered less violent resistance, and it was accomplished under a cloak of respectability that does not compare well even with the forthright, swashbuckling pillage in the West, cruel and unjust though the latter was. The frontiersman seemed to have lost some of the finesse that distinguished the operations of his no less determined forbears among the New England settlers.[5]

Berger proceeded to excoriate apologist historians "who wrote history as the proud old families of New England preferred that it should be written." Little wonder that when Leroy Bradford, district supervisor in New Bedford, sent Berger's copy to local authorities for checking, they responded that, although the material was largely accurate, "[we] do not wish our names to appear anywhere as correctors of this material on Provincetown."[6]

Berger also broke all of Washington's rules about style. The manuscript of *Cape Cod Pilot* did not undergo the state and national editing processes applied to other guidebook material, and therefore the author's self-investments were not screened out. One of the first stipulations in the American Guide Manual of 1935–and one which Katharine Kellock continued vigorously to police—concerned the effacement of authorial voice: "the impersonal style should be used, but 'we' may be used occasionally with discretion"; "Do not use 'you should see' and the 'tourist should see'; keep the form impersonal and use the declarative."[7] From the first words of *Cape Cod Pilot*, Berger puts his own and his readers' subjectivity—and its relationship to this particular place—on display:

> In the museum of the Old Dartmouth Historical Society in New Bedford there is a gilded mirror, and under it a card informing the open-mouthed visitor that here is a:
>
> MIRROR IN WHICH GENERAL GRANT AND
> ABRAHAM LINCOLN BOTH LOOKED
>
> Invariably, the attendant at the museum says, the tourist looks up quickly in the glass—and is a little disappointed at seeing only himself there.
>
> A guidebook should have better manners, I suppose, than to point back to the tourist as one of the "principal features of interest." But manners or no manners, a Cape Cod guidebook must single him out for this distinction; for within the past two decades, the tourist has stepped into the leading role; "summer business" has overshadowed all others. (1)

The author repeatedly positions himself as a reluctant guidebook writer, alluding to the unreliability of the genre and his own discomfort with the role: "I confess that I would rather not route you around like this" (295). He also voices his uneasiness at being classified with writers and artists who exploit "picturesque" Portuguese fishermen for their own creations (230–31). The continuing sparring between "natives" and "furriners"—and his own position as furriner—on the Cape allows (or reminds) Berger to pay consistent attention to racial tensions and displacements, historically and actually. Working out of this self-consciousness prevents him from adopting the "Anglo-Saxon norm" critiqued by Sterling Brown. Also, working in the service of Cape Cod inhabitants, Berger provides more sheer information about a range of racial and hybrid identities than other guidebook writers.

This characterful voice also enables Berger to read the present—especially when that means reading absence—in ways that were largely closed to writers of the more "official" state guide. The difference in the treatment of the town of Dennis is startling. Eunice Turgeon produced the field copy on racial elements in Dennis for the state guide. Faithfully following the assigned categories, she wrote under "Cultural Heritage":

> This topic is not applicable to Dennis.
> Authority: Benjamin F. Sears, town clerk, Main St., South Dennis.[8]

When Berger goes looking for race in Dennis, he finds a densely textured cultural encounter which implicates himself and, he hopes, his reader. The passage bears quoting at length:

> And now I jump, a bit abruptly, into something I suppose I shall always regard as personal, though there is no good reason for it, and I take the chance that you will go all the way with me, or at least far enough for the reward that awaits you.
>
> Of all the cemeteries on Cape Cod, the one from which I have carried away the deepest impression, the keenest consciousness of the dignity of death, and of the peace of death, is in Dennis. It has no chiseled lace, no eulogies dragging in a rhyme by the heels, no metaphysical abortions or neat slivers of faith on ice. It hasn't even any gravestones. Its single inscription is on a small slab of granite at one corner of the gateless fence around it, reading:

BURIAL GROUND OF THE NOBSCUSSET TRIBE OF INDIANS
OF WHICH TRIBE MASHANTAMPAINE WAS CHIEF.

If you go there, you will find nothing but a stone-posted iron fence, deep in the shadows of ground-pine and hemlock; nothing but the earth, thick-carpeted with fallen pine-needles; nothing but a strange, half-intelligible whisper in the boughs overhead. There is only a seclusion, a silence deeper than the silence of chiseled words, warmer and simpler and more understandable than the accented emptiness of tombs. (97–98)

In the chapter devoted to Mashpee, the dominant theme is the Native people's capacity for survival in the face of white trickery and condescension. Berger tells in considerable detail how Miles Standish (a.k.a. "Captaine Shrimpe") and other white settlers used "legal rigmarole" to trick Sachem Paupmunnuck and the South Sea Indians out of their land (345). Even Richard Bourne's missionary role is not as altruistic as the state guide and other publications portray it, since in return he gets the Christian congregation he craves. The people of Mashpee endlessly fought colonial domination: "from the beginning the white men did not feel that the Indians were competent to rule themselves—a form of anxiety that seems to come over many a conquering people when they have taken over the land of others" (349). The Natives' support in the Revolutionary War made no difference to that mindset: "After helping America win her freedom, the tribe lost its own" (350). If much of the chapter exposes white settlers' rapacity, its ending demonstrates the ignorance underpinning the white establishment's condescension. The Native people of Mashpee had sustained a Christian church on Cape Cod longer than any other group—since 1658—yet:

In 1711 the Reverend Daniel Williams, of London, died, and his will entrusted a fund to Harvard College, from which £60 a year was to be paid to "a person of prudence and piety to preach to what pagans and blacks be otherwise neglected."

Harvard chose Mashpee. (355)

In time, people of different races came together in Mashpee—Berger cites Hessian soldiers as well as Native Americans, African Americans, and Cape Verdean Americans—and this new "fusion of races" (351) carried on the fight for self-rule. Berger details the obstacles put in their path and squarely skewers historians—including one of his contemporaries—for their perpetuation of racist representations: "The historians have held these motley newcomers to Mashpee responsible for what they call a 'degenerate and degraded' condition of the town. Henry C. Kittredge refers to them as 'scum drifting to Mashpee like weeds to the Sargasso Sea'" (351). Finally the townspeople won their fight: "an act was passed in 1834 incorporating Mashpee, and authorizing the people to choose their own officers and manage their own affairs. And ever since, the 'scum and weeds' seem to have done a rather good job of it. On the 'Sargasso Sea' there have been few wrecks" (351–52). With this statement, Berger made a conscious choice to support the people of Mashpee. Wampanoag historian Mabel Avant, among others, put on record the fact that Mashpee went bankrupt and was put under the sway of a State Advisory Council only five years before the publication of this guide (Brodeur 23). Berger, unlike every other guidebook writer, concentrates on survival: "Accounts vary as to when the last full-blooded Indian died in Mashpee, but probably the pure strain was gone more than a century ago. Yet as you drive through this township, you will see people with high cheekbones, thin lips, straight hair, a red tinge to the skin. Most of the faces, it is true, are negroid, or partly so; but the exceptions are not so rare that you are likely to miss them, even in a brief drive through the scattered settlement" (353).

In making this kind of observation, Berger makes racial distinctions which, according to Marilyn Halter, writings of the period routinely ignored: "on Buzzards Bay and Cape Cod, 'white' and 'black' tended to be lumped in the same category of Portuguese 'foreigners'" (145). The government's continuing classification of its population exacerbated that invisibility: not until "the 1980 federal census forms, was it even possible for Cape Verdean Americans to officially identify themselves as such" (152). Thus were the Afro-Portuguese doubly displaced, their defining experience in America, according to Halter's analysis, the "discomfort of not belonging, the invisibility of residing between race and ethnicity" (xiv). Under the category of Portuguese, at some length in the Provincetown entry, Berger distinguishes those from the Azores or "descended of Azoreans," those from Lisbon, and those "descended of the *bravas*, a race brought into New England in whaling days from the Cape Verde Islands" (233). He acknowledges the racial prejudice among these people—"The Azorean and Lisbon people agree that the *bravas* are their inferiors, but they disagree heartily as between themselves, which faction is the superior"—as well as the "brutal treatment" inflicted on all of them by white whalers (232).

Two entries in particular can be read in conversation with contemporary articulations of racial difference. In the entry on Brewster, the guide makes a detour to the Pitcairn Islanders in the South Pacific, with whom certain citizens of Brewster had historical links. In 1936, only a year before *Cape Cod Pilot*'s appearance, Harry L. Shapiro had waded into the debate on racial hybridity—often characterized as necessarily degenerate—when his "widely publicized study of the descendants of the mutineers of the *Bounty* on Pitcairn Island concluded that the hybrids of white-Tahitian unions were more vigorous, robust, and healthy than either the average Tahitian or Englishman" (Sitkoff 192). Berger's handling of the Islanders is notably unstereotyped and respectful. Similarly treated is his story of Joe Perry, a Cape Verdean American settled in Provincetown whose family was shot at on their barge by a German U-Boat, "the first and last German shell to fall on American soil during the World War" (131). It's an amusing enough anecdote, but what is really notable is Berger's care in tracing Perry's race: "Joe Perry's people are called 'bravas,' a dark race, part Portuguese and part African, descendants of the natives of the little island group off Senegambia" (130). This description stands in stark contrast to the outcry of southern Democrats against the "Senegambian" chosen by Roosevelt to deliver the invocation at the 1936 Democratic National Convention. Senator Ellison "Cotton Ed" Smith of South Carolina walked out of the convention, protesting, "I am not opposed to any Negro praying for me . . . but I don't want any blue-gummed, slew-footed Senegambian praying for me politically" (qtd. in Sitkoff 109).

Undergirding all Berger's judgments is his respect for labor. He is at pains to expose any who secretly promote their own interests at the expense of working people: venal members of the Massachusetts legislature, who put their kickbacks before the well-being of sailors; "Our Congressmen," who understand little of sea-going (245); "The politicians of Provincetown," who care less about fishermen (282); the sea captains who take credit for their crews' efforts. One of the guide's functions is to name the contribution of labor which the public record erases: "You will not find any reference to acts of cruelty at sea on stones that mark the graves of ship commanders, naval or merchant" (48). Similarly with Captain Hatch of Eastham, who set a sailing record with his clipper ship, *Northern Light*: "When he arrived in Boston, he admitted that he had 'strained the ship dreadfully.' He said nothing about straining the ship's people, nor does the stone in this cemetery have any word of the crew, in its commemoration of the 'Astonishing

Passage,' and 'Achievement Won By No Other Mortal Before Or Since'" (183). Berger also corrects the record in the direction of labor. He says, for example, that ascribing the shutdown of the Sandwich glass industry to "labor trouble" is a misrepresentation (18). And fishermen are not picturesque loafers. They "are grossly underpaid, always have been, and probably always will be. Fishing is definitely skilled labor" (236).

In this guide, race figures not as an antiquarian relic but as one feature of workers whose value is present and continuing. "The *bravas* were good whalemen, and their descendants are good fishermen" (232). The Portuguese fishermen can spin a yarn as deftly (and at the same time as) they plait a trawl line or tar a net. There is admiration for the very different skills of seiners with Italian crews; trawlers with Portuguese, Irish, and Nova Scotians; the glassmakers of Sandwich; the submarine crew who suffocated to death off the shores of Provincetown; the endlessly brave and dedicated Coast Guard. The illustrations in *Cape Cod Pilot* reinforce this attention to labor, representing the work of mixed-race cranberry harvesters (Fig. 15), net menders (Fig. 16), Coast Guard (Fig. 17), and artists (Fig. 18). As chapter 5 shows, Berger's appreciation for working people's skills derives partly from his valuing writing as skilled labor. Moreover, mixed or hybrid or "fused" racial identities become the norm. Berger himself does some racial "crossing" in his own language, for example using plantation language to describe the situation of the Mashpees who are relegated to "the overseer system" (350) or exposing the hypocritical language of Mayflower Compact I, which allowed for slavery under another name.

Berger sustains, simultaneously, a breezy, jocular tone and a critique of class, colonialism and race relations on—and sometimes beyond—Cape Cod. Comical stories abound: the Yarmouth captain who proposed honoring his wife by renaming her after his ship; the prim Wellfleet boardinghouse keeper, cited on the tour of the Cape's "Bay Side" and "Back Side," who shocked her visitors by advising them that sun-bathing is best on the back side; President Cleveland, lost and soaking in the Sandwich woods, who "knocked at a lonely house in a clearing. A voice from aloft asked what he wanted. 'This is the President,' Cleveland said. 'I'm lost, and I'd like to stay here tonight.' 'Well,' came the answer, 'stay there.' And down went the window" (16–17). Berger even manages to raise a wry smile in his endless tales of how pilgrims went about "flimflamming the Indians" (292). Finally, though, the most impressive feature of this vibrant social scene is

Fig. 15. "Cranberry Harvest" by Cabeen, *Cape Cod Pilot.*

that it owes as much to Native, Portuguese, African, and mixed-race Americans as to the Yankee captains and art and theater colonies which tended to dominate Cape Cod's public image.

Reviewers greeted *Cape Cod Pilot* with near unanimous enthusiasm. The one negative review came from Henry C. Kittredge, the historian whom Berger accuses of racism in his chapter on Mashpee.[9] The Boston and New York press applauded the guide for its energy and irreverence. In the words of Lewis Gannett: "I never expected to read a guidebook through, every word of it, from page one to bibliography. But that is just what Jeremiah Digges's 'Cape Cod Pilot: A Loquacious Guide' . . . beguiled me into doing." And, he notes, "Mr. Digges's sympathies . . . are always with the Indians."[10] Even anti–New Dealers were won over, one of them to the point of reconsidering his wholesale dismissal of work relief. Ending an enthusiastic review, F. N. Finney wrote of the volume: "I only have two objections to it. I used to hate guide books, but Digges has dimmed that hate. So there's one less hate to enjoy. But the worst of it is that 'Cape Cod Pilot' has made me positively urbane about the WPA—at least the Massachusetts WPA."[11]

Fig. 16. "Net Menders, Provincetown" by Cabeen, *Cape Cod Pilot.*

Fig. 17. "The 'C G's' Go Down to the Sea" by Cabeen, *Cape Cod Pilot.*

Fig. 18. "Artists, Provincetown" by Cabeen, *Cape Cod Pilot.*

In terms of the Mashpee, people of color generally, and the very concept of "race," *Cape Cod Pilot* includes everything that the Massachusetts state guide omitted. A critical difference was that Berger pursued the category on which the project was founded—that is, the worker. He valued Native American townspeople, Portuguese American fishers, Cape Verdean American whalers, and Anglo-American sailors as fellow workers. Berger's respect for and interest in difference as a living category also infuse the entire guide. In *Cape Cod Pilot*, the people of Mashpee have a vibrant past, a distinctive present, and the capacity to survive the condescending manipulations of the Anglo-American establishment. Although in one sense Berger's work broke all the rules established by Washington editors, in another it embodied the project's deepest commitments—to workers, to "forgotten men and forgotten races" (to quote Roosevelt), and to discovering a hidden America.

7

ARMENIANS AND ALBANIANS IN MASSACHUSETTS

In terms of providing a public platform for minorities, the Massachusetts project had a considerably better record on Euro-American groups than on Native and African Americans. Although no statistics for project employment by ethnicity exist, employees' surnames suggest a sizable and widespread presence of non–Anglo-Americans who, in time, were assigned to document the corresponding immigrant groups across the state (Mangione, *Dream* 277–78). The canvas was huge: according to Ray Allen Billington, "Massachusetts, with over four and a quarter million people, has a population which is 65% of foreign birth or of foreign or foreign-mixed parentage. This is the second largest percentage with a foreign strain recorded for any state in the Union" (*Armenians* n.pag.). From the production of local field copy through to the publication of the state guide, voluminous detail appeared on statistical records, cultural activities, histories, and contemporary circumstances—of Portuguese, Irish, Jews, Italians, French Canadians, Syrians,

Norwegians, Swedes, French, Greeks, Finns, Chinese, Japanese, Russian, Scots, and Estonians, among others.

From early on, national editors realized that the detailed town and city copy was uncovering a diversity of European communities and practices beyond anyone's previous appreciation. Wanting to circulate fuller, more textured accounts of this diversity than the state guides could accommodate, they committed to what they called "racial surveys" across the country. In Massachusetts, Charles Goldenberg was assigned to spearhead this work from early 1937. He soon moved up from professional to supervisory rating as he directed, collated, arranged, and wrote up the voluminous research from across the state.

In the early days, George Cronyn, in Washington, D.C., coordinated this activity under the title "Pockets in America." Its orientation—later critiqued by the national folklore and social-ethnic studies editors, Benjamin Botkin and Morton Royse—spotlighted and preserved immigrant groups whose distinctive presence in America was in imminent danger of vanishing. One description reads, "'Pocket communities' include religious groups and foundations, ethnic 'islands' that still maintain some of their interesting customs, communities of national stock that have been isolated and retain some of the early American characteristics."[1] Cronyn requested from each state "a terse but vivid description of any unique or peculiar circumstance: a festival, a survival of old-world customs, a street or section given to a distinctive social or racial activity."[2] The letter signed by Harry Hopkins, designed to front nationality surveys in this series, spoke of "tracing the contributions and influences on American culture."

From summer 1938, when Alsberg brought Botkin and Royse on board, the vocabulary and emphases changed. The new title, "Social-Ethnic Studies," signaled the new belief in what we would now call the cultural construction of social identity: "The emphasis is on ways of living and cultural diversity with special reference to population distribution and change."[3] Sounding at times as if he was talking directly back to the "Pockets" project, Royse wanted workers to capture the dynamic process—the "two-way street"—of acculturation as the significant quality: "The ethnic group should be viewed as an element absorbing traits from all other elements in the community, while at the same time stamping the community with Old World markings. Studies should be functional, stressing cultural backgrounds and activities, not peculiarities and 'contributions.'" He asked that workers precisely *not* "overstress the separateness and peculiarities of a group."[4]

Both the Cronyn and the Royse initiatives provoked reams of community descriptions, and Massachusetts editors negotiated with a range of Euro- and Eurasian American organizations to sponsor free-standing volumes.[5] The untimely closing of the project meant that only two books saw publication: *The Armenians in Massachusetts* (1937) was a product of the "pockets" initiative; *The Albanian Struggle in the Old World and New* (1939) emerged directly from the social-ethnic studies approach. In considering these volumes, I am most interested in the dividing line of 1938: that is, the shape such ethnic representations took before and after the accession of Morton Royse as social-ethnic studies editor. The contrast between *The Armenians* in 1937 and *The Albanian Struggle* in 1939 demonstrates the difference between preserving the past and enabling the future.

PUTTING ARMENIANS AND ALBANIANS ON THE MAP

The precarious geocultural position of Armenians and Albanians made these guides—particularly with the U.S. government imprimatur—meaningful events in establishing their cultural identity and acceptability. In their homeland, both groups were fighting to survive under oppression and genocide. Neither group had territorial security in what was then termed "Asia Minor," both having been in diaspora for centuries with intermittent and only ever partially successful attempts at nation-state status. Culturally, as small and somewhat dispersed immigrant peoples, their identities within the dominant Anglo culture of Massachusetts were equally threatened. Armenian Americans fitted Owen Wister's classic racist epithet of the "dingy whites" in America (qtd. in Guterl 6), having to fight for their recognition as Caucasians-in-the-making and therefore their entitlement to American citizenship (Jacobson 108, 109, 129). As far as Albanian Americans were concerned, they were practically an unknown quantity in America: "Most young people believe that their lot as Albanians is worse than that of other second-generation youth in America. 'Americans don't even know where Albania is,' they say" (*Albanians* 102). Although Armenians and Albanians had been coming to the United States since the late nineteenth century, they were rendered invisible by the 1930 census, which listed these people as Turks or Greeks (*Armenians* 34, *Albanians* 4).

A comparison with African Americans in the state is telling. Numerically, both groups had a considerably smaller presence than Blacks: at that time, there were approximately 22,000 Armenians in Massachusetts—about the number of Blacks in Boston alone at that time—and about 10,000 Albanian Americans in the state (*Armenians* [13], *Albanians* 3).[6] Economically, it was a stretch for the Armenian and Albanian Historical Societies to sponsor these publications. In fact, the Armenian Society ended up defaulting on its debt to the publisher (which did not prevent the society from proposing to the project two additional, larger-scale publications for Armenians in the United States at large). As groups approaching the mantle of "whiteness," however, they were determined to take advantage of the opportunity for cultural legitimation symbolized by government sponsorship. The primary field workers—Armenian American Vahan C. Vahan and Albanian Americans G. M. Panarity and Vango L. Misho—enjoyed the strong support of Charles Goldenberg, Joseph Gaer, and Frank Manuel.[7] Indeed, Manuel became quite impatient with Royse's repeated revisions of the Albanian volume.

Rupert Emerson of Harvard University, in the introduction to *The Albanian Struggle*, articulates an agenda which rings true for both volumes: "The pleasant myth of a single and homogeneous United States—represented, perhaps, by the symbol of a shrewd but genial Uncle Sam—has been too often shattered to need further attack, but there has been a vast gap between our general sense that this is a land peopled by many races, nationalities, and creeds and our knowledge of the actual lives and ways and dreams of the peoples who have come here" (v). The guides literally put these communities on the map, globally and within the United States. The guides' maps, historical narratives, and ethnic lineages delineate their "territorial integrity" (*Albanians* 51) in Europe while cultural and political activity mark their cultural distinctiveness in America, all explicitly in the accents of cultural rescue and with the input of native informants, on and off the writers' project: "If the history of the immigrant groups is to be written—and it has been singularly neglected—data must be compiled before the early period grows dim in living memories" (*Armenians* [10]); "Only with the aid of living records, the testimony of the Albanians in this state, has it been possible to reconstruct their story" (*Albanians* 4).

These guides support the building of "imagined community," as that process is explicated by Benedict Anderson. They show how language and literature are central to these people imagining their community, their national solidarity: Armenians and Albanians invent alphabets, develop a periodical press, write textbooks, and contribute to these government guides. Within this framework, all cultural activity—religious, educational, recreational—appears explicitly political, unlike the subtextual politics which lurk in the handling of Black culture by the Massachusetts guide or *Berkshire Hills*. So, for example, "The Church has undoubtedly been the most important agency for the dissemination and preservation of culture among Armenians" (70); Albanians' "mass education movement was designed to further the nationalist cause" (39); and "Due to the political tyranny of foreign rulers who looked with suspicion upon any gathering of their young people, no matter for what purpose, the Armenians had no national sports" (43). Moreover, this confirmation of a cultural and political collectivity connects with the present in a way that *Massachusetts*' atomized treatment of historically situated Black figures does not. The incessant revision of *The Albanian Struggle* right up to a week before its appearance demonstrates the dynamic and very current relationship between the writing of the guides and the maintenance of nations. On April 7, 1939, Italy invaded Albania, and King Zog fled to Greece. Muriel E. Hawks's foreword notes: "Our book was in press when on April 7th newspapers ran headlines about dramatic events in Albania . . . we are . . . unable to take cognizance of changes occurring after the first ten days of the month" (iv); and, indeed, the occupation of April 7 appears as part of the guide's historical narrative when it appeared later that month.

That very dynamism, between community and publication, caused Alsberg a frisson of nervousness. In the case of the *Armenians*, the publication date was so close to the Sacco-Vanzetti controversy that the national director was ultra wary of any political opinions. In fact, however, when Louise Lazell, the newly appointed censor, vetted the volume, her only criticism was that it lacked attention to women.[8] *The Albanians* in one draft seemed to Alsberg altogether too partisan, and his concern brought the basic governmentality of the guidebook project to the surface: "We would be open to severe criticism from the State Department if we published anything that appeared like an attack on a Government with which the United States is on friendly relations"; "As this is to be a government publication, it will be necessary to eliminate these passages." Manuel, who had been revising the volume according to instructions from Royse for at least seven months, did not hide his dismay: "I cannot hide my misgivings that with each revision much of the zest of the original manuscript is being squeezed out."[9] Yet Alsberg's nervousness indicated that *Albanians* had indeed moved beyond the safe confines of preservationist antiquarianism and was intervening in the lived conditions of a complex ethnic group.

ASSIMILATED ARMENIANS AND HYPHENATED ALBANIANS

While the two ethnic groups had experienced similar oppression and displacement, and clustered around similar urban centers (including Boston and Worcester) in Massachusetts, their representation in the two guides was very different. Both guides sought to heighten the profile of the immigrant groups in the state, but in the first case as a "pocket" of contained culture and in the second as a participatory, social-ethnic force.

The Armenians in Massachusetts brings Armenians to America in distinctly individual terms. Earlier Armenian history—twenty-five centuries on the borderland between Asia and Europe—is told in a brisk narrative which treats the Armenians as a group—sometimes an independent nation, sometimes a scattered people subjugated by greater powers. Once the account arrives at the nineteenth century and Armenian settlement in Massachusetts, it becomes a taxonomy of individual contributions. The first settler, a servant named Garo or Garabed, brought to Worcester in about 1867 by an American missionary, left his employ when he discovered that he could make more money in one day at the local wire mill than he made per month in service. Soon others followed him into the mill. The late nineteenth century brought Michael Tophanelian, founder of the Armenian Club in Worcester which led to the first Armenian church in America, in 1891. Then the first Oriental rug merchant arrived in Boston; subsequently a family of cymbal makers established a plant at Norfolk Downs. And so on. Even group formations are identified in terms of individuals: the leaders of patriotic organizations, political factions, and the apostolic and protestant churches in Massachusetts; the publishers and editors of the state's numerous and faction-ridden Armenian newspapers; the successful athletes to emerge from Armenian American sports federations. As the list of individual achievement lengthens, and becomes less representative of wider community patterns, the guide begins to excavate pockets within the "pocket" of Armenian American life. The guide declares that "Armenians take no prominent part in the political life of Massachusetts" (40) and "The Armenian Theatre, as such, is practically non-existent in the State" (110) but, in both cases, proceeds to dredge up individual exceptions. The pressure of Louise Lazell is evident in the few women's names tacked on to accounts of organizational, sporting, and cultural achievements. The one confident cultural mark is explicitly a single exception: "The only characteristic of Armenians in contemporary Massachusetts that is definitely Armenian is their cuisine" (133).

The sense of this limited pocket of individual achievement is reinforced by the guide's self-referentiality. All the consultants thanked in Billington's preface appear as notable Armenian Americans in the volume. Dr. Varaztad H. Kazanjian, whom the volume features as a world-famous plastic surgeon celebrated at the Harvard Dental School, wrote the foreword. Vahan C. Vahan, the project employee who was the main writer on the guide, writes himself into the record with some prominence: he is identified as a founding editor, in 1932, of the *Armenian Mirror*, the community's first English-language newspaper, and as one of two Boston men who head up the list of Armenian American writers in English in Massachusetts, with his well-received *History of Armenia* in 1936.

For all this roll call of achievement, the volume's structure is profoundly assimilationist. The emphasis on individual contributions never challenges America's coherence as a nation. Indeed, the shift over time from cultural separation to assimilation figures as unambiguously progressive and mimics a New Deal "rise of America" narrative. Early immigrants came to America as a temporary measure to earn money to support, and ultimately return to, families at home. They had no interest in learning the language or customs of their new country, "they had no class consciousness, took no interest in labor unions, and showed no dissatisfaction with their working conditions" (31). This isolationism, in the opinion of the guide writers, made them responsible for their own mistreatment—"subjecting themselves to natural criticism and prejudice" (144)—by more established Americans and by their own countrymen: they "were victimized by ruthless opportunists of their own race who served them as translators and guides" (35). After World War I, the Kemalist regime in Turkey did away with any form of Armenian political power, and permanent settlement in the United States began to look like the only route to survival. Putting new efforts into belonging to the larger society, Armenian immigrants have changed from "'undesirable aliens,' in isolation" to making "remarkable progress in their endeavor for self-adjustment" (144). Their assimilation is reported in unabashedly positive terms: "The Armenians as a group, always sensitive to an environment superior to that of their origin, are rapidly merging into the American pattern" (145). In religion, superstition, language, cultural habits, political allegiances, "the American-born generation seems to have a preference for American institutions" (122).

From beginning to end, then, the authors of *The Armenians in Massachusetts* accept that this is a record for the archives, historical preservation of a people who are inevitably vanishing. Ray Billington's preface states that "the slow process of assimilation is inexorable" ([9]). Early on, the text concedes: "At the present time a united, free, and sovereign Armenia exists only as a dream for her nationals" (23). And the work ends elegiacally: "Industry, loyalty, endurance and moral fortitude are qualities that should endure even when ethnic identity has vanished" (145). An editorial in the *Armenian Mirror* (December 15, 1937) welcomed the book as "an attempt to preserve for all time a record of the contributions of our race to the culture of America, no matter how humble that may appear to be," by "a liberal and far-seeing administration" which "has done more for the cause of conservation than any previous administration—yes, conservation of natural resources, of human values, and of historic sources and records."[10]

In contrast, *The Albanian Struggle in the Old World and New* brings alive the reciprocal tension represented by the hyphen in Albanian-American. April 1939 was a highly fraught moment, politically, for Albanians, with their recently revived state—envisioned and heralded as a democratic achievement—under the autocratic rule of King Zog, then invaded by Mussolini's fascist regime. Also, of course, *The Albanian Struggle* had been reconceptualized and thoroughly rewritten under Morton Royse's social-ethnic guidelines, away from the puffery of individual "patriots" and toward the collective participation and integration of ordinary people.[11] The result reads more like a social history with guidebook and novelistic characteristics than a roll call of individual achievement. It also conveys more of the conflicted relationship between Albanian and American.

There is no clear arc of assimilation in this guide's version of history. Again, the starting point is the thirteenth century B.C., from which point these people—the oldest inhabitants of the Balkan peninsula, they claim—are constantly buffeted by war and invasion, submerged into the Turkish empire in the modern period, but continue their fight for independence. Here, however, the European story merges seamlessly with the American chapter. Massachusetts figures as an outpost of Albanian nationalism, hosting fierce battles between political factions and intensely nationalistic religious activity among Moslems and Christians, literary developments, and cultural activity. For many previously dispersed, rural Albanians, entering into the close quarters of Massachusetts mill and factory towns brought them into solidarity as "conscious Albanians" (vii). The movement back and forth between the two countries—money, arms, people—continues up to the present. An emerging (and reemerging) independent Albania owes much to American resources, with money, a new national flag, military outfits, parliamentary procedures and support, pressure groups, and educational textbooks exported from the New World to the Old. "The greatest spiritual achievement of Massachusetts Albanians has undoubtedly been their struggle for an independent fatherland. It is not too much to say that the creation of the Albanian state was largely their work" (81–82). One wave of emigration back to Albania occurred in 1908 after the success of the Young Turks' revolution fomented confidence in the return of Albanian power, another after World War I with the reestablishment of an independent Albanian state. In both cases, disillusionment with the course of developments led Albanians back to America, with the intention of permanent settlement after 1920. Even then, ongoing engagement with Albanian politics is strong, with the organization Vatra continuing to work, from Massachusetts, on behalf of a liberal Albania. Generational shifts are complex, too. While women become more independent in America, they also are the major preservers of Albanian culture, and younger Albanian Americans vacillate between Old and New World models in, for example, marriage customs.

The Albanians describes a very similar racism to that delineated in *Armenians in Massachusetts* with a very different attitude and arc. These immigrants, like their Armenian counterparts, intent at first on making money to send home, then on individual betterment, generally lacked labor solidarity or a shared class consciousness with their fellow workers. The racism they encountered is partly explained by this isolationism, but not at all excused. On the contrary, put into the mouth of one on the receiving end, the sting of racism is more keenly felt by the reader: "one old immigrant reminisced, 'We could not stir out of our *konaks* without being tomatoed or otherwise assaulted by rowdyish children and dago'd or god-damned by their fathers'" (99). In this account—and it is one of many uncomfortable truths—racism is not a thing of the past: "the harsh slum America which has been the bulk of their experience has done little to win them over" (viii); "Comparatively few Albanians . . . are enjoying a decent American standard of living"; "The older Albanian immigrants who are approaching the end of their days in these miserable flats have found little reason to accept America" (98).

The guide works hard to bring the reader into the experience of displacement and alienation, with first-person point of view and imagined scene-setting. The first response of a 1905 immigrant, "shrinking and bewildered" at life in the mill towns, becomes imagined in direct speech: "'This is not my country,' he reasoned; 'I have not come to stay. How the American people live, why they act and think as they do—these problems are not my problems'" (32). Perhaps because a combination of Albanian and non–Albanian Americans authored this guide, the pronoun usage is much less stable and confident than in many WPA publications. In the same paragraph, the reader is assumed to be part of the "we" of culpable, non–Albanian Americans—"Prior to 1912 few of us knew what manner of men Albanians were or even where Albania was"—and seized as "you"—"If you had ever encountered a newly arrived Albanian peasant . . ." (3). This repeated onslaught on the reader's awareness of the racism, poverty, and alienation suffered by immigrants eventuates in a questioning of America that the Armenian volume does not remotely approach. *Armenians* describes immigrants "who either by choice or necessity have sought, acquired, and enjoyed the hospitality of this great Commonwealth for about half of a century" (143). *Albanians* communicates a much more hollow sense of citizenship: "The Albanians of Massachusetts are ceasing to regard the traditional customs of their homeland as living reality. But have they found substantial values to replace what they are losing?" (97)

While individuals are named in this narrative—the first settlers from

Korcha and Katundi, key nationalist leaders Fan Noli and Faik Konitza—it is not a story of individual achievement. Throughout, the focus is on social formation and conditions with, for example, a quite complex appreciation of how ethnic societies and clubs deliver both isolationist and assimilationist effects. The very characterization of Albanian Americans *as* a society, rather than atomized individuals, amounts to an implicit claim for their impact on America. The vision of the future is not of a race mixing and melting into dominant America but a more active picture of immigrants' children coming "to realize that a new culture is in the making in America, and that they may join the other races of the world in helping to build it" (112).

Royse was manifestly proud of *The Albanian Struggle*: "the book squares up tolerably well with the best of the local guides, and is as good a job as has been done in the whole field. . . . There won't be any hullabaloo about this one little volume on an obscure element, but a series of such booklets will give added significance to each individual volume. It will eventually tell a story that has never been told, and couldn't have been told without the amazing set-up known technically as the Writers Project."[12] As it turned out, the volume had made it out just under the wire. Six months later, the *Saturday Review of Literature* lauded the book's dynamic representation of ethnic diversity in elegiac tones: "Such an extraordinarily interesting study of one small element of our heterogeneous population makes it seem all the more regrettable that Congress should have curtailed the useful activity of the Federal Writers' Project" (qtd. in Mangione, *Dream* 284).

The contrast between these two narratives suggests the shaping power of WPA guides. Both are progressive productions that use the authority of governmental imprimatur to compensate for the omissions in another government document: the census, which renders these immigrants' true ethnicity invisible and hides "the flesh and blood reality" "with the cold aid of statistical tables" (*Albanians* v). *How* the guides bring Armenian and Albanian Americans alive in their cultural specificity depends—as in the case of Native and African Americans—on the cultural classifications in operation. In the case of *The Armenians in Massachusetts*, the guide amounts to more nostalgic remorse, an elegiac documentation of a vanished race. *The Albanian Struggle in the Old World and New* takes on a more life-giving task—to provide rhetorical and material support to minoritized peoples, to record the highly conflicted relations between newer and "Old Stock" immigrants and, in the process, to help keep diversity and respect for difference alive.

8

MEMORY-MAKING IN SUDBURY, AUBURN, AND SPRINGFIELD

City and town guides had a different dynamic, again, from any of those considered so far. As local publications, they were relatively free of state and national oversight, but they did not have the independent vision of a Josef Berger or the solidarity of purpose of an ethnic or racial community.[1] These publications tended to be controlled by local cultural organizations—anniversary committees, chambers of commerce, city governments—whose agenda was to consolidate community identities in the face of centralized, bureaucratized, and corporate takeover—in other words, to bolster their communities in the face of threatening modernity. This chapter explores how the WPA guides to three very different towns enabled memory-making strategies which would preserve Sudbury's investment in the past, Auburn's investment in individuality, and Springfield's investment in modernity.

The issue of memory-making comes forward more insistently at the local than at the state or national levels. Whereas state publications seem to intervene in the more professional and academic domain of history-making, local guides aspire more to the status of what Pierre Nora calls *lieu de mémoire*: a memory place "which by dint of human will or the work of time has become a symbolic element of the memorial heritage of any community" (*Realms* 1: xvii). Nora understands memory places as compensatory strategies in a modern world that has lost its traditional continuities: "*Lieux de mémoire* exist because there are no longer any *milieux de mémoire*, settings in which memory is a real part of everyday experience" (*Realms* 1: 1). In the case of the local WPA guides, the mark of their collective memory-making is, first, their emphasis on territoriality. In the words of another foundational memory-studies theorist, Maurice Halbwachs, "most groups . . . engrave their form in some way upon the soil and retrieve their collective remembrances within the spatial framework thus defined" (156). More succinctly, Nora states the principle that "memory fastens upon sites, whereas history fastens upon events" (*Realms* 1: 18).

Second, the guides are more interested in continuity than chronological rupture or distance. They eschew the kind of critical perspective encouraged by history writing. Halbwachs distinguishes collective memory as "a current of continuous thought whose continuity is not at all artificial, for it retains from the past only what still lives or is capable of living in the consciousness of the groups keeping the memory alive" (80). The guides inculcate that continuity partly by demonstrating an unbroken line of descendants from a town's foundational moment to its present, partly by showing the continued existence of its territorial borders, and partly by producing a narrative connection for a sequence of moments.

Third, and most powerfully, local guides ally themselves to commemorative, bodily practices. Paul Connerton's central argument about social memory is that "images of the past and recollected knowledge of the past . . . are conveyed and sustained by (more or less ritual) performances" (3–4). The guides with the most powerful memory-making capacities are those which most closely approximate the embodiment of ritual, what Connerton calls "acts of transfer that make remembering in common possible" (39) and what Michael Kammen has explored in the specific context of 1930s' enthusiasm for pageantry and community performance. Although, as written forms, the guides cannot literally sediment habit-memory in the body (Connerton 72), they can approximate bodily enactment. Some guides incorporate into their presentation the community's ritual pageantry, while all of them draw their readers into the community, through detailed physical routes, the rehearsal of local genealogies, the delineation of iconic events, and an invitation to group membership invoked by the pronominal "we." All of these gestures of inclusion contain within them, of course, implicit and occasionally explicit exclusions.

SUDBURY

In a real—if not quite literal—sense, the writers' project guide to Sudbury saved that town from the voracious Henry Ford. *A Brief History of the Towne of Sudbury in Massachusetts, Together with the Programme of the Exercises enacted in Commemoration of its Three Hundredth Anniversary 1639–1939* is the clearest example of the writers' project enabling local agency in the community-building process. The volume is also, as its title suggests, the closest the project came to embodied memory-making. That the guidebook remains a living part of Sudbury's cultural identity is suggested by the Sudbury Woman's Club revising it, as a community improvement project, in 1968 and then the Sudbury Historical Society doing further revision for the 1987 edition.

Around 1920, Henry Ford embarked on the collecting of Americana designed to create "his own institutions of memory and patriotism," as Michael Kammen calls them (351). From the beginning, this entrepreneur's conservationist efforts were at one with his triumphs as a technocapitalist. Because his framework was national, his methods assembly-line, and his vision of power corporate, he felt able to move the pieces of his historical reconstruction around at will, using the sheer force of his buying power to remove buildings and artefacts from their historical locations to add to the ideal assemblages which he concentrated on selected sites. His historic artefacts, like his employees and his manufactures, were replaceable parts in Ford's huge, efficient machine, which manufactured history as zealously as automobiles, and in the same name of education and progress.

This was the vision informing Ford's response when, in 1923, a Sudbury stockbroker approached him about buying shares in the historic Wayside Inn, extant as a hostelry since 1716, made famous by Longfellow's *Tales* of 1863 but now fallen on hard times (Garfield 48). After a fast and surreptitious trip to the inn, Ford bought the whole property, then set about not only renovating the building but remaking its entire surroundings of nearly 2,000 acres: "Within two weeks he had purchased more than a dozen neighboring homes and farms in order to isolate and cleanse the inn of modern anachronisms and potential encroachment" (Kammen 354); " 'to provide a fitting frame for the picture and keep hot dog stands and peanut wagons out of the front yard,' as he put it" (Garfield 52). Four years later, he moved the Redstone Schoolhouse (of "Mary had a little lamb" fame) from Sterling, Massachusetts, to the Wayside Inn grounds, funding the education of sixteen local schoolchildren from grades 1 to 4 in the old-fashioned schoolroom (Garfield 52). In 1928, he sawed the Parmenter-Garfield General Store in half and moved it with teams of oxen from Sudbury town center to a spot near the Wayside Inn. And in the same years he rerouted a substantial section of the main Highway 20—at a cost variously estimated between $288,000 and $368,000—away from the front door of the inn (Garfield 53, Butterfield 59, Goodstone 26). His ambitions growing with his achievements, he next attempted to buy up all the water rights along Wash Brook in Sudbury so that he could turn the Charles O. Parmenter Grist Mill into one of his "village industries"—in this case, manufacturing Bakelite dashboard parts—and he tried to take over the planning for Sudbury's new town hall (Garfield 54). Piece by piece, he was imposing his template of a functioning community on Sudbury, reshaping the town as a demonstration of national origins, "to show how our forefathers lived and to bring to mind what kind of people they were" (qtd. in Kammen 354).

At this point, the community started to rebel. The Wash Brook project, in particular, cut across Sudbury's distinctive historical organization, by which "meadow rights" determined voting privileges and other access to power. Ford's buying up of meadowlands along the river could be seen as an effort "to reorganize the ancient proprietorships, which were first established upon the town's incorporation in 1639" (Garfield 49). In 1930, the town "politely rebuffed" Ford's offer of a town hall site (Garfield 56), and then the continued refusal of one meadowland holder to sell his water rights caused the collapse of the Wash Brook project, "leaving the townspeople, especially speculators who bought up useless meadow land, at each other's throats" (Garfield 49). While maintaining ownership of the Wayside Inn, Ford lost interest in Sudbury as a project, concentrating his cultural ambitions in Dearborn, Michigan, where, as the biggest employer in the state, he had the power to assemble Greenfield Village out of the assorted Americana that took his fancy. "Sudbury would not become the Utopia that Ford and some people envisioned and, as far as the majority of the townsfolk were concerned, it was just as well" (Garfield 74).

Five years later, when project writer George Williams—local to but not, I think, resident in Sudbury—wrote the field copy on the town for the state guide, he sounded distinctly irritated with the townspeople's lack of gratitude to Henry Ford. Williams made Ford a central figure in almost all his topic papers on Sudbury—history after 1789, history prior to 1789, noted personalities, education, philanthropy, historic houses, scenic description, even racial cultural heritage. Under that last heading, Williams argued: "Little, if any, cultural heritage has been felt as a result of new blood from other races"; "Mr. Henry Ford has endeavored to build up culture . . . a cultural benefit which is all too slightly recognized by the natives of the town. (Personal investigation)."[2]

Some of the cultural values informing the town's resistance to its takeover by Ford were on display in the pageant mounted on July 2–4, 1939, in celebration of the three hundredth anniversary of Sudbury's founding. This was a major event—"More than $1,000 of depression-era town money, not to mention hundreds of hours of volunteer work, had been plowed into this birthday party"—and it attracted a crowd of 20,000 people, the largest attendance at any event in the town's history.[3] The celebration consisted of a series of historical pageants. Townspeople dressed up as Puritans to reenact the first church service held in Sudbury. The next evening they put on the garb of seventeenth- and eighteenth-century forebears to participate in a costume ball of quadrilles and other period dances. The third day consisted partly of a historical parade, with floats representing scenes from the town's beginnings, passing chronologically from the "First Survey of Sudbury Meadows, 1633" through scenes of land purchase, home-building, the town's incorporation, the building of the first church, King Philip's War, the building of the first school, and the revolutionary battle at Concord, to "Peace and Prosperity." The *Boston Post* declared, "the history of the progress of the town developed as the floats moved on, like the pages of a book being turned" (qtd. in Garfield 95).

At first sight, the ideological markings of the tercentenary celebration match Ford's principles. It consistently emphasized patriotism, myths of origin, the linearity (hence inevitability) of progress, and the unity of the local and the national—all hegemonic emphases of which Ford would have approved (and he did, indeed, contribute the resources of the Wayside Inn to the event). But the differences between the pageant's and Ford's reconstructions are significant. Unlike Ford's efforts, the pageant demonstrated the continuity and collectivity of memory-making in the ownership of the commemorative process, its embodiment, and its relationship to place.

Most obviously, the planning and implementation of the commemoration were handled by committees of community members, not orchestrated by a corporate leader in hierarchical relationship to local employees. Certainly, class and other structures of power came into play in the formation of these committees, but they were consistent with the town's history—many of the members' family names echoing those of the settlers—and with its current social organization. The *Wayland Chronicle* first lists the names of all committee members, then comments: "These were the committees who planned the celebration but working with them, carrying out the hundreds of details, that have made this undertaking the grand success it has been are men, women and children, all doing their bit to help. . . . This has been a truly community enterprise and each person in the town may well feel a personal pride at its success."[4] A notable feature was the greater prominence of women's culture than in Fordist reconstructions. Women took ownership of several events at the tercentenary: local women wrote the two plays which opened the celebration, many women participated in the organizing committees, women designed the homemade puritan costumes, and generally the pageant gave considerable attention and value to domestic forms such as the communal lunch, historical homes, children's education, and family life.

The commemorative rituals designed by these committees and reported by local newspapers also emphasized the embodiment of memory, in people and place, very much in the terms set out by Paul Connerton as crucial to the making of social memory. Participants are repeatedly marked as "direct descendants" of the town's settlers, carrying their lineage in their names, their costumes, and their bodies. So, for example, the march to the church was "a procession of Puritans, composed of the church choir and descendants of original Sudbury settlers."[5] The preacher who read from the 1639 sermon of Jonathan Edwards was identified as a direct descendant of the seventeenth-century pastor of the First Parish Church of Sudbury Township. The tercentenary ball was in the hands of "Albert Haynes, descendant of a Sudbury founder and dancing master at the Wayside Inn."[6] One float, "Sudbury Men on Way to Concord Fight, 1775," was manned by "descendants of original volunteers."[7] The historic coach and horses lent by Henry Ford transported the five oldest descendants in the parade. The casts of the opening theatrical performances were all settlers' descendants (Garfield 93). And both the program and the *Marlboro Enterprise* of July 3, 1939, listed sixteen ancestral names represented by members of the pageant. Similarly, organizers closely matched the sites and routes of parades and performances to historical locations. This sense of historical authenticity was very different from Ford's, which insisted on accuracy of technological detail—the grist mill he had constructed at the Wayside Inn, for example, had to conform precisely to eighteenth-century specifications in design and materials (Goodstone 28)—but treated location, the historical ties of place, ownership, and local use as infinitely malleable in relation to his design.

The power of these reenactments as "acts of transfer" building community and collective memory is elucidated by Connerton. He argues that ritual commemorative ceremonies do not *remind* participants of mythic events but *re-present* them in "ceremonially embodied form" (43): "Rites have the capacity to give value and meaning to the life of those who perform them" (45). The emphasis on the genealogies and lineages of the participants accords with Connerton's assessment of embodied memory: "Every group . . . will know how well the past can be kept in mind by a habitual memory sedimented in the body" (102). The symbiotic group bonding enabling and enabled by cultural memory also played out in the display of community-building between Sudbury and its neighbors. Stories in the local press repeatedly show the citizens of Marlboro, Wayland, and Framingham (all localities which, historically, had broken away from Sudbury) entering enthusiastically into the tercentenary: "Wayland Salutes Sudbury On Birthday Which Both Share"; "For many long and pleasant years the towns of Sudbury and Wayland were one in name and therefore have a common history and interest. . . . Citizens of Wayland are proud to take a part in the Sudbury Tercentenary Celebration."[8]

Predictably, all the demonstrations of continuity and collectivity also worked to police the margins of cultural insiderism. The marginalization at work shows through only once with clarity, but the moment is telling. In describing the puritan church service, more than one newspaper described the participation of Native peoples, "direct descendants" of a different order. The *Framingham News* described the authentically costumed "Chief Eagle Claw of the Sioux tribe, who with his two sons slithered through the underbrush to the very door of the church, there to cast baleful glances at the retreating backs of the rear guards." The *Marlboro Enterprise* reported "two full-blooded Indians, Chief Eagle Claw and his son, Eagle Feather of the Sioux tribe from the Mohawk Indian Trading Post in Concord."[9] The anachronism now seems glaring, the Sioux being a plains tribe whose clothing and headgear were most inappropriate for the topography of the northeast. The mistake is more understandable in this period of "pan-Indian" revivalism when Native peoples, seeking increased visibility across the country, would borrow each other's regalia and forms of cultural display. Nevertheless, the lack of press interest in these ethnographic details contrasts sharply with the minute attention to Anglo-American residents' puritan heritage. If this performance was a staging of King Philip's War, it once more erased the Wampanoag people. Clearly Native peoples continued to exist on the margins, well outside the circle of authenticity, self-validation, and group identity of the collective memory-making exercise.

The Sudbury guide took on all the cultural baggage suggested by the tercentenary exercises. In many ways, this publication was coterminous with the pageant. The book opens with a double claim of authorship, one by the Sudbury Tercentenary Committee (with full membership list) and the other by the Massachusetts Writers' Project (with a naming of the local guide authors, as permitted by the rules for local WPA publications). This sign of collaboration is closely followed by the five-page program for the event, as printed prior to its staging—with details of the pageants and places, participation by descendants, a list of the sixteen ancestral names that will head the procession to church, and so on—which has the effect of a script for a performance to unfold in the guidebook's pages. That sense of the performative carries through to the closing pages of the guide, which consist of a written approximation of a speech act: a letter from the mayor of Sudbury, England, responding to a communication from the chairman of the tercentenary committee and pledging allegiance and a living memory of the towns' common origins.

The pageant, as a collective memory-making exercise, gained in several ways from its inscription in the guidebook. First, the guide's chronological organization converts the linearity of the pageant—its procession of floats and so on—into the "meaningful narrative sequences" which Paul Connerton identifies as crucial to remembering (26). The chapters unfold in the same chronological order as the 4th of July parade, often with the exact scenes or reenactments from the pageant (such as the community lunch in the interlude between church services) described as part of the guidebook narrative. Also, although the periodization is longer, the pacing of events—with more than 80 percent of the book focused on stories of puritan, colony, and revolution—suggests the same emphasis as the pageant: the history that "really matters" is all pre-1800. These narrative sequences also underscore the myth of progress to which the pageant gestured. Third, the pageant's reenactments gain the permanence of the published word, including a kind of fixity that protects this version of history from contestation, especially given the low-key declarative language of the guidebook genre.

Above all, the guidebook strives for continuity, in a seamless narrative which admits of no dissension during the first two centuries of the town's existence. The thoroughness of the guide's whitewashing of the colonial and revolutionary eras becomes evident in contrast with Sumner Chilton Powell's 1963 Pulitzer Prize–winning account of Sudbury's settlement, *Puritan Village: The Formation of a New England Town*. Where the guide represents collective action—community meetings, elections, building, and the like—as consensual, Powell probes the factionalism and dissent that go unmentioned in the guide, structuring his account around "a violent dispute [which] broke out in Sudbury, Massachusetts, in 1655–1657" (xix–xx). Essentially a generational conflict, it opened up "serious stresses and strains in the new ideal state of Sudbury" (xix) with, interestingly enough, the second generation rebelling against the founding fathers by invoking English authorities that the first generation had thrown off in the self-determination of the new country. Powell's treatment of military history is particularly thought-provoking, given the emphasis on military events in the guide (and other reconstructions of the town's history): "the crisis which the town had to face was not a military one. It lay deep within its own heart" (115). None of these ruptures is hinted at in the guide, which willingly gestures to the disciplinary rigors of the puritan regime, but not to any sense of internal dissension. Only once the town is well into the nineteenth century does the guide admit the presence of religious schisms, documenting the "ecclesiastical disturbance" which "divided [Sudbury] into hostile camps" from 1823 (48). Karal Ann Marling has demonstrated how the colonial revival was a protected species in the thirties, a source of patriotism, pride, and optimism that was badly needed in a period of devastating poverty and frightening violence. It is consistent with her analysis that both the guidebooks and the various pageants of the period privilege seventeenth-century beginnings and eighteenth-century revolution as heroic eras. Only the periods beyond those are fair game for criticism. Any celebratory effort had to believe in the rightness and unity of the colonial effort, and the guidebook follows the pageant in papering over any possible cracks.

That emphasis on continuity is undergirded by a much quieter, yet fundamental, attention to continuity of place. Immediately after the tercentenary program, the guide opens with a triple representation of the site of Sudbury: a map demarcating its boundaries in 1698 and 1939, a 1660 quotation from Samuel Maverick describing the position and aspect of the town, and a narrative of the site's founding. From that point on, the guide consistently traces the links between historical and contemporary locations, often in personal terms which show that the past is very much present in the daily and domestic life of Sudbury. So, for example, "The *Major Thomas Brown Garrison* was built about 1660; . . . it stood a few rods east of the Framingham Road (now Fred Ham's farm). The *Goodnow Garrison* was south of the Boston Post Road near the East Sudbury station, now a part of Aubrey Borden's house" (23). The guide consistently names current owners of historic properties, with many architectural photographs captioned "still owned and occupied by descendants." In this context, "Mr. Ford" as owner and operator of the Wayside Inn does not loom any larger than any other property owner. The guide positions him neither as the prime architect of the town nor as a major disturbance to it (as he figures in Garfield's later guide to Sudbury). The links to the present work to sew places into collective memory and attach that memory firmly to the descendants and inhabitants, the "insiders," of the town.

The continuities accumulate in the guide, strengthening the sense of a normative, delimited local community. Continuity of voice, for example, is provided by numerous quotations from letters and personal documents from times past, as well as the inclusion of tales that "old people still tell" (5). In giving a human face to governmental regulations, forms of settlement, and so on, that use of voice also folds in difference. For example, the "Indian deeds" are individualized with a characterization of Karte or Cato, who gave Sudbury settlers a deed for the land occupied by his tribal group. The consistency of population size from the Civil War to the present is taken as a sign of stability, not stagnation, as is the occupational emphasis: "By 1875, as now, the main business of Sudbury was farming" (56). As well as the past being continuous with the present, the local is coterminous with the national—the interests of the one are those of the other: "Sudbury Saves Massachusetts" (24); its citizens repeatedly show "the true 'Spirit of '76'" (52). The summative chapter which ends the volume—"Sudbury Today"—opens by reiterating the effect: "Sudbury today wears the aspect of a sheltered community. The process of change over the centuries has been one of graceful translation rather than rude substitution" (57). To a degree that sounds defensive, the chapter repeatedly denies any decline in Sudbury's fortunes. The town is "'old-fashioned' only in the best sense" (58).

Within this conservative memory-making, the one mark of progressive difference is, as with the tercentenary celebrations, the role of women's culture in the guidebook. Women played a larger role in the making of this guide than in the state production. By 1939, the director of the Massachusetts Writers' Project—who signs off on the book—is a woman, Muriel Hawks; three of the four credited project writers are women; and more than half the tercentenary committee members are women (although, both on the project and in the tercentenary organization, chairmanship roles go more often to men). Marianne Hirsch and Valerie Smith have discussed the cultural power inherent in a woman becoming "an agent of memorial transmission" (2), a role which enables women's perspectives and material contributions to be sewn into the social fabric. In this case female agency seems to have made its mark on the emphasis of both pageant and guide on settlement. Most colonial reenactments are military, with women and children literally standing on the sidelines, waving off the menfolk who see the real action of the event. In Sudbury's commemoration of 1939, military scenes are overshadowed by attention to home-building, domestic skills, and the family unit, and the guide (like the pageant) depends heavily on women's skills for its creation. The geopolitical coordinates of the guide are also feminized, in terms which are conventional but take on additional resonance in this context, as "the Mother Town of Sudbury" (46 and elsewhere) struggles to establish its independence from "the Mother Country" (37 and elsewhere). Within this female-demarcated space, the only individualized reference to an African American in the guide concerns a woman. In the mid-eighteenth century, it is said, "The town fathers met 'to see what the town will do with regard to Dido, a negro woman who is now upon charge in this town,' and 'to make strict inquiries who brought Dido into town'" (36). The reference remains undeveloped and its purpose unexplained, but the mention does mean that Dido is named and remembered within this inscription of the town's collective memory.

The reverberations of these efforts at collective memory-making, with all the complexities around power and local community, continue. April 19, 1975, saw the bicentennial celebration of the opening battle of the Revolution. Sudbury's commemoration was not entirely militarized. Organizers pressed the Redstone School (now owned by the town) back into service to enable an educational reenactment very similar to those of 1939: "children from the Sudbury schools, dressed in colonial costume, once again sat at the desks and learned lessons taught hundreds of years ago"; "children attentively listen to their teacher, living the history they are learning" (Goodstone 30, 31). One of the architects of the event makes clear the self-consciousness of this embodied memory-making: all the participating pupils, teachers, and guests were asked to sign their names on pages which would be bonded to the back of hornbook lessons and preserved in the school house, so that "they can return years from now with their grandchildren and point out their names" (Goodstone 31). That such a memory-making exercise was a priority for the town is suggested by the citizens' decision to support it despite funding being denied by the Massachusetts Bicentennial Commission.

At the same time, a few miles north of Sudbury, other townspeople were engaged in the military wing of the commemoration and, with nice irony, in full support of another Fordist regime. Playing a key part in the bicentennial reenactment of the revolutionary battle at Concord were the Sudbury Minute and Militia Companies, dressed in full colonial garb to retrace the march of two hundred years before: "Colorful in their assorted farmer's garb, enthusiastically marching to fyfes and drums, Sudbury's trail blazers were chosen Presidential Honor Guard by the Secret Service and would later be positioned along the walkway as a buffer between the roped off crowd and President Ford" (Goodstone 10). The pageant was organized around the arrival of President Gerald Ford, who had the unhappy task of memorializing America's triumphant act of war right at the fag end of the catastrophe in Vietnam. As he spoke from his podium—surrounded and protected from the crowd by Sudbury's proud militia—Ford was drowned out by the yells of the People's Bicentennial Commission. This group—a leftist, populist organization opposed to governmental and corporate control of national remembrance—had 20,000 members on hand. They charged en masse down "the Patriot's hillside," banners aloft ("Economize Democracy"; "John Hancock never sold life insurance"; "Don't Tread On Me") and accusations roaring (Goodstone 9, 12–13). As this extract from their manifesto opens, it could easily be targeting Henry Ford. As it ends, it could just as easily have the Federal Writers' Project—or the entire New Deal—in its sights:

> Corporate America has conceived a Bicentennial plan to manipulate the mass psychology of an entire nation back into conformity with its vision of what the American life should be. The strategy will be to speak of the greatness of America to those who feel insignificant; . . . to speak of patriotic commitment to those who feel isolated and confused. The long-range goal is to convince people that the problems facing America can be solved by existing institutions. (Qtd. in Bodnar 167)

While the Sudbury participants are not recorded as being on the side of resistance, their community had already played its part in creating and sustaining the *lieu de mémoire* from which opposition could be staged when they "politely refused" Henry Ford. One wonders if any theme park could have provided a site so resonant as this for resistant remembering.

AUBURN

The role played by *A Historical Sketch of Auburn Massachusetts* (1937) as a bulwark against the corporatization and disappearance of the town is graphically demonstrated nowadays in the Auburn Public Library. Auburn itself is hard to find, what was once a town now disappeared into the vast suburb spawned by Worcester, its previous lines of identity at best blurred, at worst eradicated, by a hodgepodge of motels, fast-food outlets, and businesses supporting the needs of a bedroom community dominated by white-collar commuters. The library sits within this commercial maze, an unremarkable, sparely designed concrete building at the comfortless intersection of several highways, hemmed in by the Auburn Mall, a Comfort Inn, and several other featureless commercial buildings. Tucked into the rear of the library, a small room turns out to be the Local History Room, housing surviving publications, photographs, and other materials of archival interest still valued by those who work to protect the town's identity. Within this small holding, three copies of *A Historical Sketch of Auburn Massachusetts From the Earliest Period to the Present Day with Brief Accounts of Early Settlers and Prominent Citizens*, Sponsored by the Auburn Centennial Committee, Written and compiled by the Federal Writers' Project of the Works Progress Administration for the State of Massachusetts (1937)—one original and two photocopies bound into folders—have pride of place. The guide is one of the very few materials from the 1930s in the room, and its continued citation in local histories suggests that it remains a prized resource for those in the know.

The sense of Auburn's imminent disappearance was already palpable in its one brief citation in the WPA guide to Massachusetts. On Tour 11, From New Hampshire Line to Connecticut Line, appears this entry:

> Left from Stoneville on a road skirting *Dunn Pond* is AUBURN, 0.8*m.* (Town, alt. 560, pop. 6535, sett. 1714, incorp. 1837), at first named Ward, for Artemas Ward, popular Revolutionary officer. Confusion between the words Ward and Ware caused the change in 1837 to the present name, probably suggested by Goldsmith's line, "Sweet Auburn, loveliest village of the plain."
>
> Agriculture, the original occupation, was supplanted by industry that died out as the town became a residential suburb of Worcester. (543)

Perhaps in the face of anonymous suburbanization, the town initiated a publishing project, announced as the foreword to the *Historical Sketch of Auburn*:

To celebrate the One Hundredth Anniversary
of the Act passed by the
Great and General Court
on February 17, 1837
to change the name of the town from Ward to Auburn
the townspeople
at a meeting held February 4, 1937
elected the following general committee
who are publishing this brochure

(Actually, it is a sixty-five-page book.) At this point, there follows a list of thirteen names, with their committee positions, headed by "MISS M. ELIZABETH HEWITT, *Chairman*."

This opening, with its emphasis on names—the naming of the town as the act of origin, the naming of each member of the sponsoring committee—is symptomatic of the work as a whole. The Auburn guide is much less structured according to narrative sequence than the Sudbury guide. "The Story of Auburn" is told in a single chapter, after which the organization becomes thematic: "Churches and Congregations," "Education," "Manufacturing and Agriculture," "Military Affairs," "Biographical Notes," and "Points of Interest." The book concentrates on reviving and returning to collective memory a plethora of names. The operation is both recognizable as and more than Connerton's notion of names as "a socially legitimate currency of memories" (3). The names are bridges between the individual and the collective, the personal and the public, but they are also a means of cultural survival, the materials with which the town resists its own erasure. Geographically, the "territorial changes" (23) of the past centuries are charted and reconnected with the present mainly through the recovery of place names—the first, Nipmunk names; the "mother towns" from which Auburn separated; the name change, with the petition of 1836 and its granting by the Commonwealth of Massachusetts in 1837 fully quoted; and the identification of parishes, congregations, school districts, and industrial areas.

The biggest press of material comes with the naming of people. As in the case of Sudbury, this memory-making is something of a closed hierarchy. Those whose acts made the public record at some point from the seventeenth century to 1937 (*Early Settlers and Prominent Citizens,* as the book title says) the guide now records and honors once more. Those whose lives and deaths went unremarked then are equally without mark in this volume. That said, the act of recovery aims, like Sudbury's, to create a chain of embodied continuity. Whenever possible, the lists of names explicitly link the past to the present. The original residents of Worcester, Sutton, Oxford, and Leicester who petitioned for a separate precinct four times in the eighteenth century (seventy-five men and women are named) stand as the impulse directly responsible for the existence of present-day Auburn. The eighty named minute men who served in the Revolutionary War appear within a taxonomy of military engagement which also names eighty-one Civil War veterans and the 175 men and two women who served in the recently ended "World War" (that is, World War I). The representatives from Auburn to the General Court are named from 1782 to 1935, the postmasters from 1833 to 1935, the town clerks from 1778 to the present, the pastors of the Congregational Church from 1784 to the present, similarly the deacons, the pew holders, the librarians, and so on and so forth—thousands of names held together by the thread of historical narrative. And, of course, some of those surnames reverberate with the committee members' listed in the foreword. This guide has been forged in the most literal of senses out of that continuous lineage.

These thousands of names amount to a community of "insiders," a lineage for the town to shore up against its incorporation. This impetus, evident both in the 1937 guide and in Auburn's community pageant of that year, is quite different from previous and subsequent memory-making celebrations. For example, the town's 1928 sesquicentennial celebration had been much more driven by self-promotion: "BOOST AUBURN FASTEST GROWING TOWN IN THE COUNTY," as the bunting on Holstrom Brothers' delivery truck blared for the 1928 parade (*Happy Birthday Auburn*, n.pag.). In more recent times, Auburn's public officials have devoted considerable attention and resources to Pakachoag Hill as the launching site of the first liquid-propelled rocket, developed by Robert H. Goddard, on March 16, 1926. "This invention was the forerunner of our present space flights and in honor of this event, Goddard Memorial park was established at Drury Square"; it is now one of only two Auburn sites on the National Register of Historic Places (*Happy Birthday Auburn* [3]; *Auburn Guide* 11). This event goes unmentioned in the WPA guide. The site's significance concerns the mark Auburn made on the national and international scene, whereas the guide's primary interest is the marks made by Auburn's "cultural insiders" within the community—their imprint on community formation and survival.

The exclusionary side of this impetus shows up again around racial difference. The list of eighty-one Civil War veterans, painstakingly identified by full name, regiment, and rank, ends with this notation: "2 colored Volunteers were furnished by the state" (51). A state or national editor added this note at the eleventh hour, just as the guide went to press, and no record survives of the source for the information. It does, however, graphically expose the racial privileges of individuation. Nameless and powerless—the "volunteers" under the state's control—people of color are the cultural outsiders in this endless taxonomy of worthy citizens. It is also relevant that, in the mixture of "races" and "thirteen different nationalities" (34) which we are told several times have merged harmoniously together in the town, no mention is made of Black Americans. The handling of Native Americans is exclusionary by a different method. Representatives of the tribes of "the Nipmuck Country" (5) whose lands were taken for settlement in the seventeenth century are painstakingly named, along with the Christian Indian villages from which they came. The purpose of this naming, however, is to map Native places onto colonial place names and to record the handover of the land to the settlers. After the close of King Philip's War at the end of the seventeenth century, no more is heard of Native peoples. They are quietly excluded from the guide's drive for cultural survival.

Given the primary drive of the guide toward naming (or explicitly failing to name), it makes sense that the centennial celebrations to which the publication is linked appear at the end of the volume. No visual display could recover the number and detail of names included in this volume; even war monuments name only those who have died in service. The program and the local press coverage also make it clear that Auburn's pageantry was much less invested in the authenticity of descendants and reenactments than Sudbury's. The main historical pageant of the week-long celebration begins in the symbolic: "Miss Auburn" and her retinue welcomed visitors, including "Miss Columbia" "symbolically representing the United States," a prologue immediately followed by "Epoch One—The Ballet of the Seasons" in which "the Spirits of Nature at play present the allegorical Dawn of Creation"(62). The myth of origin here is more typological than historical, and that generalized celebration of existence continued to weave in and out of more localized representations of early settlers, the first school, the naming of the town, military engagement, and so on. Tellingly, and again in contrast to Sudbury, children enacted most of the rituals which received press attention. The whole event has more the feel of a fancy dress parade or children's fête than the historically precise reenactments mounted by Sudbury's citizenry. One feature that is similar to the Sudbury event is the appropriative representation of Native peoples. The "Indians" in this case are white members of Worcester lodges with names of Swedish and Italian origin. The local press photographed them in plains-type headdress and reported a lineage which jumbled together tribes from western, eastern, and southern regions of the country, a confusion that again contrasts markedly with the painstaking reconstruction of white family lineages: "Members of the Quinsigamond and Cherokee Tribes of the Red Men and the Oseola Council of Pocahontas of Worcester will take part in the historical pageant on Saturday night representing the visiting tribes in the Indian scene where John Elliott preaches to the Indians on Pakachoag hill."[10]

Significantly, women's culture marks this pageant and guide much less than the Sudbury work. While women—often girls—perform in the pageant, men receive much more credit for its organization. The guide's emphasis on recovering the names of town officials, churchmen, soldiers, and other public figures means that women receive comparatively little attention. All the "Biographical Notes," for example, focus on men (with, on occasion, their wives mentioned within the entry), and the grave of Clara Barton (Red Cross founder), which is listed in the points of interest, does not figure in the guide's discursive text. There is, however, one woman whose role seems to have been key in establishing the preservationist and localist emphases of the guide. Miss Elizabeth Hewitt, "a local resident who was interested in Auburn's history and geneologies," served as "chairman" of the guide's sponsoring committee (Belding and Weiss-Belding 4). Recent records reveal that one item on the anniversary program—"House Party," lantern slides of Auburn homes—was also the work of Elizabeth Hewitt, who put together a slide show of "what were then considered to be the historic places in town" (Belding and Weiss-Belding n.pag.). Hewitt is now credited with attempting to instill in individual homeowners like herself a sense of responsibility for the preservation of historic Auburn, presumably a role similar to her part in making the guide happen. The necessity and tenuousness of the achievement are suggested by the fact that the Auburn community directory no longer lists local celebrations—only Independence Day on July 4 and Memorial Day on May 30—and by those flimsy, well-thumbed photocopies of the *Historical Sketch*.

Newspaper stories of the period offer one final impression of the Auburn project as a self-protective exercise, creating a historical record through names and bodies while sealing this circle of cultural insiders off from the discontinuities of modernity. Throughout June 1937, cheek by jowl with the coverage of the Auburn pageant, the local press carried daily coverage of WPA strikes—the theatre project workers on a hunger strike in New York City and, less dramatically, Massachusetts Writers' Project employees attached to the Boston, Worcester, Springfield, and New Bedford offices staging a work stoppage in the face of savage quota cuts. The authors of the Auburn guide would have been attached to the Worcester district office and therefore part of (at the very least aware of) these labor disturbances. Yet there is no hint in the Auburn writers' work that those events are part of the context for this guide, that they have any relevance to the memories of this place.

SPRINGFIELD

It was one of the Federal Writers' Project's most often quoted boasts that it didn't do boosterism. Katharine Kellock was particularly scathing of any claims in guidebook copy which amounted, in her judgment, to chamber of commerce puffery. From Washington's perspective, too much local control inevitably meant that local pride took over, and local pride could only mean bombast and boosterism (see Bold, *WPA Guides* 29–30). Yet by 1941, priorities had changed. The federal organization had been disbanded, farmed out to those states willing to sustain project work, with much more decision-making happening at the state and municipal government levels. *Springfield, Massachusetts*, by the Massachusetts WPA Writers' Project (1941), came out of this changed disposition of power, and indeed it is one of the most boosterish guides produced on the project. What Kellock and her colleagues underestimated, however, was the complexity of the cultural work done by local self-promotion. Where they could see only trivialization and commercialization, the Springfield guide does something more interesting. It cuts across the cultural lines policed by *Sudbury* and *Auburn* to produce an image of the city combining Fordist enthusiasm for the corporate version of history with a resuscitated story of colonial origins that had become invisible in the cityscape. In other words, it gives to the community a memory of past and present which combine to guarantee a secure, commercially profitable future.

The guide opens by saying that any pre-nineteenth-century history is now largely invisible—erased by the speed of modernization and change in the city: "Not a single house, probably not even a tree, of the seventeenth century remains, and traces of the eighteenth century grow fewer as the years pass" (11). The nineteenth and twentieth centuries predominate architecturally, in layout and in modern conveniences such as street lighting. The guide quickly launches into a reconstruction of the years since 1635 when William Pynchon went west to the Connecticut Valley and founded the settlement (Agawam, later Springfield) in 1636. Although some of the episodes in this account are similar to those included in the Sudbury and Auburn guides, the pace and direction of this tale of rapid growth and expanding trade are very different. Springfield's colonial past moves along at a quick clip. There are no long detours through lists of names, as in the Auburn account, and the arrival point is not the historical glory of Sudbury but the achievements of now.

To this degree, the guide seems to conform to the vision of the federal office which, in 1938, circulated a memorandum requiring that local city guides move away from their "inadequate" form and toward an emphasis on growth and progress: "The Rise of the Cities," in the memo's Beardian language.[11] The first chapter of the Springfield guide—"Growth of a City"—echoes those directions, as does its steady story of progress, improvement, enlargement, and modernization: "Secure upon the foundation of its history . . . it has learned from the past and it looks eagerly toward the future" (84). The guide also credits government for key initiatives in that growth. For example, the federal government's establishment of the Armory in Springfield in 1794 "set the pattern of Springfield's future: an industrial community, a center for skilled workmen, a cosmopolitan city of many races and creeds" (15). The government continues to be credited for its WPA projects and built structures which enhance the town—music, playgrounds, recreation programs. The double introductions to the Springfield volume work in the opposite direction to those in the Sudbury volume. Here, municipal and project personnel strive to credit each other as the true creative force: Roger L. Putnam, mayor, credits the writers' project with "the real writing task" while Muriel E. Hawks announces the volume as "a portrait of Springfield, by Springfield.' . . . Through the medium of the Massachusetts WPA Writers' Project, the community has created a self-portrait replete in detail" (although she does also name writers' project members). Both forewords stress the co-operative, collaborative effort.

Springfield city government initiated the guide not in the context of an anniversary or a pageant but with an eye to attracting a skilled workforce to the city. In the mayor's words: "It has been written so that you may see why we are so proud of our city, and with the hope that you will become interested in Springfield as a place to live, as a place to work, and as a place in which to do business." Much of the time the text sounds like standard promotional prose, stressing the city's amenities—educational, recreational, housing—and this emphasis brings with it an enthusiasm for the corporate which becomes one of the main structuring principles of place, according to this representation. For example, as with the other local guides, taxonomies predominate, but here the ostensibly inclusive lists are neither of individuals' names nor of historical events, but of social statistics, census data, industries (over three hundred "manufacturing concerns" are listed [57]), insurance companies, banks, educational institutions, retail establishments, and so on. The cited names have influence: major retailers, donors, benefactors, corporate heads such as "Stanhope E. Blunt, once a commandant of the Springfield Armory, a former park commissioner, and one of the city's benefactors," after whom a park is named (28); local manufacturer Nathan D. Bill, who gave the city two playgrounds; George Walter Vincent Smith, a successful importer and manufacturer, who donated the Art Gallery and its major collection; and Daniel L. Harris, railroad executive and one-time mayor, one of the founders of the Museum of Natural History. One of the few memorial sites is the William Pynchon Memorial Building, which contains "a progressive record of Springfield's development and history" (36). The guide clearly targets its audience when it promotes corporate bodies as the primary employers, the donors of excellent recreational facilities, and the cause of the superior housing stock (since the influx of skilled workers in the nineteenth century, the guide tells us, Springfield has been designated the "City of Homes" [20]). Most of what we hear of the Civil War is the "boom times" it afforded the Armory (50); "Other cities suffered depression after the Civil War, but Springfield had struck its industrial stride" (17). There is no mention of a depression in the 1930s. And, of course, the current war overseas is good news for Armory employment once more.

The categories for valuing these achievements also owe much to modern methods of measurement. Repeatedly, conditions of life in Springfield compare favorably with American averages derived from new social science data: tables documenting the incidence of crime per capita, hospital beds per population, and other quantifiable measures of success. The guide cites social scientists as the most modern authorities on several occasions: for example, "Social scientists have succeeded in establishing the fact that recreation makes for both physical well-being and mental health, and by decreasing crime and disease generously repays society for its expenditure upon recreational facilities" (25). City planners—the Park Commission and the like—are a concordant presence, credited with creating such a harmonious and well-adjusted environment. In this climate, gender figures as a social science category, a way of analyzing the local population. So, in addition to the more familiar histories of women's clubs, institutions for women's education and reformation, and so on, there appears a lengthy breakdown of working population by gender in various industries, professional and semi-professional fields, and agriculture (57). To a degree, the Springfield guide makes gender newly visible, yet there seems no particular valuing of domestic or women's culture. Ultimately, the emphasis is not on the domestic but the commercial, and most information is turned toward an appreciation of "the city's houses of business" (66). What matters above all is the "balance" and "stability" of "The Mercantile City" (59). The Eastern States Farmers' Exchange, for example, is celebrated not in terms of socialist value or even because of its traditional methods but because "the system obviously saves money for the consumer" (60).

Cumulatively, this guidebook presents a site which is both local *and* corporate in its identity, a town so invested with simulacra—according to the guide's account—that they constitute its lived experience. The guide presents several scenes that encapsulate this hybrid identity. First, in Forest Park, two scenes are conjoined in a typically Fordist compression of historical and physical perspective: a life-sized Christmas crêche which "draws thousands of reverent visitors" is flanked by "the dinosaur tracks brought from Holyoke" (26). Next is the village of Storrowton, a "New England Colonial Village" situated within the city's annual agricultural fair, the Eastern States Exposition, itself invented as a private corporation "founded by a group of prominent Springfield citizens" in 1912. "Given by Mrs. James J. Storrow of Boston, a vice president and trustee of the Exposition," the village has all the marks of a corporate, Fordist reconstruction:

> Since 1927, 11 Revolutionary and post-Revolutionary buildings have been removed from their original sites and reassembled here board by board and piece by piece, so that gradually Storrowton became just such a village as once stood among the hills and valleys of early New England. Its farmhouses, meeting-house, school, store, tavern, and blacksmith shop come from different States and are of varied styles that include the gambrel-roofed Phillips House built in Taunton in 1767, the square Gilbert farmhouse built in West Brookfield in 1794, the 100-year-old white church from Salisbury, New Hampshire, and the little red schoolhouse that had stood in Whately, Massachusetts, since 1810. Together they surround the village green, preserving for posterity the peaceful charm of an early New England village scene. (75)

This scene is positioned as the finale of the discursive part of the guidebook, with the implication that the account has come full circle, rhetorically, from the opening scene of three hundred years earlier.

Finally, there is the mock architecture which dominates the town itself. The massive "Municipal Group" in Court Square ("the heart of Springfield" [77]) consists of neoclassical twin buildings, one an auditorium, the other an administration building, "with identical Corinthian porticoes," between them a Florentine campanile three hundred feet high ("the unit is an impressive monument to civic pride" [77]). Other buildings mimic Italian Renaissance style: the city library of marble, the George Walter Vincent Smith Art Gallery of Pompeian brick trimmed with terra cotta, the Museum of Natural History, the Elks Home. Of a different style again are the Georgian colonial William Pynchon Memorial Building and college buildings, the Italian Gothic churches, and the English Gothic churches which imitate the originals in Springfield, England. The guide lists only one modern building, the Springfield Trade School: "a newly constructed building of steel faced with limestone . . . it is well-equipped with the latest facilities for training" (82). Artificial histories and mock reconstructions dominate the city, defining its reality and its values. In the emphases of the guide, these simulacra constitute a lived sense of the place as "the good life."

The darker side lurks, unexamined, in the contrasts which subtend this representation of the good life. For a reader with any knowledge of Massachusetts, the guide's repeated insistence on the city as a place of skilled workers, with its high proportion of single-family dwellings, evokes a close contrast with the state's troubled mill towns. The guide is at pains to stress that, for all its modernity, Springfield has neither "the harassed activity characteristic of many modern communities" (11) nor the congestion "of an industrial city." Without saying it in so many words, the guide emphatically demonstrates that this is not New Bedford, Fall River, Lawrence, or Lowell: "Most of its factory buildings are scattered; only a few are concentrated in the North End near the river. There are no mile-long brick and stone mills flanked by acres of factory tenements. No mass exodus of workers fills the streets at the screeching of a hundred whistles" (11–12). Similarly, the stress on friendly labor-management relations inadvertently evokes suppressed memories of the city's own past and others' present labor troubles: "There have been no serious labor disturbances within recent years, and Springfield has acquired a reputation for friendly industrial relationships between employers and employees" (57).

Among all the textual suppressions, this guide's treatment of racial diversity provokes, perhaps, the greatest sense of discomfort. The three guides' attitudes to race comport directly with the cities' memory-making investments. Thus, *Sudbury*, dedicated as it is to the preservation of colonial history, never addresses non-English immigration. *Auburn* acknowledges and celebrates what it calls the "new racial strains" (23) in its midst, but insists that "the various segments of Auburn population have fused into a fairly homogeneous whole" (24). This attitude allows the guide to present a roll call dominated by English names as if that collective history proves the natural superiority of "Yankees." *Springfield* is the guide which most needs the marks of ethnic diversity in order to prove the city's cosmopolitan modernity. And, indeed, its interest in ethnicity proves to be decorative: "On the windows of offices and shops are printed Irish, French-Canadian, Polish, Scotch, Italian, Jewish names—and Saint-Gaudens' reminiscent *Puritan*, from his site on State Street, confronts the modern city" (11). The guide does not pursue ethnic patterns in its treatment of residential neighborhoods, industrial occupations, or the daily pattern of people's living and working conditions.[12]

Springfield also implicitly denies a Black American population, omitting them from every statistical list in the book. The 1930 census is cited in a way which avoids acknowledging African Americans: "almost one-fourth of the city's population was foreign born. Of the native white of foreign or mixed parentage, the Irish are shown as the largest racial group, followed closely by the French-Canadians, the Italians, and the Poles. Scotland, England, Russia, Sweden and Germany are represented in lesser numbers" (18). But the absences and repression return as logical contradictions which disturb the harmony of the text. The unacknowledged Black population appears three times in the guide. John Brown, living in the town before the Civil War, had African Americans as neighbors: "When Frederick Douglass, the Negro orator and scholar, came to Springfield he found the champion of his people living in a cottage near the shacks occupied by free Negroes" (17). The list of church congregations in 1940 includes Black worshippers: "Two of the Baptist, two of the Methodist, and one of the Congregational churches have Negro congregations" (4). And among the city's clubs and cultural organizations appears the Dunbar Community League for Negroes (46). The guide wants the patina of cosmopolitanism offered by racial diversity. What it does not want is living Black presence.

In all of this—the inculcation of memory rather than the recounting of history, the drawing of the reader into collective memory, the sleight of hand whereby apparent remembering masks actual forgetting—these guides enact a shift in scale, from the national to the local. While the guides tend to position places within national narratives of triumphant modernity, they consistently value the local as the work's primary raison d'être. In the process, these guides can also make space for marginalized cultural presences which are more speedily passed over in the state guidebook: women's culture often plays a larger role in both process and product at this level; the forgotten names of those who have served their communities are returned to the record; more rarely, disenfranchised groups—striking workers, people of color—are included in the local story. The three guides' power and resistance to centralization lie in this giving of identity and voice. Their range can be schematized as a spectrum: at one end is a guide which helped a town to resist theme-park status; at the other is a city which embraced simulacra as a means of surviving the future. The guides go from the felt continuities of *lieux de mémoire* to the essential discontinuity of "hallucinatory re-creations of the past"(Nora, *Realms* 1: 12). Nora's terms are useful in this analysis because they evoke the double-edged potential of collective memory-making: on the one hand, resistant to the anomie and loss of localized power in the conditions of modernity; on the other hand deeply interested in maintaining and sustaining cultural insiderism, preserving local cultural hierarchies and racialized exclusions. This operation is fundamental to the social and political fabric. In Paul Connerton's analysis, "control of a society's memory largely conditions the hierarchy of power"; "the struggle of citizens against state power is the struggle of their memory against forced forgetting"(1, 15). The versions of cultural memory endorsed in the guides to Sudbury, Auburn, and Springfield quietly play out that struggle one more time.

THE PERFECT STORM: THE NEW ENGLAND HURRICANE OF 1938

When Sebastian Junger titled the 1991 hurricane which drowned the *Andrea Gail's* six-man crew from Gloucester, Massachusetts, "the perfect storm," he was referring both to the climatological phenomenon and to his own writing opportunity. So with the hurricane of 1938. It issued from an equally unexpected conjunction of forces, and it provided the opportunity for the perfect worker-writer publication. *New England Hurricane*, the collective photo-text published less than six weeks after the storm and one of the most popular project productions, drew particularly on the accumulated expertise of the Massachusetts Writers' Project. Material poured into the Boston office from field writers adapting their guidebook and life history techniques to the coordinates of this disaster. Muriel Hawks and Frank Manuel finetuned their sleight-of-hand editorial techniques, producing a highly shaped text which read like a gathering of individual voices. In many ways, this publication pulls together the strands running through this study: the book positioned WPA writers as conduits between their local community and the larger reading public, it won them public plaudits as both workers *and* writers for the first time, and it enabled them to convert their own localities, and their own identities within them—ordinary working lives made strange and extraordinary by disaster—into *lieux de mémoire*.

THE NEW ENGLAND HURRICANE

On September 21, 1938, a tropical hurricane veered off its predicted course, traveling at unprecedented speeds up to 186 miles per hour. It joined with incessant rainfall and a massive storm wave to devastate an unwarned, unseasoned, and unbelieving people all across New England—a region which had not been hit by a hurricane for over a century. According to Junger, "The waves generated by that storm were so huge that they literally shook the earth; seismographs in Alaska picked up their impact five thousand miles away" (129). The storm killed 680 people and destroyed $400 million of property (Allen 349).

The New Deal had become very practiced at recording disaster in terms that redounded to the credit of the administration. The Farm Security Administration was only the most famous example of the alphabet agencies skilled in documentary, combining what James Agee labeled "the central instrument of our time"—the camera—with succinct, pointed captions and more discursive commentary (9). Under the visionary direction of Roy Stryker, the Historical Section—Photographic of the FSA produced thousands of images of rural distress which powerfully communicated the human face of the Depression while persuading the public that federal intervention was not only necessary but effective. While other agencies did not achieve the aesthetic and political sophistication of the FSA photography project, many of them—such as the United States Department of Agriculture, the Civilian Conservation Corps, the National Youth Administration, and the Federal Art Project—also relied heavily on photography and photo-texts to communicate their mission, their clientele's needs, and the results.[1] The cumulative impact of that repeated documentary narrative—from displacement and despair to relief and recovery—was particularly strong at this moment in mass media, with the newly widespread popularity of radio and cinematic newsreels and the launching of the photo-magazine *Life* in 1936. Government photo-texts made sense of economic conditions in human terms, helped people to feel that they belonged to a larger community of suffering, and provided reassurance that the New Deal was not only aware of the problems but addressing them.

New England Hurricane fit this model of representation-as-relief in both its production methods and its textual dimensions. The project boasted that its response time broke all records. When Frank Manuel, regional director for New England, conceived of the book, he knew that speed of production would be crucial for sales, partly because of competition with other "souvenir" publications but also because the project needed to be visibly responsive to community needs. It needed to make sense of events for a people still in shock, to communicate the dimensions of the disaster and the succor being offered by government virtually as it happened. By September 28, he had convinced Henry Alsberg to back the plan; then he fired off directives to state editors across New England who, in turn, instructed their district supervisors to direct their field workers in immediately gathering this material and forwarding it to Manuel in the Boston office. Muriel Hawks joined Manuel in urging Alsberg to remove bureaucratic impediments to the book's production: "Unlike most of our books, the success of *New England Hurricane* depends upon its early publication."[2] When the book appeared, on November 4, 1938, press releases and reviews made a point of its production speed: "It has been reported that the whole project was in the hands of the printers 18 days after it was conceived"; "the book's sponsors claim that it is the fastest job of publication the world has ever seen."[3]

Press releases also positioned the book as a service to the community in its gathering of survivors' voices. The guidelines which Manuel circulated to state directors in Connecticut, Rhode Island, Massachusetts, New Hampshire, Vermont, and Maine repeatedly stressed the need for verbatim material. To John B. Derby, Connecticut director, he wrote that the aim was to record: "A mass reaction to a significant phenomenon"; "We want descriptions of the hurricane from the mouths of all sorts of people, preserving their similes, respecting their tall stories." To Teresa Heidel in Vermont, he described the book as "our attempt to gather living material on one of the greatest disasters ever experienced in our region." State directors then translated these priorities for district supervisors. Muriel Hawks wrote to Leroy Bradford in New Bedford, for example: "Will you inform other workers in your district also that I want them to write down at once any dramatic impressions they have of things they actually saw or to jot down as literally as they can accounts they have had from other people?"[4] Again, this emphasis shaped reviews, as the press lauded the project for bringing together the contributions of two hundred WPA writers into one coherent account: "A 40,000-word manuscript had been prepared from first-hand conversations and reports of WPA writers whose own homes had been flooded"; "The volume was prepared by WPA writers who were actually 'on the spot' everywhere throughout the hurricane area"; "From all sections of New England came proof that the 'experiment in co-operative writing' was running as smoothly as a greased gyroscope."[5]

As usual, these representations of collective authorship hid as much truth as they revealed. The "greased gyroscope" wasn't running quite as smoothly as advertised. First, gathering survivors' stories so soon after the disaster presented a considerable challenge. A week after the hurricane hit, Bradford told Hawks: "First person accounts are practically impossible at the present time because those involved in them are still under medical care because of the shock."[6] Another field worker—it sounds like Nellie Coombs—wrote to the editors: "I have had to get this (information) mostly from newspapers and what few things I could pick up from people who had contacts there (Cuttyhunk Island and Martha's Vineyard). Sorry I can't give you any verbatim reports, but it's a long swim to the islands, and furthermore, the water's too dern cold."[7] The material which field workers submitted—from their own experiences, or based on interviews or gathered via more remote hearsay—was usually not nearly snappy enough for Manuel. He and Muriel Hawks raided submissions for a turn of phrase here, a sentence there and occasionally a direct quotation, melding the fragments together into a succinct, almost newsflash style which remained true to workers' observations but did not sound very like any of their voices.

Project publicity also emphasized the larger cooperation among producers in securing information and images: the book publishers, newspapers, government agencies, numerous public and private groups, utility companies and the like. Again, the jostling behind the scenes belied this story somewhat. The publishers—Hale, Cushman, and Flint of Boston—particularly infuriated Manuel by horning in on the editing process. First, they excised material without his permission, abrogating the agreement that he had last say on content and that text would run to about one hundred words per page (in the event, many pages held less than half that amount). Once the book proved to be an overwhelming success, the publishers also began to play down the role of the writers' project, representing themselves as masterminds, editors, and authors of the work. So strong was the analogy between the book's harmonious collectivity and the mending of shattered communities that Manuel could not afford to go public with these contractual breaches. He concluded plaintively to Alsberg: "I am disturbed at the treatment we have received at the hands of this publisher, but I frankly don't see what can be done about it"; "I do not see how I could possibly have been more explicit, both in the contract and in subsequent agreements."[8]

Textually, the shape of *New England Hurricane* also fit the familiar New Deal disaster-and-recovery pattern. Tracing an arc which begins and ends with emphasis on cooperation, most of the book reads like Maren Stange's characterization of FSA documentary: "These images poignantly document the massive and irreversible breakdown of traditional . . . life" (Daniel et al. 3). Page by page, words and pictures document the course of the hurricane as it swept a path through New Jersey, New York City, and Long Island, smashing into the south coast of Connecticut, Rhode Island, and Massachusetts, up through these states into New Hampshire and Vermont, then glancing off into Maine and on up into Canada. One piece of wreckage follows another: house upon house shattered, boats innumerable heaved up onto bridges and streets, cars crushed by lampposts and trees, streets flooded with floating houses, streetcars, automobiles, and lumber. These images still dominate an eye-witness description of the scene forty years later: "Everywhere—on the docks, in the street, at the beach—normality was harshly transposed: the boat was aground, the house was afloat, the living were dead, the landmark had disappeared" (Allen 315).

Point by point, the account reads like an anti-guidebook, taking the reader on a geographical tour not of a community's accomplishments but of its losses. The route here does not conform to Katharine Kellock's highway of progress: "A well-written tour provides a guide to the rise of civilization in the country through which it passes."[9] Here, the route follows the swathe of destruction caused by the hurricane. In this landscape, modernity is reversed: one photograph shows a paved highway ending abruptly in a landslide of rocks and fallen trees; the caption reads, "The Mohawk Trail has in part returned to the wilderness" (156). In another part of Massachusetts, "Residents of NEWTON learned to do without modern conveniences; for days lights and telephones were out of commission" (176). And the commentary accompanying images of smashed mills sounds ominously like a return to

Fig. 19. Medfield Unitarian Church and Norwood First Baptist Church, *New England Hurricane* (photographs from the files of the *Boston Globe*).

the depths of the Depression: "Wings of local mills were clipped. Industrial establishments were rendered useless" (160). The very church spires and houses celebrated in the WPA guides are toppled, askew, ripped open with their innards exposed. Monuments, smashed and displaced, are "embarrassed" (77; Fig. 19). Landmarks are marked only by their disappearance: in New Hampshire, a stone bridge donated by local benefactor Edna Dean Proctor is now "a gaping hole" (202), and the Shaker Bridge at Enfield, "built by the Shaker community in 1849, was washed away" (209). The very identity of Windsor, Connecticut was threatened with erasure: "a tobacco town since 1640. . . . Today the crop is gone" (124).

Visually, this is a crazy landscape in which water and land are confused, roads are ripped away, boats end up over rather than under bridges. At Oakland Beach, Rhode Island, "cement foundations were ripped up and scrambled in meaningless forms on the land's surface" (55). At Bay Springs, Rhode Island, "Some dwellings were so expertly twisted off their foundations that nice distinctions between front door and back door could not readily be made" (73). Some photographs are literally illegible. With familiar structures collapsed, there is no sure ground from which to calculate scale and perspective (Fig. 20). The commentary—again in diametrical contrast to the guidebook rhetoric—repeatedly demonstrates the folly of humankind attempting to control nature: in Hartford, Connecticut, among the flotsam bobbing about in the flood, a waterlogged sign with its entirely irrelevant warning,"NO Trespassing" (123); on Misquamicut Beach in Rhode Island, heaped with the fragments of buildings and possessions, the only item to survive intact a crazily tilted sign reading "Persons Coming on this Beach in Bathing Suits *and* Changing in Cars *IS NOT ALLOWED.* ORDER BY LAW" (46). Or, most explicitly: "*Saunders Cottage* at Misquamicut was sliced in two, and half its stone fence was mowed down. Only a gate post was spared, to serve as an anchor for a 'Private property, no crossing' sign. Man proposes . . . " (42).

Some of the reparation offered by *New England Hurricane* is in the very act of representation, the "making it real" of documentary for a disoriented and devastated people.[10] The photo-textual layout encourages the reader to make connections between italicized or upper-case words and the images to which they refer, often leapfrogging intervening text and images to pursue the thread of commentary. And occasionally, a subject in a photograph will stare out at the reader in knowing complicity at the record which is being made. The degree of disorientation is communicated by Everett S. Allen, remembering

Fig. 20. Somewhere on the southern coast of Cape Cod, *New England Hurricane*.

his own experiences of the hurricane, in New Bedford. His account is worth quoting at length since it demonstrates how closely the project account answered the need for sheer confirmation of events:

> I walked the docks and beaches during the following days, attempting not so much to discover the truth of why it had happened as to accept the reality of what had happened. If the dark wildness of Wednesday remained unbelievable (Thursday dawned benign, quiet, its water characteristically gentle), the miles and acres of destruction over which I crawled and stumbled were equally incredible even when one walked them in the unforgiving light of day.
>
> It takes some time to sort out an experience like this. If you have seen the sea sun-sparkled and glassy, clear and clean, swirling about the bare feet of a child and have watched it in the same place, only hours later, dirty, ugly, and as high as a two-story house, crushing things and people, it stretches the mind to accept the contradictions.
>
> And there are so many other things—the row of boathouses, shops, and shanties, silvered by generations of weather, that had been a fundamental of childhood; it might not have been so bad if something had been left that was recognizable, but as it was, the buildings were gone, the land on which they stood was gone, and the land remaining was so alien in form as to repudiate and confound the memory. (352)

The project account both represents and enumerates these losses—"New England counted its dead. Six hundred eighty-two men, women and children. Many others still in hospital. Almost 700, released from hospitals, convalescing at home. . . . Seventy-two million feet of wire down. Four hundred miles of cables. Thirty-one thousand poles. Eighteen thousand cross arms. Over a quarter million telephones out of service" (218). At work here is what Michel Foucault calls the "power of enchantment" of "the mere act of enumeration" (*The Order of Things* xvi), an effect which has a particular charge in the period, according to David Gelernter: "The thirties are mesmerized by numbers" (18, 40).

The book also offers more direct antidotes to confusion and despair. Intermittently, the overwhelming accumulation of destruction is relieved by a joke, a story of heroism, or, in most typical New Deal style, images of men (and very occasionally women) at work. Sometimes smiling, sometimes visibly exhausted, these workers embody the counteraction to the hurricane's destruction. In Connecticut, "master *organists* labored amid the rocks to make repairs" to a railroad switch box at Niantic (22) and "men, working night and day, dredged a channel" to float a lighthouse tender off railroad tracks in New London (26). In Rhode Island, "restaurant workers and store clerks . . . worked courageously at the seemingly hopeless job of cleaning Providence" (62), while in Newport, "rescue workers struggled along in rowboats from door to door, offering transportation to hysterical mothers and children" (85). In Massachusetts, Monson factory workers were detailed to flood work (126), "all night men worked at the North End dike" in Springfield (137), Chicopee "workers in the city's sixteen large industrial plants joined their efforts to those of municipal employees" (141), while in Lowell, "windowless factories gaped down on exhausted volunteer workers" (192). Once or twice—as nurses and as members of the WPA sewing project—women also visibly do their bit.

The power of cultural memory-making also informed the book's impact. Even more than the guidebooks, *New England Hurricane* functions as a *lieu de mémoire*, Pierre Nora's memory place which permanently inscribes the impact of the hurricane, fixes remembrance of the loss before it is cleaned up and absorbed into the future. The need for the compensations of memory-making was overwhelming. Immediately after the hurricane, Everett Allen found himself unable to remember his familiar cityscape—the land "so alien in form as to repudiate and confound the memory" (352). The Associated Press circulated a story lamenting, "The greens and commons of New England will never be the same. Picture postcard mementos of the oldest part of the United States are gone with the wind and flood. The day of the 'biggest wind' has just passed and a great part of most picturesque America, as old as the Pilgrims, has gone beyond recall or replacement" (qtd. in Allen, jacket cover). More succinctly, Bernard De Voto declared: "The face of New England had been changed forever" (qtd. in Allen 351). Publicity press releases promised that the volume would keep memory alive: "Unlike the vaguely remembered hurricane of 1815, the 1938 disaster has within the pages of this profusely illustrated volume a definitive biography which will be studied with interest by this and succeeding generations."[11] In quintessential memory-making form, remembrance is channeled through the bodies and experience of insiders—the local writers, amateur photographers, eye-witness interviewees whose impressions constitute the substance of the record and the shared bedrock of community rebuilding. The text also represents embodied memory, ventriloquizing the voices of aged participants who have the authority of long historical reach: "Old Daniel Harry, full-blooded Indian chief, declared the catastrophe was the 'wuss I ever did see,' surpassing the famous gale of 1869" (51); "Old Vermonters declared that they never had seen such wind, and if it ever died out they didn't want to see another" (211). And sometimes the text embeds memory by simply asserting it is so: "In New London history the day is by now as deeply engraved as that other day of terror when the British under Benedict Arnold burned the city" (23). Frank Manuel was determined that the book should function as "a living record of New England's darkest day."[12]

The ultimate relief comes at the end of the narrative, in quintessentially New Deal form. The alphabet agencies rush in with succor. The WPA dominates the rescue operation, recovering bodies, clearing streets of wreckage "with trucks, tractors and Diesel-powered shovels" (75), gathering debris, shoring up dams, dikes, and sandbags, repairing bridges, sewing garments for flood victims, establishing refugee centers and playrooms for homeless children, beginning the work of reclamation. (In fact, the taxonomy of governmental relief was considerably longer before the publisher silently cut it just prior to publication, too late for the enraged Manuel to reverse.)[13] The WPA also cooperates with the Civilian Conservation Corps, the National Youth Administration, the National Guard, the American Legion, the Red Cross, and other public and private agencies: "The labors of State officials, municipal agencies, private individuals, and the Federal Government are joined together to enhance New England's prospect" (220). And, climactically, Harry Hopkins, WPA administrator, arrives on his white charger at top speed from Los Angeles to Boston: "'There are sufficient funds to meet this emergency,' said Mr. Hopkins. 'We will do whatever needs to be done'" (188). This declaration is accompanied by the only head-and-shoulders portrait in the book, as anxious officials crowd round Hopkins to hear his forceful pronouncements. All this leads to the final reassertion of progress: "*Huracan*, the evil spirit of the Caribbean, had been exorcised. In past ages, disaster was followed by plague and mass emigration from the stricken areas. Men despaired of rebuilding when flood, fire, and wind had obliterated their handiwork. Modern civilization is more resilient. It recovers with amazing speed from the havoc when nature's forces are let loose" (218). With this government at the helm, the book can even find a silver lining: on the beach resorts of Long Island and the southern New England shore, "the ill wind may bring the proverbial good, once communities have recuperated from their first shock. There are earnest proposals that the seaside resorts pass zoning laws. The New England Council hopes to persuade owners to build cottages further inland instead of at the shore's edge. The open expanse of beach will be beautified; the houses rendered more substantial. Errors of a century's haphazard building may now be rectified. The federal government is cooperating with local bankers to make funds available for reconstruction. . ." (219–20). The whole effect fits Daniel and Stein's description of "the characteristic 'documentary' style of New Deal publicity—a style that *looked* candid, intimate yet non-intrusive, even as it promoted the value of forceful, bureaucratic government intervention to shore up a stagnant economy" (Daniel et al. ix).

That this is a distinctively New Deal documentary narrative is proven by comparison with other souvenir publications. Amateur and professional photographers took thousands of images of the hurricane and its effects. Over four hundred appeared in *New England Hurricane*. Reynolds Printing of New Bedford also selected four hundred from the three thousand submitted for its souvenir booklet *1938 Hurricane: Pictures from Falmouth to Fall River and New London Areas Mostly in and about New Bedford*, then printed several hundred more the next year in its *1939 Edition Picture Book* of the 1938 hurricane, announcing *Mostly new large unpublished before and after photos in vicinity of New Bedford, Cape Cod, Marthas* [sic] *Vineyard*. The *Standard-Times Morning Mercury* reproduced more than seven hundred in *The Com-*

plete Historical Record of New England's Stricken Area September 21, 1938. And those accounts comprise only a selection from the New Bedford area. One motif is common to them all: their fascination with the radio and the role of short-wave enthusiasts in keeping communication lines open during the disaster and, by extension, their own role as modern agents of communication. Otherwise, their presentation is distinctively oriented according to different agendas. Most obvious is the almost complete lack of attention to the WPA in all the other booklets. "Hurricane Souvenir—1938," the account put out by the *New Bedford Standard-Times* ten days after the hurricane, is intent on proving the "traditional courage" of communities that will pull them through to "triumph over nature's destructive work." While the booklet names several relief and other organizations that leapt into action in response to hurricane damage, there is no mention of government aid, far less the WPA. Reynolds Printing, again a New Bedford outfit, does not present its *1938 Hurricane Pictures* as authoritative, instead describing the work as part of a conversation with the community and with other booklets. The text explains how other publications outdid them in speed, it includes many more photographs and names of local individuals than *New England Hurricane*, and, in eighty-four pages, it mentions the WPA only once. Other accounts were, like the project publication, more institutionally based. The New England Power system, for example, put out a special issue of its periodical *Contact*. Like *New England Hurricane*, this account strives to celebrate the work of its employees, but that emphasis is not balanced by detailed coverage of the destruction. The booklet stresses the positive almost exclusively, documenting the loyalty, cooperation, and efficiency of its employees; detailing how the New England Power system met the challenge; mounting individualistic heroic narratives within a corporate framework: "It was a situation which taxed the self-reliance and individual capacity of all the men who make the fabric of our organization" (12); and including a two-page photographic tribute to the crews, who are lined up against their vehicles in heroic pose. For a hurricane publication, as one newspaper review remarked, "The cheery tone of the account is surprising."[14] Similarly, the Red Cross reports documented the mechanics and costs of providing relief while stressing "the courage, self-reliance and self-help attributes of the people of those states" (v). Everett S. Allen's autobiographical account of 1976 understandably personalizes and narrativizes the experience more strongly than the writers' project. Tellingly, however, he also allows the individual voices of survivors their place in the collective story, not editing and bracketing voices to the degree that project editors did. The writers' project version of the hurricane took a distinctive shape with nicely balanced attention to destruction and governmental reparation.

Also distinctively New Deal in orientation was the volume's reception. This time, local communities did not object to their representation. The work sold at a furious pace. The first printing sold out on the day of publication, three more printings sold in the next two weeks, a total of seven printings in all, and in its first week of publication, it was listed fifth in popularity among all nonfiction in New England and twelfth in nonfiction in Boston.[15] Moreover, its authors received public plaudits as both writers *and* workers for the first time. The *Boston Traveler*, for example, aligned WPA writers with other relief workers, both groups working to help communities to recover from disaster: "Here is another refutation of the story of WPA leaning on its shovels. . . . we should not forget that while WPA writers were producing the book in record time, 110,000 WPA workers were acting as shock troops of disaster, saving life and property and helping restore order out of chaos."[16] Burton Rascoe, writing in *Newsweek*, criticized the writers' status as workers only to the extent that he didn't know whom to thank for the excellent writing: "By far the best written book out of about twenty I've encountered lately has something peculiar about it. Credit is given to practically everybody except the ones who wrote it." Alfred Lucarotti, writing in *Gazetta del Massachusetts*, echoed the praise: "It is commendable literature by commendable writers. Sheer drama of the big New England blow, full of human interest stories and as vivid an account of human misery in the raw as I have ever seen chronicled anywhere. Members of the Writers' Project have done themselves proud with this slice of earthy drama; a true-to-life plot laid in locales familiar to all New Englanders."

THE HURRICANE IN MASSACHUSETTS

How it felt to document the hurricane as a project writer we can best tell from Massachusetts. The Massachusetts section of *New England Hurricane* carries its own distinctive emphases, with more class analysis, more emphasis on lives lost, and more attention to the ethnic dimensions of the disaster than in any other part of the volume. The minute the hurricane hits the coast of southeastern Massachusetts, the text begins to notice the unemployed: "At Ocean Grove, poor man's beach resort, unemployed textile workers, who in depression days had made this a year-round residential district, retreated foot by foot before the onslaught of wind and water. Dozens of jerry-built cottages collapsed and were whirled away, leaving the bare, bleached bones of their concrete foundations to mark former sites" (87). While the commentary never becomes a fully developed class analysis, the attention to economic difference and its consequences is continuous. As the hurricane passes through the vicinity of Fairhaven, for example:

> the most pathetic victims were the poor who made up a large portion of the Harbor View district. This was a colony of over 100 small houses, most of them originally summer residences, converted into year-round homes by former New Bedford wage-earners who turned to the sea and its fish as a means of livelihood when industrial activity slackened. The flimsy frame dwellings were smashed to match wood and flung haphazardly in either direction, far inland or out to sea. (98; Fig. 21)

The sheer difference in scale from the damage done in Boston's comfortable quarter implicitly exposes class privilege: "Beacon Hill's crowded residential section gave the wind no chance for spectacular destruction. Blinds hung by one hinge. Flower pots lay in alleys" (188). Similarly, attention to ethnic difference goes beyond the single picturesque "full-blooded Indian chief" in Rhode Island (51) to notice a more systemic impact: damage near the Fairhaven–New Bedford Bridge particularly affects "anchorage for large numbers of Portuguese fishermen" (95) while, in Southbridge, "with factories deluged, the large French-Canadian population was thrown out of work" (165).

These emphases were in large part due to writers in the New Bedford district office, whose careers we followed in chapter 5 and who covered the first impact of the hurricane on Massachusetts' southeast coast. Their unedited submissions on the hurricane show how the crisis that tested the project's capacities also stretched the resources of individual writers, bringing to the surface both the potential and the limits of writers come to their craft by project employment. Comparing their submissions to the published book reminds us once more of the management of voices—which so easily shades into the exclusion of voices—at which the project became proficient.

Some of the New Bedford writers made no contribution to *New England Hurricane*. Julia Keane was absent during the hurricane, attending the Los Angeles convention of the American Legion Auxiliary. She did make a public response to the hurricane in a *New Bedford Standard-Times* story about her

Fig. 21. Harbor View, Fairhaven, *New England Hurricane* (photograph from the files of the Works Progress Administration, Massachusetts).

which appeared simultaneously with the publication of *New England Hurricane* in November 1938. It is a peculiar piece in that, published two months after her trip to Los Angeles, it uses that event only as a launching point to discuss her missing the hurricane and her fears about its imagined effects—again, entirely omitting any mention of the WPA publication or of her employment on the project. Frank McKenna had by this time crossed the line, to the "worker" side of the WPA. Gone from the project, he contributed to hurricane relief as the local administrator assigning WPA manual workers to clear the debris and help the homeless. Elsie Moeller continued to resist the worker-writer perspective. Her copy was highly formulaic and melodramatic, an account of a one-legged man breaching the storm to rescue a group of nuns, all with the help of a local ghost.[17] No part of her submission seems represented in the published volume.

Nellie Coombs, on the other hand, wrote extensively on the effects of the hurricane—in Bourne, Westport, Martha's Vineyard, and Cuttyhunk Island. Her class analysis of its effects is acute and sustained, and it did make its mark on the published guide, contributing to the distinctive class emphasis of the Massachusetts section. While many workers simply noted that the hurricane robbed rich and poor alike, Coombs noticed the crucial difference: "a man may lose his summer home or cat boat and it is a monetary loss on the pleasure side of the ledger. But when a fisherman loses his boat, or his shanty with all his equipment, then it is more than money he loses. He has lost whatever opportunity he had to make money." She also noted the disproportionate effect of these crippling losses on the Portuguese American community. She displayed a nice eye for irony, around, for example, the submerged signs on West Beach at Westport, with their feeble warnings against dogs, speeding, and trespassing; "But the sea paid no more attention to man than it did in the days of King Canute." Out of her engagement with the human costs of the hurricane came stylistic experimentation, as she developed an almost Whitmanesque voice to introduce odd, ironic, and absurd tales of the storm's whimsy:

> This is written in protest against the endless streams of adjectives splashed with abandon through column after column of type. This is a breakdown in the ability to receive any more information of sorrow, death, and destruction. . . .
>
> I sing of stuff and nonsense—scraps from the ever-increasing number of side-issues relating to the hurricane. And I sing this in a spirit of respect for the people who could live through the hell of that day and night and yet find time to tuck away in a corner of their brain the humorous side of the tragedy.[18]

Leroy Bradford was the other deeply invested contributor. Of all the project writers in the southeastern section, his engagement with the hurricane was the closest, in both physical and writerly terms. At the time, Bradford lived on low-lying ground near the Acushnet inlet in Fairhaven, an area that was swamped with wind and water, and his brush with death was close. When Muriel Hawks invited personal contributions from field workers, his reaction was heartfelt:

> Your suggestion that we turn in material on the recent hurricane comes as a decided relief. I thought I was a hard boiled newspaper man for I've covered disasters without number but this one seems to have left those of us who were close to it in a blue funk. I have been trying to write Cape copy for the past few days, only to tear up sheet after sheet. . . . At the present writing it seems as though Fairhaven was hit as hard as any place. They are still digging bodies of neighbors and friends out of the debris. We are still using candles for illumination at home.[19]

He turned in quite a lot of material on the hurricane—on Ocean Grove, Falmouth, Fairhaven, New Bedford—and all of it sounds distinctly unlike his other project writings. It is engaged with quotidian texture, "editorializes" expansively, and speaks in a voice of commitment rather than of obligation. He also approaches—though more gingerly than Coombs—a political analysis of class, noting the very different effect of the hurricane on wealthy housing and summer residences compared to the demolition of holiday shacks to which people in straitened circumstances had reverted as their only homes during the Depression. It is his treatment of Ocean Grove, for example, that Manuel included in the published version, edited down by half but retaining some of Bradford's original phrasing and his overall political emphasis. Particularly characteristic of Bradford is an emphasis on hubris, the laughing incredulity of residents which often led to their deaths. One photograph of faces pressed up against the window of the New Bedford Yacht Club, for example, carries exactly the feel of Bradford's perspective on human vulnerability (Fig. 22): "The New Bedford Yacht Club was plucked bodily from its foundation and scattered in broken wreckage on the surface of the New Bedford–Fairhaven bridge. This occurred 15 minutes after the photograph of the club was taken; members may be seen peering at the storm from windows. All escaped" (93). Again, this atmosphere permeates the book's coverage of southeastern Massachusetts. This writing by Bradford, as excerpted and adapted in *New England Hurricane*, is the closest he came to developing a worker-writer perspective in print.

One of his contributions focused, at Hawks's request, on his own experience of the hurricane. The singularity of Bradford's response to this assignment is telling. Most project writers responded with alacrity to the invitation to write personal narratives. For once they could put their own adventures at center stage, become the heroes of their own stories, and they made the most of the opportunity. Emily Moore in Worcester was typical in detailing her valiant fight through the storm to reach her eighty-year-old mother and two sons, written in terms which accentuate both the hurricane's power and her own determination:

> I had lost my hat, my hair was soaking wet, my clothes were wet, I must have been a sight to behold, but that gave me no concern. I had one objective —get home. I took to my heels, looking backward and sideways, ducking pieces of slate which was being blown from the nearby roofs, tripping first over one thing, then another, knowing all the time I could never get to my street as a huge tree had fallen across, completely blocking my way. . . . As

Fig. 22. The New Bedford Yacht Club, *New England Hurricane* (photograph from the files of the New Bedford Standard-Times).

> I neared the tree, wondering whether I could crawl under, go around, or what I should do, a woman yelled, "Look out—that tree." I looked back and saw an enormous tree and it looked just as if it was falling from the sky. In my fright and excitement I jumped over the tree that had fallen, something I never in the world could do again, for from the way it was across the street it was four or five feet from the ground.[20]

Bradford, in comparison, seems to have experienced considerable difficulty writing himself into his field copy, able to position himself only as an ineffectual observer. His account stages him as spectator three times, each time getting closer to a realization of his vulnerability. First he stops on the New Bedford–Fairhaven Bridge to watch the storm. Then he runs home and fetches his wife and son to move down onto Marine Park, filled-in land on the edge of the bridge, to get an even closer view. Then the three rush home to change into oil skins so that they can get out of the car into the storm. On their last trip back, they discover that the bridge is now impassable. They make it only as far as the high school steps, from where they watch the denouement of the disaster:

> cars are showing only their tops above swirling, filth-laden waters. Over the surface of the New Bedford-Fairhaven bridge go careening large motor and sailing craft, carrying away a large section of the railing on both sides of the causeway. Motor cars are stalled and either totally or partially submerged on the surface of the bridge. Several are actually being swept from the bridge surface. . . . Then and only then, comes the realization that a catastrophe is being enacted in front of our eyes.[21]

Finally they return home once more, to a place bereft of light and warmth—"Another aid of modern life has failed us"—cut off from electricity, gas, and communication beyond their immediate neighbors, shaken by the realization of how foolishly they had skirted disaster.

The community from which Bradford speaks is one of vulnerable spectators. His family rush to the scene, seeing only "fun" and "a lark" in the disaster. "Nor are we alone in our fool hardiness"; scene after scene shows groups of neighbors clustered together, right on the edge of danger, unaware and careless. Finally, the account winds down to the dank and dark aftermath, as the tide recedes, the wind lessens, and the community finds its domestic security gone:

> Huddled close together in one room of their chill home, illuminated only by flickering candles, we find friends who had raced from one point to another when danger actually existed, now, when the disaster had passed, actually terrified at the thought of leaving their homes.
>
> "Why didn't they leave when they had a chance?" Why didn't hundreds, yes, thousands of others flee for high land instead of remaining around? Plain morbid curiosity is one part of the answer, ignorance, is the remainder.

In producing himself as part of this scene, Bradford is a family man whose domesticity is threatened, a member of a community pulled together partly by its vulnerability and ignorance, and a spectator who recognizes his own and others' foolishness without having the capacity to act on it.

What he is not is a government writer. At the beginning of the account, he relates leaving "the office" without clarifying what the office is, without ever engaging with his identity as a WPA writer, and without ever mentioning the other WPA workers who come to the rescue. His positioning again stands in contrast to his project colleagues'. Nellie Coombs begins her personal account by noting that she was working on the Portuguese history the morning of the storm; then she traces her movements to the genealogical room on the third floor of the New Bedford library. Later in the account, she playfully stages herself writing the very piece we are reading. At the height of the storm, recording the experience by candlelight, she tells us: "Every time I pressed the space bar, the light flickered." Further afield, Wade Van Dore in Southfield described how, as the weather worsened, "I tried to concentrate on my W.P.A. writing assignment of the week, but with difficulty," while Frederick Krackhardt in West Berlin describes how he began the day interviewing unemployed mill and carpet workers, then delivers a nicely metaphorical image of himself struggling home in the storm "holding my manuscript case against my chest as a shield."[22] All of them also pay attention to the achievements of WPA rescue and rehabilitation workers. Bradford could write a personal account only by excising his project identity and the WPA context generally. Conversely, as we have seen in chapter 5, his project service and writing routinely excise personal conviction or voice.

Of course, excision of individual voices was at the heart of project editors' technique, reviewers' impressions to the contrary. Katherine McKinzie is only the most explicit in assuming the presence of individuated voices: "What made *New England Hurricane* exciting reading was the inclusion of articles from project workers who experienced the wrath of the storm" (134). In fact, the pace, cross-cutting between text and image, and the symbiosis in that process could only have been achieved by a strongly central editorial hand which managed multiple voices according to a New Deal agenda. WPA writers did not include in their unedited contributions the paean to the WPA which is so pronounced at the beginning and end of *New England Hurricane*. They did not shape their observations according to its triumphal arc. The book molded their voices every bit as much as it shaped communities, using the means of modernity (speed of production, radio) and governmental organization (especially WPA relief measures) to deliver a more hopeful future.

POSTSCRIPT

As so often in WPA publications, the omissions in *New England Hurricane* carry a racial complexion. For all the stories of bravery, terror, and tragedy in this guide, not one concerns a person of color. There are no stories of the Cape Verdean Americans whom Mary Heaton Vorse described so vividly resident on the New Bedford waterfront, despite the battering the storm gave that location. We hear nothing of the Mashpee clinging to their strip of land on Cape Cod abutting the ocean. A single figure, in a photograph of windswept, laughing Bostonians, may—tantalizingly, for a reader looking for race—be African American, but the caption does not acknowledge racial difference. Yet images of the Black community weathering the storm were available: the front-page photograph of the *Hartford Courant Magazine* issued soon after the disaster, for example, shows a group of Black children sleeping in improvised quarters, refugees from hurricane damage.[23]

And at least one Black woman did die, although it took forty years for her story to be published, as told by one white man to another. Mrs. Josephine Clarke was from Jamaica, come to Massachusetts to work as a maid to a wealthy white family with a summer residence on Martha's Vineyard. Nellie Coombs told the story of her drowning in her field copy, though Coombs, working from secondhand accounts of the hurricane on Martha's Vineyard ("it's a long swim to the islands, and furthermore, the water's too dern cold") clearly did not know that the victim was Black: "At Chilmark the cook at the home of Mr. and Mrs. Benedict Thielien [*sic*] lost her life when the family, attempting to sail a small boat across the rising waters to safety[,] capsized."[24] Only in 1976 did the story see publication, in Everett S. Allen's *A Wind to Shake the World: The Story of the 1938 Hurricane*.

Allen described the event as he had heard it from Benedict Thielen. This account, in its intermingling of gender and race against the shattered landscape and its eerie transference of blackness to the face of the white Mrs. Thielen, vividly represents the horror that the New Deal management of landscape was designed to repress. This is the scene of the drowning of Mrs. Josephine Clarke:

> The poor frightened black face rises, then disappears in the gray whirling water. . . . I must let go my hold on this dark reaching hand. . . . I see the dark face sink in the water, then rise again. . . . I see my wife swimming slowly ahead of me. The other face is gone. . . . My wife turns about, and her face, her mouth, is smeared with black mud. . . . The wind cries all night long around the house, and every time you close your eyes you see the immense slavering arch of the oncoming wave, the yellow spittle dripping down, and a dead face in the sullied waters. (Allen 261–63)[25]

This image, in its racial lineaments and its textual suppression, reminds me of the dead Black man standing guard over Captain Kidd's treasure, whom

De Voto singles out in his review of *Massachusetts*, of the ghostly Black quarry workers of Great Barrington in *The Berkshire Hills*, even of Sacco and Vanzetti in the silently revised guide to Massachusetts. Here, again, in Josephine Clarke's drowning, the ghost of what is "beyond the pale" haunts the governmental reassurance offered to shattered communities by the WPA guides.

EPILOGUE: THE LEGACIES OF THE MASSACHUSETTS WRITERS' PROJECT

> It's almost stunning to remember that the U.S. government once directly employed destitute writers.
>
> Henry Kisor,
> *Chicago Sun-Times Book Week*
> September 10, 1989

The WPA Arts Projects constitute one of the great "what if?" moments in U.S. cultural history. In 1938, Congress considered two bills to convert the Federal Arts Projects into a permanent bureau of arts and letters.[1] What if these bills had succeeded, creating a continuous stretch of federal arts sponsorship from the 1930s till now? Would the paradigm of "work"—the arts as socially useful labor—have changed the history of U.S. arts funding? Would funding paradigms be more collective, more community oriented, and more inclusive of marginalized groups than those instituted by the National Foundation on the Arts and the Humanities in 1965 as a reward system for individual artistic and scholarly merit? For all the multitude of rich publications produced by the writers' project, even more materials went suppressed or unpublished. The list of unrealized works to which Massachusetts writers contributed include "Portrait of the Negro as American," "Go Down Moses," "Negroes in Massachusetts," "We Work on the WPA," "Living in New England," "History of New

England Women," and "The Portuguese in New England," not to mention field workers' papers on Black Boston, Black abolitionists (male and female), Mashpee Indians, workers' narratives from a great spectrum of racial and ethnic experience, living lore, and working slang. What if all these manuscripts had reached publication at the time? They would have circulated as living contributions to contested and neglected areas of the state's culture, rather than as the historical curios their belated publication makes them. How might they have changed the state's public culture, enriching the representation of class with the differences of race, ethnicity, and gender and offering varied paradigms of collective creation and collaborative voice? What if Henry Alsberg had survived as national director, to see through an experiment that, by 1938, had clearly become the most ambitiously revisionist project of literary labor and cultural representation ever launched in American history?

Of course, the writers' project is not entirely forgotten. Since the lively project memoir of Jerre Mangione, national coordinating editor, was published in 1972, half-a-dozen scholarly monographs have appeared, by an international array of scholars from different disciplines and approaches.[2] WPA guides have been recurrently reprinted and excerpted for anthologizing.[3] More volumes of unpublished project materials—life histories, workers' interviews, folklore, African American and other cultural studies—have appeared, and the Library of Congress American Memory collection has put the massive archive of ex-slave narratives and other WPA oral histories on line.

Yet examples of broader cultural amnesia remain legion. In the 1960s, as public debates heated up around the nation's "second major cultural experiment"—the legislation that would eventuate in the National Endowment for the Arts and the National Endowment for the Humanities—supporters did their best to quash any association with "the specter of the WPA" (Larson 208, 91). Throughout the 1990s—as the NEA fought to survive the culture wars, decency debates, and inexorable defunding—the arts projects remained very largely absent as a historical reference point. "The American artistic community will long remember 1989–90 as the year that art became hard news," pronounced Ted Potter, implying that 1939 never happened (41). "For the first time, a substantial portion of the electorate had come to feel it had a personal stake in the expenditure of government arts dollars," judged Stephen Benedict in 1991 (15–16). Only recently have NEA and NEH officials inched toward the proposition that public funding of the arts could learn from the WPA experiment. In 1998, William J. Ivey, NEA chair, celebrated the endowment's recent stay of execution by Congress by announcing his vision of "a New Deal without the Depression, with murals painted all over the country and music composed" (qtd. in Henneberger). Jerrold Hirsch has argued that some of the writers' project vision was reborn—again in unacknowledged form—in the efforts by William Ferris, NEH chair, to establish regional humanities centers between 1997 and 2001 (*Portrait* 236–37).

The legacies of the Massachusetts project are there to be found. In the 1930s, Bert Loewenberg claimed that the project was making a lasting mark on Massachusetts' public culture: historical societies and cultural organizations—Jewish, Irish, Armenian, Albanian, Portuguese, Franco-American, and Jamaican, among others—were mushrooming across the state. The published guides were the first to put so many of the state's working people, political minorities, racial and ethnic communities, and multicultural histories on what, after the Second World War, became the tourist landscape. Even the controversies—over the representation of Sacco and Vanzetti, the state's labor history, racial diversity, individual communities' images—constituted a salutory "going public" of cultural questions which too easily remain moot. We can hypothesize that the battles lost and won around publicly funded representation touched the consciousnesses of all those—writers, editors, readers, reviewers, interviewers, interviewees—involved in the production and circulation (and suppression) of project material. This epilogue posits some concrete evidence of this legacy in two parts. First, I trace the afterlife of project publications, some of which function like ticking time bombs, and the subsequent careers of some employees who came to realize the project's unfulfilled potential. Then I turn, in more personal vein, to the search with which I began this book—for the visible marks left by the project on the state's cultural landscape. This search finally takes me to Lowell and Lawrence, the mill towns on the Merrimack River, which, with federal and state funding, continue the memory work begun by the project seventy years ago.

PUBLICATIONS AND CAREERS

The continuing impact of the project's labors is suggested, first, by the intermittent reprinting of published (and occasionally first printing of unpublished) materials. *Massachusetts*, *Cape Cod Pilot*, *Sudbury*, *The Berkshire Hills*, *Whaling Masters*, *The Armenians in Massachusetts*, and *Boston Looks Seaward* have all been reissued over the years, with varied introductions which suggest that their impact ranges, at different moments, from revisionism to antiquarianism to nostalgia. In 1980, Ann Banks unearthed a few of the Massachusetts life histories for inclusion in *First-Person America*. In 1988, the magazine *Spinner: People and Culture in Southeastern Massachusetts* resurrected a treasury of unpublished manuscripts by New Bedford project writers, an act of respect for grassroots writing too often quashed by the project's editorial hierarchy.

Another way of measuring potential impact is to consider the publications aimed at children who came to adulthood in the 1960s. As well as *Old Newbury Tales* (discussed in chapter 2), the project produced various leaflet series for schoolchildren with explicitly educational and consciousness-raising mission. One such series, "Stories of Massachusetts," was reported in the local press in 1941:

> The leaflets were produced under the sponsorship of the Boston school committee and were printed by the students on school presses at Roxbury Memorial High school, Boston Trade school and the Boston Continuation school.
>
> The entire series is designed to teach students in Boston public schools something about the social, economic, and cultural history of their own community. This idea has the approval of most educators who have long deprecated the fact that the teaching of local history is almost entirely neglected in the American school system, largely due to the fact that materials for teaching this subject are not available. Textbook writers find this field financially unprofitable because in most cases the potential circulation of the books is extremely limited. In this way the Writers' Project hopes to make a real contribution to the community in which it works.[4]

At that point, twenty titles had appeared, with another thirty projected. Some are notably revisionist in orientation. Number 16, for example, concerns "Phillis Wheatley—Slave Poet of the Revolution." While the pamphlet positions Wheatley within established categories—"slave," "poet," "Revolution"—it also introduces to schoolchildren a figure who would not enter academic literary canons for another forty years and who has come to challenge established literary histories, categories of aesthetic value, and assumptions about textual sophistication. The pamphlet makes good the rather empty gesture to Wheatley in the guide to Massachusetts.

There is also a long list of writers and public intellectuals whose careers were enabled by employment on the Massachusetts project. For some, the project simply served to keep body and soul together while allowing them to stay in the writing game. Pulitzer Prize–winner Conrad Aiken, so disdainful of project procedures and left-wing politics, is the most emphatic example. An employee of a very different order—Eunice Turgeon, New Bedford field worker who participated in the local writers' union and the project's social life—would also insist fifty years later, "It was a stop gap job for me," between college and a career in the navy (qtd. in Donaghy and McCabe 23). For others, documenting the archives, life histories, folklore, memories, and working vocabularies of their local communities brought alive what poet Muriel Rukeyser described as "the key to the '30's": "the joy to awake and see life entire, and tell the stories of real people" (qtd. in Penkower 243). For some, project activity provided models of cultural engagement which set them off in new directions.

Several members of the state office developed careers consonant with their project experience. Ray Allen Billington, second state director, sustained a distinguished academic career, producing a long list of scholarly volumes and becoming the preeminent historian of the American frontier. Several of his projects make explicit his continuing commitment to public culture. For example, in collaboration with Bert Loewenberg and Samuel Brockunier, he wrote *The United States: American Democracy in World Perspective*, in the foreword to which (penned in July 1938, soon after he left the project), he declared: "The historian is and must be today above all a social scientist with a public responsibility" (v). In the 1960s, an international network of professional associations and foundations commissioned Billington to produce *The Historian's Contribution to Anglo-American Misunderstanding: Report of a Committee on National Bias in Anglo-American History Textbooks*. During the same period, he served as president of the Organization of American Historians. Bert Loewenberg, assistant state director, also sustained an academic and scholarly publishing career. Among the accomplishments for which his project experience would have prepared him were his directorship of the Center for Continuing Education at Sarah Lawrence College, 1965–1969, and his final, posthumously published study, *Black Women in Nineteenth-Century American Life: Their Words, Their Thoughts, Their Feelings*, which he edited with Ruth Bogin. As a woman with a commitment to women's history, Grace Kellogg—former state editor in the Boston office and perpetual thorn in her male colleagues' side—had a much harder time trying to establish a foothold in the academy. In 1951, she returned to graduate school "after my husband's death, presumably, from the academic point of view, with my faculties impaired by prolonged domestication." She proposed writing a master's thesis on Edith Wharton's life and work at the University of Vermont, a subject which the graduate council promptly rejected as lacking literary significance and archival weight. In tones familiar from her project correspondence and armed, perhaps, with the experience of those battles, Kellogg continues her story:

> I had set my heart on Mrs. Wharton. . . . As a youngster I am sure it would not have occurred to me to challenge the decision of the wise Council . . .. As a woman with a goal in mind and a determination to achieve it I could not be so easily downed. I stuck to my guns. . . . Grudgingly I was permitted Edith Wharton. . . . My thesis cut quite a swath. At the close of my last Oral, the Chairman of the Examining Board walked down the corridor with me. "I've been reading Master's Theses for thirty years" he murmured in my ear—"and this is *the first exciting one* I've ever had." (311–12)

In 1965, almost thirty years after she first proposed her history of New England women, Kellogg published *The Two Lives of Edith Wharton*.

Some throughlines can also be detected in the subsequent careers of district employees. As discussed in chapter 5, the Provincetown contingent sustained writing careers before and after their project service. Josef Berger's publications—adult and juvenile, fiction and nonfiction—remained oriented toward labor and what later became known as "history from the bottom up." In 1938, mainly on the strength of *Cape Cod Pilot*, he won a Guggenheim award to work on a study of Portuguese fishing people in Gloucester.[5] In later life, Berger continued to publish working people's histories and stories, sometimes in collaboration with his wife, Dorothy Berger. As their introduction to the collaboratively edited *Diary of America* puts it: "For the measure of America's greatness, read the historians. . . . But for the heartbeat, go to the people" (vii). George Willison also survived as a popular historian. For thirty-odd years after the project ended, he published numerous trade and popular books, many of which mount revisionist treatments of America's colonial and revolutionary history. Among other topics, he took on the pilgrims, Virginia, Patrick Henry, and Pittsfield, Massachusetts, as well as "Cliff's Notes" study guides to American texts. As far as I can trace, Elsie Moeller was the only New Bedford field worker to achieve book publication, with her travel memoir, *Pack a Bag*, in 1955. Otherwise, her published work seems to have consisted of articles in the local press. Some careers—including those of the writers of color—are even more difficult to document. Zylpha Mapp, the field worker in the Boston district office who researched the Black press, became, according to an obituary, "a prominent Baha'i, educator and human rights champion."[6] She traveled globally in humanitarian service, served as professor at Makerere University in Uganda and other African institutions, taught in Massachusetts schools, authored educational works for schools in Botswana, and edited the memoir of her husband, Robert Robinson, *Black on Red: My 44 Years Inside the Soviet Union*. Edythe Mae Gordon, who fought to retain her employment in the Boston district office, published two more poems in 1938, then disappeared from the public record. Despite recent scholarly excavations, "nothing is known of her life after 1941" (Roses and Randolph 510).

These, then—publications on and beyond the project and employees' working careers, only a tiny fraction of which are sketched here—are legacies to set against amnesia and regret. Vincent McHugh, for example, formerly of the New York City Writers' Project, wrote to Jerre Mangione in 1968: "The whole WPA experience seems to have gone uselessly down the drain."[7] Paul DeKruif said it well when he wrote in his 1941 foreword to the WPA guide to Michigan: "We, working Americans, have built signboards for you." The Massachusetts Writers' Project taught writers to recover, preserve, and document the often undervalued details of local life by interviewing mill operatives, old seamen, former slaves, service workers, and craftspeople; exploring archives, libraries, and personal papers; and detailing architectural, material, and vernacular culture. It encouraged writers to recognize their commonality with other workers on the breadlines and to develop voice and visibility for underrepresented social groups out of this alliance. Project writers' research excavated a wealth of hidden histories and suppressed stories. Their writings were invigorated with the glimmerings of a "proletarian poetics" (Rabinowitz 190). And their collective activities showed the government the tremendous worth—and complexity—of putting its money where its mouth was in support of cultural work. At best, the results gave new life to the most varied range of voices Massachusetts had to offer: Sacco and Vanzetti, Captain Joe Antone, Phillis Wheatley, Mashantampaine of the Nobscusset tribe, workers of all ethnicities—Mashpee, Armenian American, Albanian American, African American, Irish American, Italian American, Lebanese American, Syrian American, Anglo-American, "Black" and "white" Portuguese—made available by WPA writers to be heard by a newly expanded public. These voices continue to enrich Massachusetts' meanings.

LIVING HISTORY IN LOWELL AND LAWRENCE

In Lowell and Lawrence, mill towns on the Merrimack River heavily marked by postindustrial decay, I finally found the evidence of the legacy for which I had been searching in towns and cities across the state. On the face of it, Lowell and Lawrence are not a large part of the writers' project story. There is no WPA guide to either city, only their descriptions in the Massachusetts state guide. Approximately fifty years later, however, government funds supported cultural memory-making efforts in both cities, and the results look uncannily like unfinished business from the 1930s. The Lowell "living history" experience feels like a three-dimensional version of the silently revised state guide, Lawrence more like the road not taken when the project was closed down.

The essays on Lowell and Lawrence in the Massachusetts guide are quite different. "Lowell: Company Founders and City Fathers" tells the story of Lowell's "rapid rise to industrial eminence" in the early nineteenth century, charting the technology, capital, and working conditions which went into the making of this new textile city and "huge company town" (261). A quiet skepticism about this industrial triumph of human regulation colors the language of the entry—in, for example, the description of company agents "luring thousand of immigrants into the maw of the hungry, growing city" (261)—and then becomes explicit at the end: "The peak of the city's industrial development was achieved in the period of artificial prosperity preceding 1924. After 1924 there was a general decrease, ending in the devastating debacle of 1929. . . . By 1934 it seemed to have entered the upward grind toward recovery" (263). The tour of Lowell includes no mills—focusing instead on the standard fare of parks, statues, educational institutions, and houses—as if the industrial buildings were not a historical legacy in which the guide-makers took pride.

The whole orientation of "Lawrence: Warp and Woof" was more worker-centered and more confrontational than the Lowell essay. The guide trumpets Lawrence as "Massachusetts' only 'made city'" and uses it as the paradigmatic mill town elsewhere in its copy. The entry quickly moves through the founding of the town by the Essex company in the mid-nineteenth century, stressing the costs for workers:

> The abnormally rapid growth of the town, coupled with the focusing of its builders' attention upon industrial production rather than on social evolution, naturally resulted in unfortunate living conditions. Sanitation, proper

heating, and ventilation were lacking. Overcrowding, low wages, and long working hours prevailed. Little consideration was given in the design of factory buildings to the health or safety of the operatives. (251–52)

Then several paragraphs are devoted to the famous Bread and Roses strike of 1912, including names of organizers, Anna LoPezzi—an Italian worker killed by police—and the findings of the congressional committee which exposed the inhuman working conditions. The account ends with thirty-eight local trade unions in existence and attempts to diversify the city's economy. Of the ten points of interest on the tour, over half focus on mills, canals, dam, working parts of the mill town. Most quietly resistant is the entry on the town's common, which names as "vigilantes" those who opposed the workers' efforts at better work conditions: "Near the pond stands a large wooden flagpole which commemorates the Flag Day celebration held by the vigilantes in protest against the strike of 1912" (253). Several paragraphs on the 1912 strike also appear in the "Labor" essay.

The Lawrence entry was one of many that went down with the Sacco and Vanzetti controversy discussed in chapter 3. On August 20, 1937, as the controversy broke, the *Lawrence Tribune* printed an open letter by the secretary of the Lawrence chamber of commerce to Governor Charles F. Hurley, protesting the representation of the city in the guidebook and citing facts and figures to prove the city's industrial zeal and its conformity to the NRA code. The headline blared: "Lawrence Protests WPA Guide Book Reference." As a result of this and other protests, in the silently revised edition of 1938 the descriptive paragraphs on the 1912 strike in the Lawrence essay disappeared, to be replaced by an account of the ways in which the city's businessmen have responded to unemployment, stirred up civic pride once more, and join hands with "professional men, service clubs, and labor organizations" (252). "These co-operative efforts resulted in the formation of the Lawrence Industrial Bureau," whose successes in reclamation and industrialization are thereafter recounted (252). In the revised "Industry and Labor" essay, a reference to the Lawrence strike survives, though in shortened form. And the entry on the flagpole on the common has reversed its sympathies. The revised language implicitly endorses the celebrators (previously "vigilantes") in opposition to the IWW strikers: "Near the pond stands a large wooden flagpole which commemorates the Flag Day celebration against the demonstrations of the I.W.W. in the strike of 1912."

In 1933, the National Park Service joined the federal intervention into the cultural life of the United States. In that year, the government expanded the park service mandate beyond parks and wilderness areas to centralize the management of historical landmarks and sites into one system which would standardize both the selection and interpretation of commemorative sites. This standardization set new yardsticks of "national" significance and "professional" methods of presentation, terms which, as John Bodnar has noted, carried with them powerful but unacknowledged class affiliations:

> Since park service programs were administered by middle-class professionals, the link between the traditional middle-class promotion of progress and patriotism was actually reinforced. The state in other words not only began to consolidate its already considerable power and use it in the discourse over memory, but it advanced some of the class interests of those who were intimately tied to that power for over a century. (170)

Bodnar also discusses how the schematization of collective memory-making by the National Park Service in the 1930s amounted to "the triumph of the nation-state" as arbiter of the "nationally significant," holder of jurisdiction over the sites selected for funding, and prime symbol of the sites' meanings in their public presentation (191); "the process of nation building . . . formed the basic narrative structure of park service ideology" (204). In this context, it is telling that, in 1978, the federal government passed legislation to create Lowell National Historical Park. Although the 1937 Massachusetts guide attributed more "firsts" to Lawrence than to Lowell (and "firsts" were a central qualification for national significance), it was Lowell that the legislation seized on as "our nation's first great industrial city," ideally positioned to tell the story of the industrialization of "the young nation" (as the promotional brochure "Lowell National Historical Park" declares). Perhaps Lowell was also more amenable to incorporation by a middle-class perspective than its unruly sister town ten miles down the road—and perhaps their contrasting representations in the 1937 WPA guide contributed to that impression.

The refashioning of Lowell into a National Historical Park has resulted in an experience that is as close as I can imagine to walking into the (silently revised) guide to Massachusetts. If, as the guide literature suggests, you "begin your visit at the Visitor Center at Market Mills, the former Lowell Manufacturing Company" and "see the Park's introductory video, 'Lowell: The Industrial Revelation,'" the first sign is the rhetoric of a narrative which has all the hallmarks of Federal Writers' Project language: "Lowell's story *is* the story of industrial America." In measured tones, the male narrator delivers a smooth narrative of the city's rise, stringing together a series of incompatible terms—"machines, power, capital, labor" or "capital, technology and labor"—without acknowledgment of the fundamental fissure represented by those very different interests. The narrative cloaks itself in a New Deal–type "balance," perceptible in its quietly insistent progressivism, in the involvement of academics in the film's making, in the trajectory of rise, decline, and revival aided by government agencies (often expressed, as in the guidebooks, as a coalition of community and government).

To step out of the visitor center is graphically to realize how guidebook rhetoric and reconstruction contain and change a place's identity. The city feels like a representation of itself, one of Nora's "hallucinatory re-creations of the past" (*Realms* 1: 12), turned into a "living museum" in more ways than its architects intended. The park service has refurbished and mapped out the entire town center, with signs designating several cotton textile mills, worker housing, 5.6 miles of power canals, operating gatehouses, churches and parks. The result carries the faintly antiseptic air of managerial efficiency, the feel of a place reshaped, cleaned up, and interpreted by standardized protocols of presentation. The relationship of these refurbished structures to the commercial buildings amongst which they sit—restaurants, shops, businesses—is also reminiscent of the local guides' function within the 1930s' communities, boosting and sometimes protecting them from the threats of modernity. In the 1970s, Lowell had a depressed economy, with high unemployment rates and a dying inner city. It needed the boosterism of the "living history" project to resurrect its fortunes. That boosterism remains perceptible in some of the guide literature—"There's a lot to LIKE about LOWELL," trumpets one brochure—as does the economic motive driving the representation of the past. Another brochure recounts how a coalition of park service, municipal government, and university together "are preserving the past and nurturing a vigorous heritage that will continue to define the city" ("Lowell"). The success of the effort is suggested by Lowell's receiving the 1999 All-America City Award. Its tenuousness is suggested by the shabbiness and quietness of many of the commercial establishments, which contrast with the bustling museum shops, packed with goods and customers.

The park service refurbishment aims to put visitors in the footsteps of nineteenth-century textile workers and bosses, sometimes literally, as when the ranger tour guide directs her group to the shallow indentations worn into the wooden floor of Suffolk Mills and gets us to fit our feet to the traces left by loom operators who stood at their posts for fourteen hours a day. Or we encounter, in the 1830s Boott Mill boarding house, an employee dressed as housekeeper who guides us through the workers' living arrangements, while the voices of "mill girls" play over the P.A. system, individualizing their reactions to the move from farm to mill work. "Hear in their own voices, about how these women built their new lives in Lowell," the brochure tells us ("Lowell"). The effect, at least for this visitor, is more alienating than empathetic. The conditions are too clean, the voices too crisp to give a sense of the exhaustion and exploitation of the industrial city. Ironically, the physicality of the historical bodies is so absent that what imprints itself most strongly on my memory is an impression of the tour's own contradictions, rather than any embedded or embodied connection with the working people of that era.

The agenda driving this "living history"—as in the WPA guides—concerns progress, not protest, and it determinedly refuses to connect historical conditions to current inequities. So, for example, in explicating the conditions of labor in nineteenth-century textile mills, the park ranger concludes cheerily, "Are you still thinking of the good old days? . . . Not me, I like my modern conveniences." Despite her best efforts, however, the modern *in*conveniences keep intruding on the tour, the bits of the story which don't fit the narrative of progress. In its refusal to acknowledge the visible inequities of the present, the tour narrative begins to feel more like distraction than information. Delivering her spiel about the 1830s "mill girls," the guide refuses to comment on the crumbling housing stock which we can spy on our canal-boat trip, visibly inhabited by a more recent immigrant community. Her repertoire is further confounded by the crumbling infrastructure which prevents the Suffolk Mills turbine from making its scheduled demonstration run (no explanation is forthcoming; presumably the project is running out of resources to repair the seepage in the canal walls).

Similarly, the Boott Cotton Mills exhibition takes the form of a progressive narrative with typical New Deal "balance." The commentary acknowledges, then moves beyond "Lash and Loom"—"The brutal institution of slavery in America was propelled by the rapid expansion of the cotton textile industry"—to a triumphant vision of government and industry reinvestment in the contemporary city, a "High Tech Turnaround." As in much WPA rhetoric, uncomfortable facts and inequitable conditions are acknowledged, but as a pause, a stutter in the story of progress, not its fundamental undermining. Yet the finale of this exhibition *is* undercut, for those who read closely: temporary handwritten cards propped against one after another exhibit—Joan Fabrics, the New England Folklife Center—quietly declare them now closed. As much as anything, the videos, tours, and exhibitions—the bureaucratized, rationalized re-presentation of the city—are an education in how to ignore what you don't want to see, how not to notice silences you don't want to hear.

Again in close parallel to the WPA state guide, the racialized voice of dissent is relegated to the margins. Tucked into a corner at the very end of the Working People Exhibit in the Boott Mill boarding house is another video, this one produced by the U.S. Department of the Interior in 1988. This film is much less ambitious in terms of production qualities and much less trumpeted than the award-winning film splashily presented in the custom-built theater at the visitor center. Here, there are at most half-a-dozen folding chairs scattered before the tiny screen, easily missed as visitors head towards the exit sign. The video is made up of contemporary immigrants speaking about their experiences of Lowell. The structure foregrounds not just debate but tension: some speakers are enthusiastically pro bilingual education or urban development or multicultural population; some are vociferously against. For example, a Cambodian immigrant speaks gratefully of what the city has offered him; Mary A. Minorgan, an Irish American, in contrast, says "Granted we have connectors and we have shopping malls, but we don't have St. Peter's that people had and we don't have the South End neighborhood as I knew"—urban renewal tore apart her neighborhood. The narrator's voiceover still strives for balance, but the effect is much less confident and more explicit about the partiality of access to equity: "It's still a city of opportunity, if you have the tools to deal with all the obstacles." The voice which lingers longest in my ears is that of the sole African American speaker, a man who came in 1941: "The Blacks that came here are always on the bottom of the rung."

The fictiveness of progress is much more on display down the road in Lawrence Heritage State Park. As *Cape Cod Pilot* is to *Massachusetts*, so to a degree is the Lawrence state park to the Lowell national park: Lawrence puts on show what Lowell tries to suppress. Entering the Lawrence state park is an unnerving experience, for many reasons. First, the space doesn't feel particularly safe. Walking through the deserted area, past long, echoing mills that border the river, with their broken windows and dilapidated facing intermittently kept up, I feel threatened by the evident lack of attention paid them. Anyone could be lurking here. It's a completely different feeling from the restored and polished mills of Lowell, with plenty of bustling, official activity to make the visitor feel secure. And the visitor center, located in a restored 1840s boarding house, itself is so quiet. I walk into the red brick entranceway and spot a pile of photocopied leaflets. "SOLIDARITY! . . . THEN AND NOW," "17 MO FESTIVAL ANNUAL DE LA HERENCIA 'PAN Y ROSAS' " jump out from the day-glow orange and pink photocopies—there are no glossy brochures in sight here—and I put my hand out to take one, only to become entangled in a thick spider's web. No one's around, and the equipment room door is propped open, with a handwritten note stuck on it, telling "Tommy" to come upstairs to an event in the community room. I move into the exhibit hall, and a girl in an open-necked shirt and jeans takes her feet down, a bit sheepishly, from the desk. Later, when I return to ask her to turn on the exhibition video, she pulls herself reluctantly away from web-surfing, and I realize that she is in fact dressed in the understated uniform of the state park system. The shirt is regulation khaki with a small badge reading Massachusetts Forests and Parks; it's a much different presence from the national park rangers in Lowell with their sprightly green trousers, brown buttoned-down shirts, ties, and hats.

Again in something of a parallel to Berger's guide, the exhibition extends that emphasis of putting the working community first. The whole of the ground floor concentrates on representing the workers who dug the canals and dams, built the looms, and worked the mills. The video, entitled "Collective Voices," is a co-production of the Massachusetts AFL-CIO, the Commonwealth Museum, and Lawrence Heritage State Park. Its subject is the Great Strike of 1912, the powerful story of nearly 30,000 workers and the nation's continuing labor struggles. The list of immigrants on display—"Who came to Lawrence?"—includes, prominently, the African Americans so often sidelined in guidebook literatures and exhibitions. After a paragraph on immigrants from England, Scotland, Germany, and Canada, the text reads, "Blacks and Chinese also made their way to Lawrence during this period. Unlike the groups mentioned above, however, they came to Lawrence from other parts of the United States and arrived in small, isolated numbers. Blacks came from the south, before the Civil War, as part of the underground railroad. The Chinese gradually made their way east from California, arriving in Lawrence in the 1850s." The accompanying photographs include representations of both groups. The exhibition does include some standard boosterism: "From Bobbins to Computers. Today, Lawrence has a more diverse industrial base. . . . Now a variety of industries operate in mill buildings that once housed only textile manufacturing companies. Products ranging from electronic components and designer clothing to quality furniture, toys, sheet metal, shoes, pasta, plexiglass, and cosmetics are all made in Lawrence." But this rhetoric is accompanied by a repeated undercutting of investors as a type. A description of the urban planning by Boston investors in the 1840s is followed by a sketch of urban planning by state and local government agencies today, including the Heritage State Park system. It is easy to see both efforts implicated in the panel elsewhere in the first-floor exhibit: "Best Laid Plans. To the founders of Lawrence the plan for their model town was clear; people from New England would come to Lawrence and work in the mills to produce cotton and woolen cloth. They would live in carefully supervised company-owned boarding houses or well-constructed single family homes with room for a garden in the backyard. . . .[what resulted were densely packed] dangerous and often squalid living conditions."

Upstairs the irony becomes more pronounced. The massive banner draped across the stairway shouts "WE WANT BREAD AND ROSES TOO." The second-floor display opens with portraits of individual English American investors whose image, already ironized by the text on the floor below, is further undermined by their juxtaposition with panels representing the native Pennacook tribes and how they were treated by "the often intolerant English." Nearby is a child-oriented interactive panel which seems to drip with sarcasm as it puts children through Charles Storrow's decision-making process in planning Lawrence. The display sets out the investor's options for building a city, requiring users to push the button next to what they consider the appropriate choice. On the question of boarding houses, the options read:

> A. Build the boarding houses on the outskirts of town so people can farm and keep animals.
>
> B. Build the boarding houses as close to the mills as possible so people can easily walk to and from work.
>
> C. Build the boarding houses on the other side of the Merrimack River where there is a scenic view of the water.

The correct answer is B. The text lights up, pointedly explaining the hidden agenda which lurks within the apparent attention to workers' comfort:

> Good choice!
>
> Storrow put the corporation boarding houses on tree-lined streets across the canal from the mills. The close proximity meant workers could return home for meals; they could also be more easily supervised by mill owners who felt responsible for their moral, mental, and physical welfare.

Like the guide to Springfield, this exhibition involves social science explanations and charts: for example, tabulating textile companies by number of operatives and capital worth. Within a textual atmosphere of irony and double entendre, however, the visitor is apt to notice that such tables turn people into capital, exposing the dehumanizing logic of the investors yet again. The text also translates social science classifications into affective prose: the Lawrence Survey of 1912, for example, is glossed, "The blocks with the densest population were ruled by a chain of D's: Darkness and dampness and dirt; dirt and discomfort and disease; death."

In short, Lawrence Heritage State Park does not read like a standard nation-building exercise. In fact, of course, this site was deemed not "nationally significant" enough for national park service treatment. It qualified for a state program, whose aims are articulated with considerably less boosterism than was on view in Lowell. The State Heritage Program brings together "urban environmental design, historic preservation, and economic revitalization. Established in 1978, the parks celebrate the cities' heritage, encourage private development, bring people into downtowns, and create urban spaces for the whole community to enjoy." The visitor center and its environs feel community-based, both in the exhibition's emphasis and in the provision of community spaces. A room, a gallery, and a park are available for meetings and functions by community organizations. Community newspapers and leaflets in English and Spanish—one for the 4th Annual Bread & Roses Heritage Festival, another for A Public Forum on Labor History and Its Meaning for Today—are on display. Even the somewhat decayed and underresourced atmosphere seems appropriate to a town which is clearly struggling to stay solvent.

In this local memory-making, the Bread and Roses Strike of 1912 remains front and center. One of the few photocopied brochures available—"The City of Workers"—immediately foregrounds the cost of the merchants' entrepreneurial successes to the conditions of the workers' lives; moves to the Bread and Roses Strike; then directs visitors to go in the strikers' footsteps:

> History by Foot
> Walk the route that the labor strikers did in the historic Bread and Roses Strike. Pass massive brick mill complexes, some of which were the largest in the world when they were built. . . .

I take this foot tour, guided only by the leaflet, and feel the threat of the mills—their dominating size, their eerily inhuman proportions, their cavernous, echoing spaces—anew, from a different perspective now. The continuity between past and present, sustained along an axis of respect for workers, is palpable. Like Berger's guide, like the life histories and immigrants' stories gathered by project writers, this guided route—and the Lawrence Heritage State Park in its entirety—embody the perspective and conditions of those always "on the bottom of the rung." Following the theorists of social and collective memory cited earlier, we can appreciate the "acts of transfer" which this environment encourages, its immersion of visitors in the living memory of work and bodies connected to the details of this place, its organic solidarity with the past fed by "what still lives or is capable of living in the consciousness of the groups keeping the memory alive" (Connerton 39; Halbwachs 80).

I return to the visitor center and buy up their entire stock of Bread and Roses T-shirts, for the years 1993, 1998, and 2000, with their brightly colored images of workers at play and their bilingual mottoes. "They're a bit dusty; let me see if I can find a bag," says the attendant, and I leave, feeling that I am carrying with me a glimpse of how memorializing the past can feed resistant collectivities in the present, how memory—*pace* Nora—can feel a real part of everyday existence, and how government can quietly give sustenance to that effort.

NOTES

INTRODUCTION

1. The fifty state offices were comprised of one in each state, two in California, and one in New York City.

2. For further discussion of the other federal arts projects, see Bindas, Bloxom, Bustard, Contreras, Craig, Flanagan, Fraden, Gill, Harris, Kazacoff, McDonald, R. McKinzie, Mathews, Melosh, Meltzer, O'Connor, O'Connor and Brown, and Ulrich.

3. Muriel Hawks, state director of the Massachusetts Writers' Project, cited the figure of "33 publications" in a radio interview in 1941 ("Take Pride in Your Country," WMEX Nov. 10, 1941; LC FWP, A834 Massachusetts). Arthur Scharf lists only nineteen published Massachusetts project titles, along with two New England guides in which Massachusetts played a major role and two cross-regional guides which included Massachusetts project material (383–84). If we were to count all the productions overseen by the Massachusetts office—the published, completed but unpublished, and partially completed work, as well as the regional works centered in the Boston office—the total number would well exceed either of these figures.

4. Bert Loewenberg to Henry Alsberg, May 8, 1937 (Entry 20, Central Office Records, RG 69, NACP).

5. Morton Royse to Henry Alsberg, Jan. 3, 1939 (Entry 20, Central Office Records, RG 69, NACP).

6. Embarrassment may be too mild a word for some project writers' reactions. Mangione records: "A San Francisco poet, who found employment with a brokerage firm after the Project closed, never revealed her connection with the WPA in the twenty-five years she worked for the company, out of fear that her job would be jeopardized" (*Dream* 119).

7. On the New Deal's impact on America's physical landscape, see Cutler, Wilson.

8. For a trenchant analysis of the differences between history and memory, see Nora, "Between."

CHAPTER 1

1. Josef Berger to Mary Heaton Vorse, Dec. 17, 1935 (Entry 1 Massachusetts, Central Office Records, RG 69, NACP).

2. Colby to Billington, June 9, 1936 (Entry 13 Massachusetts, Central Office Records, RG 69, NACP).

3. Additional details on the administrative and editorial practices of the central office —especially the careers and ideologies of Alsberg, Cronyn, Harris, and Kellock—appear in Bold, "View" and *WPA Guides*.

4. Reed Harris, Interview, 1968 (Mangione Papers, Box 96).

5. For fuller details of the Federal Writers' Project and the American Guide Series, see also Banks and Carter, Birdsall, Bold, Brewer, Fox, J. Hirsch, Hofstra Library Associates, Kellock, K. McKinzie, Mangione, Penkower, and Schindler-Carter. Studies of specific regions and states include Bordelon, Clayton, J. Hirsch, "Culture," Mitchell, Sporn, and Taber .

6. For more on the careers and visions of Sterling Brown, Benjamin Botkin, and Morton Royse, see J. Hirsch, *Portrait*.

7. Gaer to Alsberg, July 1, 1937 (Entry 4, Central Office Records, RG 69, NACP).

8. Quoted in Mangione, *Dream* 85.

9. Artists and Writers Union of Massachusetts to Alsberg, Nov. 6, 1935 (Entry 1 Massachusetts, Central Office Records, RG 69, NACP).

10. Roderick Seidenberg to Alsberg, March 27, 1936 (Entry 6, Central Office Records, RG 69, NACP), Alsberg to Lulu Martin Scott, Feb. 11, 1938 (Entry 1 Massachusetts, Central Office Records, RG 69, NACP).

11. Billington, "Government and the Arts" 474–75. Billington also wrote privately to Mangione about anti-Semitism on the project. See Billington to Mangione, Jan. 28, 1969 (Mangione Papers, Box 1).

12. Mangione, *Dream* 86. Note, however, the *Baltimore Morning Sun* Aug. 21, 1937: "Dr. Billington is known to WPA officials [in Washington, D.C.] as somewhat of a conservative, an impression based largely on the fact that he is a history teacher."

13. Shipton to Cronyn, Oct. 30 1935 (Entry 1 Massachusetts, Central Office Records, RG 69, NACP).

14. See also J. Hirsch, *Portrait* 227–28. For example, Newsom designated Colby special coordinator of activities at the "Meeting of State and Regional Representatives for a Discussion on Objectives, Methods, Techniques of the WPA Writers' Program During the Coming Year," May 26–28, 1941. At that meeting, Colby also gave a presentation, "Training and Stimulating Community Talent through Work on National Publications." Katharine Kellock's private correspondence during April and May 1942

shows that she believed Colby to be an opportunist and a survivor (Kellock to Walter [McElroy] April 9, 1942; Kellock to Harold [Coy], May 14, 1942; Kellock Papers). When the arts projects were folded into a "cultural" section in April 1942, to be headed by Holger Cahill, Colby again survived, as Cahill's advisor on writers' activities. All the other staff—including Kellock, Ruth Crawford, and Stella Hanau—were let go, unsupported in facing a grim Washington job market, with "its heavy ban on women, especially older women" (Kellock to Harold [Coy], May 14, 1942; Kellock Papers).

15. In December 1935, Shipton cited 490 as the original quota of writers set for Massachusetts, but this figure included both writers' project and historical records survey personnel (Shipton to Alsberg, Dec. 1, 1935; Entry 1 Massachusetts, Central Office Records, RG 69, NACP). From October 1, 1936, the historical records survey became an independent project. On June 2, 1936, the *Boston Evening Transcript* reported "more than 350" writers on the Massachusetts project. The figure of 146 comes from "Our New England Guides," *Chronotype*, Westborough, Mass. Sept. 17, 1937. In April 1938, Hawks records 139 workers, of whom 7 were nationally known writers, 5 had held important editorial posts, 7 had more than statewide reputations as scholars, educators, or research workers, 28 had had at least a year's experience on a newspaper, 23 had sold material to magazines and newspapers but were not nationally known, 2 were beginning writers with promise, 13 had done a little newspaper work, and 22 had done scholarly work for which they received only local or state recognition (Hawks entries in Memorandum from Alsberg to all state directors, April 5, 1938; Entry 12, Central Office Records, RG 69, NACP).

16. Gaer to Cronyn, April 22, 1937 (Entry 6, Central Office Records, RG 69, NACP).

17. Alsberg [Kellock] to Billington, April 12, 1937 (Entry 13 Massachusetts, Central Office Records, RG 69, NACP).

18. See, for example, telegram, Billington to Alsberg, April 28, 1937 (Entry 13 Massachusetts, Central Office Records, RG 69, NACP); Alsberg to Gaer, April 26, 1937 (Entry 4, Central Office Records, RG 69, NACP); Edward M. Barrows to Gaer, April 27, 1937 (Entry 4, Central Office Records, RG 69, NACP).

19. The project had various titles. Grace Kellogg appears as the representative of the Boston local of the American Writers' Union, and Myriam Sieve is reported as presenting the "History of American Women" project to a meeting of the American Writers' Union, in *The American Writer* 1.1 (June 1936), 2 (Entry 36, Central Office Records, RG 69, NACP). Frank J. Manning, Chairman, Mass. Council of the American Writers' Union, to Harry Hopkins, June 1, 1936 (Entry 1 Massachusetts, Central Office Records, RG 69, NACP).

20. Harris to Kellogg, Feb. 20, 1937 (Entry 1 Massachusetts, Central Office Records, RG 69, NACP); Harris to Agnes Cronin, Feb. 20, 1937 (Entry 5, Central Office Records, RG 69, NACP).

21. Billington first recommended Kellogg's promotion and salary raise to Alsberg—"Mrs. Kellogg is in charge of our editorial board and is responsible for imparting to our copy the literary style that it has" (Billington to Alsberg, Aug. 31, 1936; Entry 1 Massachusetts, Central Office Records, RG 69, NACP). Then, in November 1936, Colby requested that Kellogg be made state editor on the basis of her work with copy, and Cronyn seconded the recommendation: "My records indicate that whatever satisfactory work has been done in introductory essays, cities, and tours has come through Mrs. Kellogg's editing" (Cronyn to Alsberg, Dec. 30, 1936; Entry 13 Massachusetts, Central Office Records, RG 69, NACP). By July 1939, Hawks, clearly working on Alsberg's orders, reports to him that she

is not including a position for Mrs. Kellogg in the application for exemption for the coming period (Hawks to Alsberg, June 15, 1939; LC FWP, A176). By this stage, Kellogg was a non-certified worker being paid a non-security wage of $200 per month, so that decision pushed her off the project.

22. Corresponding with Mrs. Lulu Martin Scott, regional director, Women's and Professional Projects, Alsberg judged Mrs. Hawks "not up to the job of directing the Massachusetts Project. . . . I feel that she will make an excellent assistant" (Feb. 11, 1938; Entry 1 Massachusetts, Central Office Records, RG 69, NACP). By March 30, 1939, however, Alsberg wrote to Hawks with palpable gratitude: "of all the New England states Massachusetts under your direction is perhaps outstanding" (Entry 1 Massachusetts, Central Office Records, RG 69, NACP).

23. Billington, in "Government and the Arts," speaks of her somewhat disparagingly as a political appointee.

24. Hawks to Alsberg, Jan. 5, 1939 (Entry 1 Massachusetts, Central Office Records, RG 69, NACP).

25. See, for example, Hawks to Alsberg, March 24, 1938 and April 13, 1938 (Entry 1 Massachusetts, Central Office Records, RG 69, NACP).

26. Salem was headquarters for Essex County (District No. 1), Boston for Middlesex, Suffolk, and Norfolk Counties (District No. 2) and for the City of Boston (District No. 3), New Bedford for Barnstable, Bristol, Dukes, Nantucket, and Plymouth Counties (District No. 4), Worcester for Worcester County (District No. 5), and Springfield for Berkshire, Franklin, Hampden, and Hampshire Counties (District No. 6).

27. Billington identifies wage scales as low as under $60 per month, but I believe the figure refers to southern states, not Massachusetts ("Government and the Arts" 468).

28. Aiken to Mangione, July 24, 1968 (published in *Pennsylvania Gazette* Nov. 1973, 31)

29. Bradford to Hawks, May 5, 1938 (Entry 36, Central Office Records, RG 69, NACP)

30. Goldenberg to Silveira, June 17, 1937 (Entry 36, Central Office Records, RG 69, NACP).

31. Shipton to Alsberg, Dec. 31, 1935; Alsberg [Bleiberg] to Shipton, Jan. 16, 1936 (Entry 1 Massachusetts, Central Office Records, RG 69, NACP).

32. Shipton to Alsberg, March 1, 1936 (Entry 6, Central Office Records, RG 69, NACP).

33. Report, Joseph Gaer to Alsberg, Dec. 27–31, 1935 (Entry 6, Central Office Records, RG 69, NACP).

34. Cronyn to Billington May 12, 1937 (Entry 13 Massachusetts, Central Office Records, RG 69, NACP).

35. J. Henry King to Bert Loewenberg, April 8, 1936 (Entry 34, Central Office Records, RG 69, NACP).

36. Heale 150, 165.

37. On the New Deal realignment in Massachusetts by ethnic groups, see Gamm. On the Democratic coalition, see Barbrook, Gorvine, and Huthmacher.

38. Shipton to Alsberg, Dec. 30, 1935 (Entry 1 Massachusetts, Central Office Records, RG 69, NACP).

CHAPTER 2

1. Kellock to Gaer, July 1, 1937 (Entry 6, Central Office Records, RG 69, NACP).
2. Oddly enough, there is no Massachusetts representation in Doty's *Franco-Americans*

in *New England*, a selection of life histories from the Federal Writers' Projects in New Hampshire, Maine, Vermont, and Rhode Island, published in 1985.

CHAPTER 3

1. The voluminous literature on the Sacco-Vanzetti case includes Avrich, Dos Passos, Ehrmann, Frankfurter, Jackson, Joughin and Morgan, Porter, Russell, and Weeks.

2. A more recent argument makes a similar point: "In January 1920 the Palmer raids netted hundreds of suspects in Boston and other Massachusetts towns. This image of industrial communities liberally infested with Communists and anarchists set the backdrop for the state's prosecution of Nicola Sacco and Bartolomeo Vanzetti" (Heale 154).

3. The Dedham entry also revivifies a pamphlet protesting the Lowell Commission report on Sacco and Vanzetti, circulated (and suppressed) at Harvard's tercentenary celebration in 1936.

4. The quotation is taken from a clipping enclosed in a letter from Creighton Hill to Professor Robert E. Rogers, Massachusetts Institute of Technology, Sept. 3, 1936 (Felicani Collection, Ms.2030 7A).

5. *New York Post* Aug. 21, 1937; *Boston American* Aug. 19, 1937; *Washington, D.C., Evening Star* Aug. 19, 1937; *Boston American* Aug. 27, 1937; *New York Times* Aug. 29, 1937.

6. *Boston American* Aug. 19, 1937.

7. *Boston American* Aug. 19, 1937.

8. *Boston Herald* Aug. 20, 1937. See also *Boston American* Aug. 19, 1937; *New York Times* Aug. 20, 1937.

9. *Providence* [R.I.] *Journal* Aug. 25, 1937; *Worcester Telegram* Sept. 1, 1937.

10. *Boston American* Aug. 27, 1937; *Pawtucket* [R.I.] *Times* Aug. 28, 1937.

11. Catharine Sargent Huntington to Aldino Felicani, Aug. 20, 1937 (Felicani Collection, Ms.2030 7A).

12. *New York Post* Aug. 21, 1937.

13. On November 16, 1931, Gardner Jackson wrote to Aldino Felicani that Gutzon Borglum had cast the tablet in bronze: "The question is what to do with the sculpture. I do not believe there is any point in trying to have it placed on public display in Boston anywhere. Of course, you might get some publicity by writing a letter to Mayor Curley asking him to place it on the Common" (Felicani Collection, Ms.2030 7A).

14. Letter, Creighton Hills to Aldino Felicani, Aug. 23, 1935 (Felicani Collection, Ms.2030 7A).

15. *New Bedford Standard-Times* Aug. 20, 1937. The scene is hauntingly familiar: "in 1927, the Massachusetts Department went out of its way to take a stand in the Sacco-Vanzetti case. In a 'wild uproar' at the State Convention in Fitchburg, the Legion 'applauded and expressed its appreciation to the Governor [Alvan Fuller] for his untiring efforts in the interest of justice' when he refused eleventh-hour pleas that he pardon the two 'convicted murderers.' The Legionnaires 'clapped. They yelled in one big chorus. . . . They stood, then they pounded the chairs. Then the band played America'" (Pencak 166).

16. *Boston American* Aug. 21, 1937; *Boston Post* Aug. 23, 1937; *Boston American* Aug. 26, 1937.

17. *Boston Post* Aug. 27, 1937. One account claimed that extra material had been inserted after the typescript left Hurley's hands but before it arrived in Washington D.C. (*Boston American* Aug. 21, 1937; *New York Times* Aug. 21, 1937). Another version claimed that the "Labor" essay was smuggled into the typesetter after the dummy had passed through both his and the Washington office's hands (*Boston Post* Aug. 21, 1937).

18. *Boston Post* Aug. 23, 1937. On distrust between Massachusetts and New Deal Democrats, see Kennedy, Keyssar, T. O'Connor, and Trout.

19. *Boston Advertiser* Aug. 22, 1937.

20. *Boston Globe* Aug. 20, 1937; *Boston Post* Aug. 21, 1937.

21. *Boston Post* Aug. 21, 1937.

22. *New Bedford Standard-Times* Aug. 20 and Aug. 22, 1937.

23. American Writers Union Workers Alliance to Hopkins, Sept. 9, 1937; American Writers Union to Alsberg, Sept. 10, 1937 (Entry 1 Massachusetts, Central Office Records, RG 69, NACP).

24. *Fairhaven Star* Aug. 26, 1937.

25. The paper trail of drafts (all undated) goes in the following order: "A. R. Buckley, Hist. after 1789" [Ms.] (Entry 34, Central Office Records, RG 69, NACP); "A. R. Buckley, Dedham, History after 1789" [Ts.] (Entry 34, Central Office Records, RG 69, NACP); "FEC—Buckley, SEC—Peach, ED—Kellogg, Dedham" (LC FWP, A174); "Dedham" [Final] (LC FWP, A174). Washington editors also argued for increasing the attention to Sacco and Vanzetti in the Dedham entry, attaching material on them to both the city description and the accompanying tour. The state editors resisted that suggestion. In the published version, the Dedham entry contains only one paragraph on Sacco and Vanzetti, attached to the Norfolk County Courthouse on the walking tour. The "Summary Criticism" on the Dedham copy is initialed "GMC" and "RC"—presumably George Cronyn, associate director in the Washington office, and Ruth Crawford, an editor in the New York City office with nationwide responsibilities (Entry 13 Massachusetts, Central Office Records, RG 69, NACP).

26. Billington, "Government and the Arts" 478. See also Cyr.

27. *Boston Globe* Aug. 19 and 20, 1937; *Boston Herald* Aug. 19 and 20, 1937.

28. *Baltimore Evening Sun* Aug. 19, 1937. See also *Washington, D.C., Evening Star* Aug. 19, 1937; *NYC The Sun* Aug. 19 and 20, 1937; *Cleveland Plain Dealer* Aug. 20, 1937; *Baltimore Morning Sun* Aug. 20, 1937.

29. On September 20, 1937, Ruth Crawford addressed a memo to Henry Alsberg: "The Massachusetts Guide, according to *The Transcript*, moved to fourth place among last week's best sellers in Boston" (Entry 2, Central Office Records, RG 69, NACP). The press which quoted Hopkins included *Boston Globe* Aug. 20, 1937; *Boston Herald* Aug. 20, 1937; *Boston Post* Aug. 20, 1937; *Baltimore Morning Sun* Aug. 20, 1937; *New York Times* Aug. 21, 1937; *Pittsburgh Press* Aug. 20, 1937; and *Baltimore Morning Sun* Aug. 21, 1937. The *Boston Post* Aug. 21, 1937 refuted his accusation.

30. Alsberg to Gaer, Sept. 22, 1937 (Entry 6, New England, Central Office Records, RG 69, NACP).

31. Alsberg to Ellen Woodward, Oct. 14, 1937 (Entry 5, Central Office Records, RG 69, NACP).

32. Alsberg to Ellen Woodward, Oct. 14, 1937 (Entry 5, Central Office Records, RG 69, NACP).

33. Alsberg to Lawrence Morris, March 23, 1938 (Entry 5, Central Office Records, RG 69, NACP).

34. The letter, signed by Alsberg, but composed by Reed Harris (assistant director in Washington), to R. N. Linscott at Houghton Mifflin, reads in part: "Although the decision as to whether changes are to be made in the text of the Massachusetts Guide have been left in my hands now, I do not feel that any changes should be made until you think about the whole matter very carefully. We feel that a great deal of the public-

ity we have received and the reputation we have developed may be credited to the outspoken statements in the Massachusetts book. As you know, a large number of leading educators, critics and others have commented very favorably on the book as it stands now" (Jan. 25, 1938, Central Office Records, Entry 13 Massachusetts, Box 97).

35. Linscott to Alsberg, April 25, 1938; Linscott to Alsberg, April 28, 1938 (Entry 13 Massachusetts, Central Office Records, RG 69, NACP).

36. *New York City World-Telegram* Aug. 21, 1937.

37. I have found very little information on Muriel E. Hawks beyond occasional newspaper mention during her time as state director. The 1942 Boston City Directory lists her occupation and address. My reconstruction of her role in revising the guidebook comes from two sources. A memorandum from Hawks to Gaer discusses the revised material as if she authored it on direction from above: "In accordance with your request, I enclose the essay on Industry and Labor" (Hawks to Gaer, Dec. 9, 1937; Entry 4, Central Office Records, RG 69, NACP). An undated draft press release—almost certainly never circulated—reads in part: "In preparation for this new printing, the Federal Writers' Project collected and analyzed all criticisms that have been made and combed the book, line by line, for possible errors." The circular also makes a claim that is not supported by the editorial records that I have seen: "In addition to the factual corrections, one important change has been made in the book—the substitution of an essay on labor and industry for the present essay on labor. It was the original intention of the directors of the Federal Writers' Project to have the essay cover both subjects but the pressure in getting the book out prevented the completion of the essay in time to include in the book" (Entry 13 Massachusetts, Central Office Records, RG 69, NACP).

38. The dynamic is consistent with the operation which Michel Foucault dubbed "governmentality": that is, the continuum of pressures—from institutional government to cultural forms to social and individual relations—on a population to identify as a governable unit with particular qualifications for membership (see Foucault, "Governmentality" 87–104).

39. Manuel to Alsberg, Aug. 16, 1938 (Entry 13 Massachusetts, Central Office Records, RG 69, NACP).

40. Linscott to Alsberg, Sept. 27, 1938 (Entry 13 Massachusetts, Central Office Records, RG 69, NACP).

41. See Penkower 106. Presumably Alsberg also consulted Loewenberg and Billington, the two other signatories to the preface.

42. The seriousness of the threat was proven by the closing of the Federal Theatre Project and the devolving of the other three arts projects to state control in 1939.

43. Gov. E. D. Rivers, who was feuding with Hurley about convict extradition, announced that the guide "would be considered for purchase 'so our children may be informed as to the deplorable condition of the courts and penal system in Massachusetts'" (*Atlanta Constitution* Aug. 21, 1937; *Providence* [R.I.] *Journal* Aug. 21, 1937; and *Worcester Telegram* Aug. 21, 1937).

44. Bearse vii. Bearse writes Sacco and Vanzetti prominently into the history essay and the Dedham entry and mentions them in his treatment of government, Boston, and Braintree. Kay does not alter the 1937 text.

45. Penkower discusses the pressure on Alsberg to revise the guide and the addition of the "policy editor" (106–7); Schindler-Carter mentions that "Contrary to popular opinion, the Massachusetts guide was slightly revised" (109).

CHAPTER 4

1. Indeed, over twenty years later, Ray Billington somehow believed that they *had* achieved broad representation of African Americans. He describes Black employees on the Massachusetts project: "No less thrilling was the change that occurred in the attitude of Negroes or representatives of other minority groups as the realization dawned that they were to be judged on their merits rather than by the color of their skins or the nature of their beliefs, for the WPA projects played an important, if often forgotten, role in the battle against discrimination" (471).

2. *Boston Globe* Aug. 19, 1937.

3. Sullivan 55. Ickes "had served as president of the Chicago branch of the NAACP. [Upon his appointment as administrator of the PWA] He promptly appointed Clark Foreman (white) and Robert Weaver (black) as special assistants to keep him informed on race matters, and local committees in charge of public works in particular areas were encouraged to have Negro members to keep them posted on any special problems that developed" (Wolters 186).

4. Raymond Wolters reports the statistic: "In the United States of 1930, twenty-three of every two hundred persons gainfully employed were Negroes. Of these twenty-three, nine were engaged in some form of agricultural work, six were employed in industry, six earned their living as household employees, and the remaining two were engaged in trade, the professions, or public service" (183–84).

5. Alsberg was conscious of racial discrimination, writing to Aubrey Williams about the need for a Black editor in Washington, D.C., on December 16, 1935: "I am sure that there is discrimination in the southern states against employment of negroes on the writers' project" (Entry 5, Central Office Records, RG 69, NACP).

6. For more on Brown's career and beliefs in the context of the Federal Writers' Project, see J. Hirsch, *Portrait*.

7. Shipton's communications seem evasive. He wrote to Alsberg on Jan. 15, 1936: "You will find enclosed a list of negroes who are to be employed on the Records Project. None is at present employed on the Guide because only one colored applicant had any qualifications at all, and that one was non-relief. He is now being taken care of" (Entry 1 Massachusetts, Central Office Records, RG 69, NACP). A second Black was employed during January 1936. On January 17, Shipton sent a list of four Blacks (Ernest E. Ormsby, Edythe [which he spelled "Edith"] M. Gordon, Robert H. Green, William E. Harrison) "to be employed on the Records Project" (Entry 27, Central Office Records, RG 69, NACP). On February 10, Shipton wrote to Alsberg again: "The Artists' and Writers' Union has been completely silenced. The representative of the colored element has been contacted and assured of our cooperation" (Entry 13 Massachusetts, Central Office Records, RG 69, NACP). In October 1936, the *Boston Chronicle* celebrated forty Black project employees, fifteen of them writers working on the state guide and the others skilled workers engaged as clerks and editors. Their list of writers included "William Harrison, who is working on his Degree of Doctor of Philosophy at Harvard University, and who is expecting to receive a fellowship to study at Oxford University in England; Dr. Walter O. Taylor, a well known Boston personality; Edythe Mae Gordon, A.M., Boston University, 1935; Alice T. Walton, formerly associated with the Boston CHRONICLE; Harry O. Bowles, Robert Greene, Zylpha Mapp, Ernest E. Ormsby, Edward C. Williams and Elizabeth Smith" (*Boston Chronicle* Oct. 31, 1936). Yet by December 10, Loewenberg reported to Alsberg only fifteen Blacks currently or recently employed (Entry 13 Massachusetts, Central Office Records, RG 69, NACP).

8. "Report from the Editor on Negro Affairs" (February 1937), 5 (Entry 27, Central Office Records, RG 69, NACP).

9. Brown's uphill fight continued throughout his time on the project. On June 8, 1937, he wrote in exasperation to Alsberg: "This New South (or New Midwest or New North) from which the Negro is an exile, not self-imposed in this case, is hardly recognizable. . . . if our publications are to be true guides to American life, the Negro cannot be so completely relegated to the background" (Entry 27, Central Office Records, RG 69, NACP). In 1938, the guide to Mississippi was published with its racist epithets—to which Brown's office had objected strenuously and repeatedly—intact. His editorial directions to the collectors of ex-slave narratives also suggest the depth of the problem: "I should like to recommend that the words darky and nigger and such expressions as 'a comical little old black woman' be omitted from the editorial writing" (qtd. in Mangione, *Dream* 62). As late as 1939, several southern states still employed no or very few Blacks.

10. Alsberg [Brown] to State Directors of the FWP, June 15, 1937 (Entry 11, Central Office Records, RG 69, NACP).

11. Brown, no title, no date (Entry 27, Central Office Records, RG 69, NACP).

12. Loewenberg to Alsberg, attn. Sterling Brown, Oct. 6, 1936 (Entry 13 Massachusetts, Central Office Records, RG 69, NACP).

13. *Boston Chronicle* Oct. 31, 1936.

14. Harrison is discussed in the following letters: Loewenberg to Alsberg, Oct. 7, 1936; Alsberg [Brown] to Billington, March 25, 1937; Loewenberg to Alsberg, March 29, 1937 (Entry 1 Massachusetts, Central Office Records, RG 69, NACP).

15. Information on Gordon comes from Gordon and from Roses and Randolph.

16. The surviving correspondence about Gordon's dismissal consists of the following letters: Gordon to Alsberg, July 4, 1937; Reed Harris to Gordon, July 7, 1937; Alsberg to Gaer, July 8, 1937; Loewenberg to Alsberg, July 19, 1937; Woodward to Scott, July 26, 1937 (Entry 1 Massachusetts, and Entry 6, Central Office Records, RG 69, NACP). Clearly, some of Gordon's additional approaches to upper-level administrators never made it to the archives.

17. The Massachusetts Theatre Project had a Negro unit which, among other productions, performed a Black *Macbeth* in Boston, and the Massachusetts Music Project supported Black units in Boston, Cambridge, and Springfield (see McDonald 614).

18. "The American Guide Manual," 54, Oct. 1935 (Entry 11, Central Office Records, RG 69, NACP).

19. Winnie C. Matthew, FEC Abington: Racial Groups (Entry 34, Central Office Records, RG 69, NACP).

20. Roger T. Balloch, FEC Mattapoisett: Racial Groups, Racial Cultural Heritage, Relationship of Racial Groups to Community Development, Contemporary Racial Groups Retaining Ethnic Identity (Entry 34, Central Office Records, RG 69, NACP).

21. James F. McKenna, FEC New Bedford: Racial Groups, Racial Cultural Heritage, Relationship of Racial Groups to Community Development, Contemporary Racial Groups Retaining Ethnic Identity (Entry 34, Central Office Records, RG 69, NACP).

22. Sara Tyler, FEC Wareham: Racial Cultural Heritage (Entry 34, Central Office Records, RG 69, NACP).

23. See, for example, Curtis F. Day, FEC Scituate: Relationship of racial groups to community development (Original) (Entry 34, Central Office Records, RG 69, NACP).

24. Ernest E. Ormsby, FEC Barnstable: Racial Groups; Catherine M. Vanni, FEC Barnstable: Racial Groups (Entry 34, Central Office Records, RG 69, NACP).

25. Ernest E. Ormsby, FEC Burlington (Entry 34, Central Office Records, RG 69, NACP).

26. George Gloss, FEC Holbrook: Racial Groups (Entry 34, Central Office Records, RG 69, NACP).

27. Otto Abrahamsen, FEC Harwich: Racial Groups, Racial Cultural Heritage, Relationship of Racial Groups to Community Development, Contemporary Racial Groups Retaining Ethnic Identity (Entry 34, Central Office Records, RG 69, NACP).

28. Josef Berger, FEC Provincetown: Racial Groups, Racial Cultural Heritage, Relationship of Racial Groups to Community Development, Contemporary Racial Groups Retaining Ethnic Identity (Entry 34, Central Office Records, RG 69, NACP).

29. Kellogg to Alsberg and Cronyn, May 10, 1937, says that tour wordage in the Massachusetts guide was reduced from 220,000 to 97,000 words (Entry 4, Central Office Records, RG 69, NACP). Mangione also reports Kellock writing to Grace Kellogg, May 8, 1937, that she and one assistant "checked and edited and reduced the wordage in half for over 200,000 words of Massachusetts [tours] copy" (*Dream* 64).

30. Ermin Markella, FEC North Bridgewater (Entry 34, Central Office Records, RG 69, NACP).

31. Frank L. Gallagher, FEC Roxbury: Racial elements, Groups Retaining Ethnic Identity (Revised) (Entry 34, Central Office Records, RG 69, NACP).

32. The unsigned paper "Racial Groups in Boston" reads, *in toto*: "The two large concentrations of Negroes in Boston are in the South End and in Roxbury, particularly on the dividing line. There are fourteen Negro churches in Boston, including four Baptist, three Methodist, two African Methodist, two Episcopal and one each of the Presbyterian and Congregational denominations, as well as many 'Store-front' churches of the 'Holy Rollers', Spiritualists, 'Wash-foot Baptist', and the followers of Father Divine, who meet nightly on West Canton Street. The latter sect believe their leader, in New York, has taken on the body of God, and every day they carry on his practice of feeding the poor. There are two outstanding Negro newspapers, the Guardian and the Chronicle; two weekly forums, the Community at 464 Massachusetts Avenue, and the Boston Literary at 558 Massachusetts Avenue, as well as a primitive African Art Center on Harwich Street. The Greater Boston Negro Chorus has won many prizes at the International Music Festivals held in Symphony Hall" (LC FWP, A882). None of these items of Black cultural life in Boston appear in the Massachusetts guide.

33. William Wells Brown worked in Boston as a Massachusetts Anti-Slavery Society lecture agent and wrote *Narrative of William W. Brown, an American Slave* which, Brown's own note tells us, "was first published in Boston, (U.S.) in July, 1847, and eight thousand copies were sold in less than eighteen months from the time of its publication." Of the legal and constitutional educational struggles of Blacks in nineteenth-century Boston, contemporary historians say: "The 'separate but equal' doctrine, the legal linchpin of Jim Crow in America, has its origins in the cradle of liberty, Boston, Massachusetts" (Levy and Jones vii). W. C. Nell was "one of the leading Negro reformers of the day . . . an intimate of Wendell Phillips and William Lloyd Garrison" (Levy and Jones ix). Julian D. Rainey came from South Carolina to Boston to practice law in the 1920s and became a significant figure in developing "recognition" politics and balance between Republican and Democratic power in Massachusetts (Huthmacher 121–22).

34. Du Bois talked at greater length about his sense of place and social class, as it emerged from his upbringing in Great Barrington, in *Dusk of Dawn: The Autobiography of a Race Concept* (1940).

35. "The star of the evening was a husky Negro who came out in a fantastic costume to sing 'Jump, Jim Crow,' before a wide-eyed audience" (160).

36. Eugene Holmes to Wood, April 7, 1938 (Entry 27, Central Office Records, RG 69, NACP).

37. Brown to Munson, Jan. 9, 1940 (Entry 27, Central Office Records, RG 69, NACP).

38. Sitkoff reports that "a few historians" in the 1930s began to show the role of Blacks in the abolition movement (201). He cites Lawrence D. Reddick, "A New Interpretation for Negro History," *Journal of Negro History* 22 (January 1937): 17–28, and Merl R. Eppse, *The Negro, Too, in American History* (Chicago, 1939).

39. Typescript material on Anthony Burns is filed under "The Portrait of the Negro as American" (LC FWP, A856, A860). The quoted material on Paul Cuffee and Crispus Attucks appears in an untitled synopsis signed "Professor Brown" ("The Portrait of the Negro as American"; LC FWP, A860). The quoted material on Phillis Wheatley appears in "Black Abolitionists" 12, 10 ("The Portrait of the Negro as American"; LC FWP, A856).

40. Quoting from the "Manual for Folklore Studies" which he issued on August 15, 1938, Botkin describes the relationship between folklore and social-ethnic studies on the project thus: "whereas the folklore studies dealt with 'a body of lore in relation to the life of a group or community,' the social-ethnic studies dealt with 'the whole life of a group or community,' including its folklore. Inevitably, the two sets of studies had to be closely correlated, since they fed each other, were carried on often by the same workers, and were planned jointly by Morton W. Royse, social-ethnic editor, and myself. We made field trips together to New York, Pennsylvania, and New England, and derived a great deal from our association. . . . In connection with immigrant and foreign-language groups we learned, specifically, that their true measure, as components of 'composite America,' is in their participation in, rather than in their 'contributions' (outmoded work) to, our cultural diversity" (191–92). For more information on Botkin and Royse in the context of the Federal Writers' Project, see J. Hirsch, *Portrait*.

41. Royse to Mangione, June 9, 1970 (Mangione Papers, Box 58).

42. "Supplementary Instructions 9-F to The American Guide Manual: Manual for Folklore Studies" (Aug. 15, 1938); "Supplementary Instructions 9-G to The American Guide Manual: Manual for Social-Ethnic Studies" (Aug. 15, 1938) (Entry 11, Central Office Records, RG 69, NACP).

43. See chapter 3 at note 30.

44. Jerome Blackwell, "Negroes in Mass. (Clifford Sinclair)" (July 28, 1939), 6 (LC FWP, A179).

45. Zylpha O. Mapp, "Negro Press" (Jan. 19, 1939), 13–14 (LC FWP, A882).

46. "Social History of Massachusetts" (LC FWP, A177).

47. Among other evidence of Brown's dissatisfaction with the new order is his memo to Botkin on March 5, 1940, expressing his reservations concerning Botkin's powers as chief editorial supervisor. Brown, his title changed from editor on Negro Affairs to editorial supervisor of Negro studies, wrote: "Naturally I should not like to see anyone else responsible for the writing of these books. *Finis coronat opus.*" He wanted reciprocal responsibilities between Botkin and himself: "In line with this recommendation I suggest that the title of Chief Editorial Supervisor be changed to that of Literary Adviser" (LC FWP, A869). A month later he wrote to Botkin again, protesting his classification and reduction in salary: "I believe that my services are just as valuable now as they were three years ago when I was receiving fifteen dollars per diem, and certainly as valuable as last year when I received ten dollars per diem." His salary had been reduced by $20.16 each

month, $241.92 per year. "I understand that for consultants within my rank eight dollars and eighty-eight cents is the maximum per diem allowed. I should like therefore to be classified in the next highest rank of Assistant Editor (with a salary range of from $2900 to $3500) so that my salary would not have to be reduced. I believe that I am the only person on the reorganized project to have received a cut in salary." He also pushed for more Black employees in the national office and for the promotion and a pay raise for his assistant Glaucia B. Roberts, from editorial clerk to senior editorial clerk: "She has worked on the Project since [June] 1936 with only one advance in rank and salary. She deserves better" (Brown to Botkin, April 11, 1940; Entry 32, Central Office Records, RG 69, NACP).

48. Plans for a national study of Indians and culture—possible under the supervision of Franz Boas and Ruth Benedict—did not pan out (Penkower 149).Various administrators discussed "Indians of the United States" in 1941, possibly as a series of regional books from University of Oklahoma Press with consultants from the University of Oklahoma faculty and Stella Hanau in charge in Washington, D.C., but by December 1941 that work had to be postponed because of the "all-out war effort" (Entry 211.73, Central Correspondence Files, RG 69, NACP). See also J. Hirsch, *Portrait* 38.

49. The full list of assignments under "Archeology and Ethnology" in "The American Guide. Massachusetts Project. Instructions For All Writers On Local Subjects" (Jan. 7, 1936) (Entry 13 Massachusetts, Central Office Records, RG 69, NACP) was as follows:

D-211	Earliest human remains.
D-212	Indian remains.
D-220	Indians: History and anthropology, reservations, tribal remnants not on reservations.
D-231	Earliest white settlement.
D-232	Earliest communal life, general description.
D-241	Early Folklore legends.
D-242	Other folklore (songs, dances, dress, superstitions, etc.)
D-243	Contributions to language: Names of Indian origin, Localisms.

50. "Supplementary Instructions #11B to American Guide Manual" (July 25, 1936), 12 (Entry 11, Central Office Records, RG 69, NACP).

51. "Supplementary Instructions #11 to American Guide Manual" (May 5, 1936), 7 (Entry 11, Central Office Records, RG 69, NACP).

52. Emma A. Paulding, FEC Mashpee: Racial Groups, Racial Cultural Heritage, Relationship of Racial Groups to Community Development, Contemporary Racial Groups Retaining Ethnic Identity, History after 1789 (Entry 34, Central Office Records, RG 69, NACP).

53. Thadious Davis made these remarks in a presentation entitled "The Federal Writers' Project and the Legacy of Black Writers" at the symposium The WPA and the Federal Writers' Project, November 8, 1986, Fort Lauderdale, Fla. Her second quotation is from Ralph Ellison's essay "Remembering Richard Wright."

CHAPTER 5

1. Conroy 83. On the cultural power and images of "the worker" in America, before and during the New Deal, see Brody, Gutman, Hapke, and David Montgomery.

2. Billington to All District Supervisors, Nov. 24, 1936, circulates *General Letter No. 90* from Harry Hopkins (Nov. 2, 1936) on WPA workers' "right to organize and select representatives of their own choice for the purpose of adjusting grievances with the Works Progress Administration, and [they] shall not be required to limit their choice

of representatives to persons engaged on the Works Program" (Entry 36, Central Office Records, RG 69, NACP).

3. Denning xx and passim; Szalay, *New Deal Modernism* 3. Other discussions of the strategies available to writers on the left in the 1930s include Aaron, Browder, Irr, Peeler, Pells, Staub, and Susman. In terms of the Federal Arts Projects, Denning focuses on the involvement of "plebians" and "the ethnic working-class" (44–50, 77–83). Szalay reconstructs the vision and impact of the Federal Writers' Project from the published fiction of some project writers and statements by the upper echelons of project administrators (*New Deal Modernism* 55–74; "Introduction" xxi–xxxv). There were very many project employees (such as the majority in the New Bedford district office) who did not identify with—or did not qualify for—any of these categories.

4. Unemployment in New Bedford always hit women, African Americans, and "other" (i.e., Portuguese) workers disproportionately (Wolfbein 39, 44).

5. *New Bedford Evening Standard* April 17, 1928; qtd. in Georgianna 145, 80, 83.

6. Wolfbein shows that the proportion of New Bedford's population dependent on "public assistance" (including "general relief, old age assistance and WPA") rose from 16 to 25 percent between 1935 and 1939 (37). Ironically, the New Deal exacerbated New Bedford's decline. The "wholesale liquidation of New Bedford cotton textile mills" resumed and redoubled when the NRA was struck down by the Supreme Court in 1935 (Wolfbein qtd. in Georgianna 150).

7. See "Attack on WPA Wage Planned; New Bedford Labor Group to Join Oppositionists at State Meeting" (*New Bedford Standard-Times* Aug. 7, 1935).

8. "Projects Here Vindicate WPA, Edwards Says; City Work Relief Seen by Visitors as Tribute to Mayor Ashley" (*New Bedford Standard-Times* Sept. 24, 1936; Ashley Scrapbooks, Roll 46).

9. *Fairhaven Star* Aug. 15, 1935.

10. Although local publications—the Fairhaven guide, the directory of whaling masters—were met with quietly appreciative reviews, the work of producing these books remained largely unnoticed. An article in the *New Bedford Standard-Times* (Nov. 25, 1935) works to position writers in a professional category of their own: "Selections will be made from writers or authors, who have made writing their profession; journalists and editorial workers, newspapermen, historians, research workers, art, literary and other similar professions. . . . Special writers will be used in condensing the many facts obtained by research workers. . . . Many well-known writers and newspapermen have applied for work on the project, including no less than seven who hold the degree of doctor of philosophy." (This last comment refers to the project at the national level. Large chunks of this story were clearly taken from a centrally distributed news release, but the account played differently in different locations.)

11. Later, the project office was relocated to City Hall in downtown New Bedford, a much grander building in a more formal setting than the Mary B. White School. That move could well have hardened the sense of governmental status with which some writers protected themselves.

12. Bradford to Melvin Peach, n.d. (Entry 36, Central Office Records, RG 69, NACP).

13. See, for example, the *New Bedford Times* April 11, 12, 1928; the story about Bradford's fishing trip is in the *Fairhaven Star* Sept. 21, 1928.

14. I have assembled Bradford's biography and residences from the following sources (as well as my own visits to his listed addresses): the *New Bedford and Fairhaven Directory* 1900–1960; *Fairhaven Star* Sept. 21, 1928, Nov. 22, 1929, April 4, 1930, July 31, 1931,

Aug. 28, 1931, Aug. 11, 1932, Aug. 16, 1934, March 7, 1935, Nov. 27, 1935, March 19, 1959; *New Bedford Evening Standard* Nov. 12, 1920; *New Bedford Standard-Times* Aug. 10, 1932, Aug. 28, 1932, Sept. 21, 1932, July 7, 1935, April 6, 1948, March 17, 1959, March 7, 1971.

15. See WPA conference, April 3, 1936, for the quintessentially bureaucratic role of district supervisor (Entry 36, Central Office Records, RG 69, NACP).

16. Editorial Report (Summary Criticism), Mass. New Bedford, May 7, 1937 (GWC): "Since New Bedford is a textile town, trade union organization should be given some treatment. . . . some mention should be made of the union that conducted the six months' strike described on page 5" (Entry 13 Massachusetts, Central Office Records, RG 69, NACP).

17. James McKenna, FEC New Bedford (LC FWP, A177).

18. Tripp to Bradford, July 11, 1936 (Entry 36, Central Office Records, RG 69, NACP).

19. He addressed local authorities in the name of "the directors of the project" (Bradford to Rev. Frank I. Noyer, Jan. 7, 1936; Entry 36, Central Office Records, RG 69, NACP) and repeatedly borrowed federal authority: for example, to defend bureaucratic writing protocols as "a certain procedure . . . [necessary] as in all government activities" (Memo to district employees, Feb. 19, 1936; Entry 36, Central Office Records, RG 69, NACP). See also Bradford to Kellogg, July 20, 1936; Goldenberg to Bradford, Feb. 9, 1938; Bradford to Goldenberg, Dec. 21, 1936 (Entry 36, Central Office Records, RG 69, NACP).

20. Ryder to Bradford, Jan. 31, 1936 (Entry 36, Central Office Records, RG 69, NACP).

21. Bradford to Ryder, Feb. 3, 1936 (Entry 36, Central Office Records, RG 69, NACP).

22. "I am exceedingly fond of Mr. Ryder and would be glad to see him re-employed" (Bradford to Hawks, May 5, 1938; Entry 36, Central Office Records, RG 69, NACP).

23. His position was taken over by Frank Manning, a move which, by privileging "an outsider," gave rise to some local discontent (according to the *Fairhaven Star* Jan. 14, 1937).

24. I have assembled James McKenna's biography and residences from the following sources (as well as my own visits to his listed addresses): the *New Bedford and Fairhaven Directory* 1926–1940; *Fairhaven Star* Sept. 8, 1929, Jan. 14, 1937; *New Bedford Standard-Times* Oct. 20, 1938, Nov. 4, 1938, Oct. 26, 1940; James McKenna Jr. Interview, Donaghy and McCabe 24. McKenna's obituary states that he was a member of the American Legion, but this membership was not part of his public persona in the way that it was for Julia Keane.

25. I have assembled Julia Keane's biography and residences from the following sources (as well as my visits to her listed addresses): the *New Bedford and Fairhaven Directory* 1914–1947; *Fairhaven Star* Sept. 15, 1932, June 15, 1933, Jan. 28, 1937, March 14, 1937, May 27, 1937, Aug. 12, 1937, Sept. 30, 1937, July 28, 1938, Sept. 15, 1938, Feb. 15, 1940, Feb. 17, 1938, June 15, 1939; *New Bedford Standard-Times* Nov. 3, 1938.

26. I have assembled Elsie Moeller's biography and residences from the following sources (as well as my visits to her listed addresses): the *New Bedford and Fairhaven Directory* 1939–1945; *Fairhaven Star* March 17, 1935; *New Bedford Evening Standard* May 7, 1919, June 4, 1919, March 23, 1924, Nov. 18, 1925, July 20, 1926, Feb. 11, 1927; *New Bedford Standard-Times* Nov. 2, 1936, April 10, 1937, March 20, 1955, Aug. 16, 1958; Rodman Moeller Interview, Dougherty and McCabe 25; G. Leroy Bradford, "Isabella White" (*Spinner* 69); Moeller, Jacket Note, *Pack a Bag*.

27. [Moeller] to Charles Goldenberg: "I have received my Professional re-classification. To say that I am pleased is putting it lightly for it was entirely unexpected, and I only hope to be able to live up to it" (Aug. 18, 1938; Entry 36, Central Office Records, RG 69, NACP).

28. For more details on Berger, see chapter 6. Willison was born and brought up in Colorado. From 1923 to 1928, he wrote journalism for the *Denver Express* and, from about 1926 to 1936, published stories, book reviews, and articles in the *New Yorker*, *Nation*, *New York Herald Tribune*, and *New Massses*. His books published prior to project employment included *Here They Dug Gold* (1931), concerning the Pike's Peak Gold Rush, and *Why Wars Are Declared* (1935), "a study and running argument about the basic economic-social drives toward imperialist conflict." In 1936, he was writing a play based on *Gold* (Willison to Colby, July 3, 1936; Entry 36, Central Office Records, RG 69, NACP). By 1936, Carl Malmberg had published popular fiction under the pseudonym Timothy Trent and an exposé of diet fads, *Diet and Die*, under his own name; he did editorials for the *New Masses*, and he was working on a biography of Frances E. Willard, the founder of the Women's Christian Temperance Union. He planned a study of health economics in the United States and an analysis of private relief and public welfare (Malmberg to Colby, July 6, 1936; Entry 36, Central Office Records, RG 69, NACP).

29. Berger to Alsberg, Dec. 18, 1935 (Entry 1 Massachusetts, Central Office Records, RG 69, NACP).

30. Berger to Vorse, Dec. 17, 1935; Berger to Alsberg, Dec. 28, 1935 (Entry 1 Massachusetts, Central Office Records, RG 69, NACP).

31. Alsberg to Vorse, Jan. 2, 1936 (Entry 1 Massachusetts, Central Office Records, RG 69, NACP).

32. See mimeographed bulletins and the short-lived newspaper *The American Writer*, especially for the promise of "democratic rank and file control." Over time, as the union struggled for membership, its platform became a narrower, trade unionist defense of writers' working conditions. Eventually, in 1937, it folded, never having moved in large or secure ways beyond New York City. Boston was, however, one of the few places to organize effectively and to initiate locals in several Massachusetts towns.

33. Manning to McKenna, March 29, 1936 (Entry 36, Central Office Records, RG 69, NACP).

34. Local 15 AWU Minutes, Oct. 13, 1936 (Entry 36, Central Office Records, RG 69, NACP).

35. When Linda Donaghy and Marsha L. McCabe interviewed James McKenna's son fifty years later, the son still remembered the father's role in the United Textile Workers Union during the 1928 strike and in the "New Bedford Writers' Union" (25). In contrast, in the same series of interviews, Eunice Turgeon—who had been a member of the New Bedford project and secretary of local 15 of the American Writers' Union—characterized union activity in entirely apolitical terms, as a "group"making a request: "When they were going to cut the FWP way down, a group of us went to Washington to ask them not to" (Donaghy and McCabe 24).

36. Local 15 AWU Minutes, Dec. 8, 1936 (Entry 36, Central Office Records, RG 69, NACP).

37. Local 15 AWU Minutes, Oct. 27, 1936 (Entry 36, Central Office Records, RG 69, NACP).

38. Julia Keane to John. J. McDonough, June 11, 1937 (Entry 36, Central Office Records, RG 69, NACP).

39. Keane to McDonough, n.d. (Entry 36, Central Office Records, RG 69, NACP).

40. Evelyn D. Silveira to Mary Gion, Aug. 17, 1936 (Entry 36, Central Office Records, RG 69, NACP). Tension around the application from the Provincetown project writers is legible in Local 15 AWU Minutes, Aug. 11, 1936, Sept. 8, 1936.

41. Minutes, New Bedford District Local 15, American Writers' Union, Sept. 8, 1936 (Entry 36, Central Office Records, RG 69, NACP).

42. "Yesterday, Today and Tomorrow in New Bedford, Massachusetts" (Entry 34, Central Office Records, RG 69, NACP).

43. *Fairhaven Star* Sept. 16, 1937 covers the forthcoming publication of *Whaling Masters*.

44. Hawks to Bradford, March 22, 1939 (Entry 36, Central Office Records, RG 69, NACP).

45. Royse to Alsberg, Jan. 3, 1939 (Entry 20, Central Office Records, RG 69, NACP).

46. Berger to Seph [Gaer], "Monday" (Entry 4, Central Office Records, RG 69, NACP).

47. Willison to Gaer, "Friday" (Entry 4, Central Office Records, RG 69, NACP).

48. Nathan Halper, another Provincetown project writer, took up "Mashpee Kingdom," but the volume appears not to have reached completion. Willison did complete a pilgrim history, after the project's closing: *Saints and Strangers*, published in 1945.

49. See discussion of her writing on the New England hurricane in chapter 6.

50. Hawks to Bradford, March 30, 1938 (Entry 36, Central Office Records, RG 69, NACP).

51. Bradford to Hawks, Sept. 9, 1938, Sept. 10, 1938; Hawks to Coombs, Sept. 12, 1938 (Entry 36, Central Office Records, RG 69, NACP).

52. Coombs "Captain Joe Antone, *Cape Verdean seaman*," ("We Work on the WPA" 130). This is the only publication of Coombs's two interviews. The original typescripts, dated Aug. 6, 1939, are in LC FWP, A788.

CHAPTER 6

1. J.D., "Acknowledgment," n.d. (Entry 6, Central Office Record, RG 69, NACP).

2. Alsberg to All State Directors, June 5, 1937 (Entry 4, Central Office Records, RG 69, NACP).

3. Jo[sef Berger] to Merle [Colby], June 8 [1937] (Entry 6, Central Office Records, RG 69, NACP); Berger to Book Editor, *Boston Globe* June 26, 1937; Jo[sef Berger] to Seph [Gaer], June 27 [1937] (Entry 4, Central Office Records, RG 69, NACP); Mangione, *Dream* x.

4. Alsberg to State Directors of the Federal Writers' Project, June 17, 1937 (Entry 11, Central Office Records, RG 69, NACP).

5. Josef Berger, FEC Provincetown: Racial Groups (Entry 34, Central Office Records, RG 69, NACP).

6. Frances C. Gifford to Bradford, March 14, 1936 (Entry 34, Central Office Records, RG 69, NACP).

7. Alsberg [Kellock] to Billington, July 21, 1936 (Entry 13 Massachusetts, Central Office Records, RG 69, NACP).

8. Eunice Turgeon, FEC Dennis: Racial Cultural Heritage (Entry 34, Central Office Records, RG 69, NACP).

9. Henry C. Kittredge, Review of *Cape Cod Pilot, New England Quarterly* 11 (March 1938): 192–93.

10. "Books and Things," *New York Herald Tribune* 1937 (undated clipping in Entry 12, Central Office Records, RG 69, NACP).

11. Enthusiastic reviews include May Cameron, "Tall Tales and Legend Are Woven Into an Amusing Guide Book to Cape Cod," *New York Post* July 14, 1937; "New Book Sings Fame of Cape Cod," *Boston Post* June 10, 1937; and E.C.S., "Cape Cod Log," *Christian Science Monitor* July 16, 1937. F. N. Finney's review appeared in the *Arizona Daily Star* Oct. 10, 1937.

CHAPTER 7

1. Alsberg [Mangione] to Robert Cantwell, Jan. 19, 1939 (Entry 1 Massachusetts, Central Office Records, RG 69, NACP).

2. Cronyn to State Directors, July 7, 1937 (Entry 5, Central Office Records, RG 69, NACP).

3. "Supplementary Instructions 9-G to The American Guide Manual: Manual for Social-Ethnic Studies" (Aug. 15, 1938), 3 (Entry 11, Central Office Records, RG 69, NACP).

4. Royse uses the phrase "two-way street" in a letter to Mangione, June 9, 1970 (Mangione Papers, Box 58); the next two quotations are from "Manual for Social-Ethnic Studies" (Aug. 15, 1938), 4–5, 9 (Entry 11, Central Office Records, RG 69, NACP).

5. See Goldenberg to Alsberg, April 6, 1938 (Entry 1 Massachusetts, Central Office Records, RG 69, NACP); *Boston Globe* March 23, 1937; Loewenberg to Alsberg, May 8, 1937 (Entry 20, Central Office Records, RG 69, NACP).

6. The *Worcester Telegram* Dec. 6, 1937, reports 3,000 Armenians in Boston, 4,500 in Worcester.

7. Eaton and Anabel Woogmaster also worked on *Armenians*. The foreword to *Albanians* additionally credits Charlotte L. Busby, Emile LaRue, Jane K. Leary, Emily B. Moore, Evelyn Palmer, William Raymond, John Thornton, Ray Tucker, Edward C. Williams, Anabel Woogmaster, and Helen Sullivan Mims.

8. See Woodward to Lawrence Morris (attn. Alsberg), Oct. 25, 1937; Alsberg to Hawks, Oct. 25, 1937; Hawks to Alsberg, Oct. 28, 1937 (Entry 13 Massachusetts, Central Office Records, RG 69, NACP).

9. Alsberg [Coy] to Manuel, Jan. 16, 1939; Editorial Report on "The Albanians in America," Jan. 14, 1939 (LC FWP, A2); Manuel to Alsberg, Jan. 27, 1939 (Entry 20, Central Office Records, RG 69, NACP).

10. A rather cryptic note from Frank Manuel indicates that there was also some negative press: "the Hairenick Press which published the book reviewed the volume unsympathetically in its newspaper" (Manuel to Alsberg, June 4, 1938; Entry 13, Central Office Records, RG 69, NACP).

11. Editorial Report on State Copy, "The Albanians of Massachusetts," May 2, 1938 (Entry 34, Central Office Records, RG 69, NACP).

12. Royse to Alsberg, Jan. 3, 1939 (Entry 20, Central Office Records, RG 69, NACP).

CHAPTER 8

1. In February 1937, the central office circulated a memorandum explicitly eschewing a uniform pattern for local guides. State directors continued to play a role in production, and the national office still signed off on the final manuscript ("General Memorandum on Supplementary Instructions #15," Feb. 10, 1937; Entry 11, Central Office Records, RG 69, NACP).

2. George L. Williams, FEC Sudbury: Racial Elements, Racial Cultural Heritage (Entry 34, Central Office Records, RG 69, NACP).

3. Garfield 91; *Framingham News* July 5, 1939, 1.

4. *Wayland Chronicle* July 7, 1939, 8.

5. *Framingham News* July 1, 1939, 1.
6. *Framingham News* July 1, 1939, 3.
7. *Marlboro Enterprise* July 1, 1939, 1.
8. *Wayland Chronicle* June 30, 1939, 2.
9. *Framingham News* July 3, 1939, 1; *Marlboro Enterprise* July 3, 1939, 1.
10. *Worcester Daily Telegram* June 25, 1937.
11. Memorandum on "The Growth of the Cities," July 28, 1938 (LC FWP, A787).
12. The only naming of groups is self-naming, in the list of churches and certain community organizations. Churches include Greek Orthodox, Jewish, Lutheran, Polish National Catholic, Presbyterian, Roman Catholic, and Russian Orthodox, among its 22 designations of 95 churches; community organizations include the Jewish Community Center, the Ancient Order of Hibernians, and other organizations for Irish, Armenians, French, Germans, Italians, Jews, Poles, Russians, and Swedes—as well as Yankee and English.

CHAPTER 9

1. On New Deal agencies' dexterous use of photography, see Daniel et al., Fleischhauer and Brannan, Natanson, Stott, Stryker and Wood.
2. Hawks to Alsberg, Oct. 17, 1938 (Entry 16, Central Office Records, RG 69, NACP).
3. "Book Describes N.E. Hurricane," *Montpelier Evening Argus* Nov. 15, 1938; "WPA Book Presents Story of Hurricane," *New York Times* Oct. 31, 1938, 5.
4. Manuel to Derby, Sept. 28, 1938 (Entry 16, Central Office Records, RG 69, NACP); Manuel to Heidel, Sept. 28, 1938 (Entry 16, Central Office Records, RG 69, NACP); Hawks to Bradford, Sept. 24, 1938 (Entry 36, Central Office Records, RG 69, NACP).
5. "N.E. Hurricane Book Is Issued by W.P.A.," *Brockton* [Mass.] *Enterprise* Nov. 1, 1938; *Hartford* [Conn.] *Courant* (unidentified clipping in LC FWP, A996); Stephen J. Manookian, "New England Hurricane Reappears in Book." *New Record* (undated clipping in LC FWP, A852).
6. Bradford to Hawks, Sept. 29, 1938 (Entry 36, Central Office Records, RG 69, NACP).
7. Qtd. in Stephen J. Manookian, "New England Hurricane Reappears in Book." *New Record* (undated clipping in LC FWP, A852).
8. Manuel to Alsberg, Oct. 25, 1938 and Nov. 10, 1938 (Entry 16, Central Office Records, RG 69, NACP).
9. Alsberg [Kellock] to Esther Marshall Greer, May 25, 1937 (Entry 13, Central Office Records, RG 69, NACP).
10. On documentary effects, see Foley, Renov, and Stott. The book's methods are also analogous to war reporting that makes sense of carnage by creating a shaped narrative for a public feeling the need to know. Indeed, the war analogy was made on and off the project. In *New England Hurricane*, passengers in a stalled train in Massachusetts converse on "the fate of nations. Said one passenger: 'We *did* miss not having a radio. Most of us were wondering how the Czechs were making out'" (172). Mary Heaton Vorse repeatedly parallels the hurricane's arrival and destructive force with Chamberlain's flight to meet with Hitler and the destruction of Czechoslovakia which ensued: "Two great disasters, that of Europe and that of the hurricane, were contrapuntal to one another" (329). Later, Everett Allen's memoir of the hurricane also invokes the international situation: "If the world, the nation, and I were fouled up—in suspension and transition, if you will—so was the weather" (17).

11. “*New England Hurricane* Sets Another Record,” Press Release Oct. 31, 1938 (Entry 1 Massachusetts, Central Office Records, RG 69, NACP).

12. Manuel to Alsberg (Tel.) Oct. 10, 1938 (Entry 16, Central Office Records, RG 69, NACP).

13. Manuel to Alsberg, Oct. 25, 1938 (Entry 16, Central Office Records, RG 69, NACP).

14. “Hurricane Data,” *Boston Herald* Nov. 25, 1938.

15. Hawks to Alsberg, Oct. 29, 1938 (Entry 16, Central Office Records, RG 69, NACP); “Book Barometer” for week ending Nov. 5 (unidentified clipping in LC FWP, A852); “What Boston Is Reading,” *Boston Herald* Nov. 12, 1938. The information that there were seven printings of *New England Hurricane* comes from “They Cover the Nation,” *Stoughton* [Mass.] *Chronicle* (Nov. 18, 1941) and that they printed an edition of 25,000 copies from Merle Colby, “Presenting America to All Americans,” *Publishers' Weekly* May 3, 1941, 1828.

16. “WPA Hurricane Souvenir Book.” *Boston Traveler* Nov. 4, 1938.

17. Four pieces by Moeller on the hurricane survive in typescript; see especially “Out of the Gale,” Oct. 4, 1938 (Entry 36, Central Office Records, RG 69, NACP).

18. Quotations from Coombs's manuscripts come from “New Bedford's Fishing Industry and the Hurricane”; “Story of the Hurricane Damage in Westport, Mass.” (Oct. 4, 1938); and “The Great Hurricane” (Entry 34, Central Office Records, RG 69, NACP). See also Coombs, “The Great Hurricane, Martha's Vineyard Island” and “Cuttyhunk Island” (Entry 36, Central Office Records, RG 69, NACP).

19. Bradford to Hawks, Sept. 27, 1938 (Entry 36, Central Office Records, RG 69, NACP).

20. Emily B. Moore, “Hurricane, Worcester, Personal Experience,” 7 (Entry 34, Central Office Records, RG 69, NACP).

21. Bradford, “Personal observations and reactions to the storm,” 3. Other typescript contributions by Bradford on the hurricane include “The Big Wind—Fairhaven,” “Hurricane (Falmouth),” “Hurricane—Ocean Grove section of Swansea,” “Hurricane material,” “‘The Big Wind’ Material” (all in Entry 36, Central Office Records, RG 69, NACP).

22. Coombs, “Personal Impression of the Hurricane”; Wade Van Dore, “Flood in New Marlboro, Berkshire County”; Frederick Krackhardt, “Hurricane of 1938, West Berlin, Personal Experience” (all in Entry 34, Central Office Records, RG 69, NACP).

23. *Hartford Courant Magazine* Oct. 2, 1938 (Entry 34, Central Office Records, RG 69, NACP).

24. Coombs, “The Great Hurricane Martha's Vineyard Island” (Entry 34, Central Office Records, RG 69, NACP).

25. Fascinatingly, Allen himself, who trained as a reporter—learned to observe and write—in the thirties, fails equally to *see* race even in the 1970s—well into the civil rights movement, Black Power imagery, and a general heightening of consciousness around race in America. When Allen itemizes the cultural groups making up New Bedford's population, he includes Portuguese but not Cape Verdeans; his list has exactly the lacuna identified by Marilyn Halter—since Cape Verdean Americans fall “between race and ethnicity,” in hypothetically being both, in practice they are neither. Mrs. Josephine Clarke gets noticed only at a remove—not only is she “from Jamaica,” but it is Benedict Thielen's voice, as recorded by Allen, which relates her drowning. Neither Allen nor the WPA writers, all creatures of the thirties, can grapple with the intermingling of race, class, and gender on this broken landscape.

EPILOGUE

1. Representative William Sirovich introduced H.J. Res. 79, Senator Claude Pepper and Representative John Coffee introduced S. 3296/H.R. 9102, then the three congressmen came together to sponsor H.J. Res. 671. Several other efforts to institute government departments of the arts took place from 1935 to 1939 (see *Congressional Record* and House and Senate Committee Hearings on H.J.Res. 220, H.R. 3239, H.J.Res. 79, S. 3296, H.R. 9102, H.J.Res. 671, and S. 2967). Larson (42–44) and Overmyer (191–216) analyze congressional reception of these efforts.

2. See Bold, J. Hirsch, Mangione, Penkower, Schindler-Carter, and Sporn.

3. See Hobson, O'Gara, and Weisberger.

4. *Quincy Patriot Ledger* March 20, 1941.

5. "WPA Man Winner of Big Award," *Boston Post* April 4, 1938; "W.P.A. Writer's Cape 'Guide' Wins Him Guggenheim Award," *Boston Globe* April 4, 1938.

6. Obituary, Zylpha Mapp-Robinson, *UMass Magazine Online* (Spring 2002) . Consulted November 1, 2002.

7. Vincent McHugh to Jerre Mangione, April 28, 1968 (Mangione Papers, Box 6).

WORKS CITED

ARCHIVAL SOURCES

Mayor Ashley Scrapbooks, New Bedford Free Public Library (cited as Ashley Scrapbooks, microfilm roll number).

Census Records, Genealogy Room, New Bedford Free Public Library.

Clippings File, *New Bedford Standard-Times*.

Felicani Collection, Rare Books and Manuscripts, Boston Public Library, Ms.2030 7A (Courtesy of the Trustees of the Boston Public Library) (cited as Felicani Collection).

Historical Papers, Old Dartmouth Historical Society, New Bedford Whaling Museum.

Historical Records, Millicent Library, Fairhaven.

Charles F. Hurley Papers, Special Collections, Boston Public Library.

Katharine Kellock Papers, Library of Congress Manuscripts Division, Washington, D.C. (cited as Kellock Papers).

Jerre Mangione Papers, Rare Books and Special Collections, University of Rochester (cited as Mangione Papers, Box Number).

Records of U.S. Work Projects Administration, Federal Writers' Project, Library of Congress Manuscripts Division, Washington, D.C. (cited as LC FWP, Box Number).

Work Projects Administration Central Correspondence Files, Record Group 69, National Archives at College Park, Md. (cited as Central Correspondence Files, RG 69, NACP).

Work Projects Administration Division of Information, Record Group 69, National Archives at College Park, Md. (cited as Division of Information, RG 69, NACP).

Work Projects Administration Federal Writers' Project Central Office Records, Record Group 69, National Archives at College Park, Md. (cited as Central Office Records, RG 69, NACP).

MASSACHUSETTS WRITERS' PROJECT PUBLICATIONS

The Albanian Struggle in the Old World and New. By Members of the Federal Writers' Project of The Works Progress Administration of Massachusetts. Boston: The Writer, Inc., 1939.

An Almanack for Bostonians 1939. By Workers of the Federal Writers' Project of the Works Progress Administration in Massachusetts. New York: M. Barrows & Co., 1938.

The Armenians in Massachusetts. By the Federal Writers' Project of the Works Progress Administration for the State of Massachusetts. Boston: Armenian Historical Society, 1937.

The Berkshire Hills. By Members of the Federal Writers' Project of the Works Progress Administration for Massachusetts. New York: Funk & Wagnalls Company, 1939.

Boston Looks Seaward: The Story of the Port, 1630–1940. By Workers of the Writers' Program of the Work Projects Administration in the State of Massachusetts. Boston: Bruce Humphries, 1941.

A Brief History of the Towne of Sudbury in Massachusetts Together with the Programme of the Exercises enacted in Commemoration of its Three Hundredth Anniversary 1639–1939. By Members of the Federal Writers' Project of the Works Progress Administration in Massachusetts. [Sudbury]: n.p. [1939].

A Brief History of the Towne of Sudbury in Massachusetts 1639–1939. By Members of the Federal Writers' Project of the Works Progress Administration in Massachusetts. 2nd rev. ed. Sudbury Historical Society. Rutland, Vt.: Sharp Offset Printing, 1987.

Cape Cod Pilot: A WPA Guide. By Jeremiah Digges [Josef Berger] with editorial and research assistance of the members of the Federal Writers' Project. Provincetown: Modern Pilgrim Press, 1937.

Fairhaven Massachusetts. By Members of the Federal Writers' Project of the Works Progress Administration in Massachusetts. Fairhaven: Board of Selectmen, 1939.

Here's New England!: A Guide to Vacationland. By Members of the Federal Writers' Project of the Works Progress Administration in the New England States. Boston: Houghton Mifflin, 1939.

A Historical Sketch of Auburn Massachusetts From the Earliest Period to the Present Day with Brief Accounts of Early Settlers and Prominent Citizens. By the Federal Writers' Project of the Works Progress Administration for the State of Massachusetts. Worcester: Charles D. Cady Printing Co., 1937.

Massachusetts: A Guide to Its Places and People. By the Federal Writers' Project of the Works Progress Administration for the State of Massachusetts. Boston: Houghton Mifflin, 1937.

Motor Tours in the Berkshire Hills. By Workers of the Federal Writers' Project of the Works Progress Administration for the State of Massachusetts. [Pittsfield]: Berkshire Hills Conference, Inc., 1938.

New England Hurricane: A Factual, Pictorial Record. By Members of the Federal Writers' Project of the Works Progress Administration in the New England States. Boston: Hale, Cushman & Flint, 1938.

Old Newbury Tales: An Historical Reader for Children. By Workers of the Federal Writers' Project of the Works Progress Administration of Massachusetts. [Newburyport]: Historical Society of Old Newbury, 1937.

The Origin of Massachusetts Place Names of the State, Counties, Cities, and Towns. By Workers of the Writers' Project of the Work Projects Administration in Massachusetts. New York: Harian Publications, 1941.

Selective and Critical Bibliography of Horace Mann. By Workers of the Federal Writers' Project of the Works Progress Administration in the State of Massachusetts. Roxbury, Mass.: Roxbury Memorial High School (Boys) Printing Department, June 1937.

Skiing in the East: The Best Trails and How to Get There. By Members of the Federal Writers' Project of the Works Progress Administration in New York City. M. Barrows & Co., 1939.

Springfield, Massachusetts. Massachusetts WPA Writers' Project. [Springfield]: n.p., 1941.

State Forests and Parks of Massachusetts: A Recreation Guide. By the Massachusetts WPA Writers' Project. Boston: Department of Conservation, 1941.

The State Teachers College at Westfield. By Workers of the Writers' Program of the Work Projects Administration in the State of Massachusetts. [Boston]: n.p., 1941.

U.S. One: Maine to Florida. By the Federal Writers' Project of the Works Progress Administration. New York: Modern Age Books, 1938.

Whaling Masters. By the Federal Writers' Project of the Works Progress Administration of Massachusetts. New Bedford, Mass.: Old Dartmouth Historical Society, 1938.

Winter Sports and Recreation in the Berkshire Hills. By Workers of the Federal Writers' Project of the Works Progress Administration in the State of Massachusetts. Pittsfield, Mass.: The Berkshire County Commissioners, 1937.

The WPA Guide to Massachusetts: The Federal Writers' Project Guide to 1930s Massachusetts. By the Federal Writers' Project of the Works Progress Administration for the State of Massachusetts. Intro. Jane Holtz Kay. New York: Pantheon Books, 1983.

SECONDARY WORKS

Aaron, Daniel. "Guide-books and Meal-tickets." *Times Literary Supplement* 28 July 1978. 837.

———. *Writers on the Left*. New York: Harcourt, Brace, and World, 1961.

Agee, James, and Walker Evans. *Let Us Now Praise Famous Men*. 1941. Boston: Houghton Mifflin, 2001.

Allen, Everett S. *A Wind to Shake the World: The Story of the 1938 Hurricane*. Boston: Little, Brown, 1976.

The American Writer 1.1 (June 1936).

Anderson, Benedict. *Imagined Communities: Reflections on the Origin and Spread of Nationalism*. Rev. ed. London: Verso, 1991.

The Arizona Daily Star 10 October 1937.

Atlanta Constitution 21 August 1937.

The Auburn Guide & Community Telephone Directory 2001 Edition. Worcester: Worcester Telegram & Gazette, 2001.

Avrich, Paul. *Sacco and Vanzetti: The Anarchist Background*. Princeton: Princeton University Press, 1991.

Baltimore Evening Sun 19 August 1937.

Baltimore Morning Sun 20 August 1937, 21 August 1937.

Banks, Ann, ed. *First-Person America*. New York: Knopf, 1980.

———, and Robert Carter. *Survey of Federal Writers' Project Manuscript Holdings in State Depositories*. Washington, D.C.: American Historical Association, 1985.

Barbrook, Alec. *God Save the Commonwealth: An Electoral History of Massachusetts*. Amherst: University of Massachusetts Press, 1973.

Bearse, Ray. *Massachusetts: A Guide to the Pilgrim State*. 2nd ed. Boston: Houghton Mifflin, 1971.

Belding, John, and Meredith Weiss-Belding. "Auburn: Cultural Resources Survey" [typescript] 4 volumes. 30 March 1981.

Benedict, Stephen. *Public Money and the Muse: Essays on Government Funding for the Arts*. New York: W. W. Norton, 1991.

Berger, Josef, and Dorothy Berger, eds. *Diary of America: The Intimate Story of Our Nation, Told by 100 Diarists–Public Figures and Plain Citizens, Natives and Visitors–over the Five Centuries from Columbus, the Pilgrims, and George Washington to Thomas Edison, Will Rogers, and Our Own Time*. New York: Simon and Schuster, 1957.

Billington, Ray Allen. "Government and the Arts: The W.P.A. Experience." *American Quarterly* 13 (1961): 466–79.

———, with the collaboration of C. P. Hill et al. *The Historian's Contribution to Anglo-American Misunderstanding: Report of a Committee on National Bias in Anglo-American History Textbooks*. New York: Hobbs, Dorman, 1966.

———, Bert James Loewenberg, and Samuel Hugh Brockunier. *The United States: American Democracy in World Perspective*. New York: Rinehart, 1947.

Bindas, Kenneth J. *All of This Music Belongs to the Nation: The WPA's Federal Music Project and American Society*. Knoxville: University of Tennessee Press, 1996.

Birdsall, Esther K. "The FWP and the Popular Press." In *Challenges in American Culture*, ed. Ray Browne, Larry N. Landrum, and William K. Bottorff. Bowling Green, Oh.: Popular Press, 1970. 101–10.

Bloxom, Marguerite D. *Pickaxe and Pencil: References for the Study of the WPA*. Washington, D.C.: Library of Congress, 1982.

Bodnar, John. *Remaking America: Public Memory, Commemoration, and Patriotism in the Twentieth Century*. Princeton: Princeton University Press, 1992.

Bold, Christine. "Mapping Out America: The W.P.A. Guidebooks and the American Scene in the 1930s." In *Modern American Landscapes*, ed. Mick Gidley and Robert Lawson-Peebles. Amsterdam: VU University Press, 1995. 172–96.

———. "'Staring the World in the Face': Sacco and Vanzetti in the WPA Guide to Massachusetts." *Massachusetts Historical Review* 5 (2003): 95–124.

———. "The View from the Road: Katharine Kellock's New Deal Guidebooks." *American Studies* 29 (1988): 5–29.

———. "Worker-Writers on the WPA: The Case of New Bedford, Massachusetts." *Prospects: An Annual of American Cultural Studies* 28 (2003): 1–30.

———. *The WPA Guides: Mapping America*. Jackson: University Press of Mississippi, 1999.

"Book Describes N.E. Hurricane." *Montpelier Evening Argus* 15 November 1938.

"Book on Hurricane in New England Prepared by WPA." *Washington Post* 31 October 1938.

Bordelon, Pamela G. "The Federal Writers' Project's Mirror to America: The Florida Reflection." Diss., Louisiana State University, 1991.

Boston Advertiser 22 August 1937.

Boston American 19 August 1937, 21 August 1937, 26 August 1937, 27 August 1937.

Boston Chronicle 31 October 1936.

Boston Evening Transcript 2 June 1936.

Boston Globe 23 March 1937, 26 June 1937, 19 August 1937, 20 August 1937.

Boston Herald 19 August 1937, 20 August 1937.

Boston Post 20 August 1937, 21 August 1937, 23 August 1937, 27 August 1937.

Botkin, B. A. "We Called It 'Living Lore.'" *New York Folklore Quarterly* 14.3 (Fall 1958): 189–201.

Bradford, G. Leroy, et al. *Barnacles and Bilge Water: A Collection of Old Whaling Yarns*. New Bedford: Reynolds Printing, 1941.

Brewer, Jeutone. *The Federal Writers' Project: A Bibliography*. Metuchen, N.J.: Scarecrow Press, 1994.

Brodeur, Paul. *Restitution: The Land Claims of the Mashpee, Passamaquoddy, and Penobscot Indians of New England*. Boston: Northeastern University Press, 1985.

Brody, David. *Workers in Industrial America: Essays on the 20th Century Struggle*. 2nd ed. New York: Oxford University Press, 1993.

Browder, Laura. *Rousing the Nation: Radical Culture in Depression America*. Amherst: University of Massachusetts Press, 1998.

Brown, Richard D. *Massachusetts: A Bicentennial History*. New York: W. W. Norton, 1978.

———, and Jack Tager. *Massachusetts: A Concise History*. Amherst: University of Massachusetts Press, 2000.

Brown, Sterling A. "Negro Character as Seen by White Authors." *Journal of Negro Education* 2.2 (April 1933): 179–203.

Brown, William Wells. *Narrative of William W. Brown, an American Slave*. 1847. London: C. Gilpin, 1849.

Bustard, Bruce I. *A New Deal for the Arts*. Washington, D.C.: National Archives and Records Administration/Seattle: University of Washington Press, 1997.

Butterfield, Roger. "Henry Ford, the Wayside Inn, and the Problem of 'History Is Bunk.'" *Proceedings of the Massachusetts Historical Society* 77 (1965): 58–60.

Cameron, May. "Tall Tales and Legend Are Woven into an Amusing Guide Book to Cape Cod." *New York Post* 14 July 1937.

Carby, Hazel V. "Introduction." *The Magazine Novels of Pauline Hopkins*. The Schomburg Library of Nineteenth-Century Black Women Writers. New York: Oxford University Press, 1988. xxix–l.

Clayton, Ronnie W. "A History of the Federal Writers' Project in Louisiana." Diss., Louisiana State University, 1975.

Cleveland Plain Dealer 20 August 1937.

Clifford, James. "Identity in Mashpee." In Clifford, *The Predicament of Culture: Twentieth-Century Ethnography, Literature, and Art*. Cambridge: Harvard University Press, 1988. 277–346.

Cohen, Lisabeth. *Making a New Deal: Industrial Workers in Chicago, 1919–1939*. Cambridge: Cambridge University Press, 1990.

Colby, Merle. "Presenting America to All Americans." *Publishers' Weekly* 3 May 1941. 1828–31.

The Complete Historical Record of New England's Stricken Area September 21, 1938. The Standard-Times Morning Mercury (New Bedford). n.d.

Connerton, Paul. *How Societies Remember*. Cambridge: Cambridge University Press, 1989.

Conrad, Earl. *Jim Crow America*. New York: Duell, Sloan, and Pearce, 1947.

Conroy, Jack. "The Worker as Writer." In *American Writers' Congress*, ed. Henry Hart. New York: International Publishers, 1935. 83–86.

Contact. Flood and Hurricane Issue. New England Power Association. 19.11 (November 1938).

Contreras, Belisario R. *Tradition and Innovation in New Deal Art*. Lewisburg, Pa.: Bucknell University Press, 1983.

The Courant (Hartford, Conn.) 1 November 1938.

Craig, E. Quita. *Black Drama of the Federal Theatre Era: Beyond the Formal Horizons*. Amherst: University of Massachusetts Press, 1980.

Cutler, Phoebe. *The Public Landscape of the New Deal*. New Haven: Yale University Press, 1985.

Cyr, Paul A. "Governor Hurley, Sacco & Vanzetti and the Massachusetts Guide." *Spinner: People and Culture in Southeastern Massachusetts* 4 (1988): 12–15.

Daniel, Pete, Merry A. Foresta, Maren Stange, and Sally Stein. *Official Images: New Deal Photography*. Washington, D.C.: Smithsonian Institution Press, 1987.

Davis, Thadious. "The Federal Writers' Project and the Legacy of Black Writers." Paper presented at The WPA and the Federal Writers' Project: A Symposium, 8 November 1986. Fort Lauderdale, Fla.

Denning, Michael. *The Cultural Front: The Laboring of American Culture in the Twentieth Century*. London: Verso, 1996.

De Voto, Bernard. "New England via W.P.A." *Saturday Review of Literature* 14 May 1938. 3–4, 14.

Donaghy, Linda, and Marsha L. McCabe. "In Search of the Federal Writers." *Spinner* 4 (1988): 23–25.

Dos Passos, John. *Facing the Chair: The Story of the Americanization of Two Foreignborn Workmen*. 1927. New York: Da Capo Press, 1970.

Doty, C. Stewart. *The First Franco-Americans: New England Life Histories from the Federal Writers' Project 1938–1939*. Orono: University of Maine, 1985.

Dubofsky, Melvyn, and Stephen Burwood, eds. *Women and Minorities during the Great Depression*. New York: Garland, 1990.

Du Bois, W. E. B. *Dusk of Dawn: The Autobiography of a Race Concept*. New York: Harcourt, Brace, 1940.

———. *Souls of Black Folk*. 1903. New York.: New American Library, 1969.

E.C.S. "Cape Cod Log." *Christian Science Monitor* 16 July 1937.

Eco, Umberto. *Travels in Hyperreality: Essays*. Trans. William Weaver. London: Pan/Picador, 1987.

Ehrmann, Herbert B. *The Case That Will Not Die: Commonwealth vs. Sacco and Vanzetti*. Boston: Little, Brown,1969.

———. *The Untried Case: The Sacco-Vanzetti Case and the Morelli Gang*. Foreword Joseph N. Welch. Intro. Edmund M. Morgan. New York: Vanguard Press, 1960.

Fairhaven Star 21 September 1928, 8 September 1929, 22 November 1929, 4 April 1930, 31 July 1931, 28 August 1931, 11 August 1932, 15 September 1932, 15 June 1933, 16 August 1934, 7 March 1935, 17 March 1935, 15 August 1935, 27 November 1935, 14 January 1937, 28 January 1937, 14 March 1937, 27 May 1937, 12 August 1937, 26 August 1937, 16 September 1937, 30 September 1937, 17 February 1938, 28 July 1938, 15 September 1938, 15 June 1939, 15 February 1940, 19 March 1959.

Fast, Howard. *The Passion of Sacco and Vanzetti: A New England Legend*. London: Bodley Head, 1954.

Felix, David. *Protest: Sacco-Vanzetti and the Intellectuals*. Bloomington: Indiana University Press, 1965.

Flanagan, Hallie. *Arena: The Story of the Federal Theatre*. 1940. New York: Limelight, 1985.

Fleischhauer, Carl, and Beverly W. Brannon. *Documenting America, 1935–1943*. Berkeley: University of California Press, 1988.

Foley, Barbara. *Telling the Truth: The Theory and Practice of Documentary Fiction*. Ithaca, N.Y.: Cornell University Press, 1986.

Foucault, Michel. "Governmentality." In *The Foucault Effect: Studies in Governmentality*, ed. Graham Burchell, Colin Gordon, and Peter Miller. London: Harvester Wheatsheaf, 1991. 87–104.

———. *The Order of Things: An Archaeology of the Human Sciences*. New York: Pantheon, 1971.

Fox, Daniel M. "The Achievement of the Federal Writers' Project." *American Quarterly* 13 (1961): 3–19.

Fraden, Rena. *Blueprints for a Black Federal Theatre, 1935–1939*. Cambridge: Cambridge University Press, 1994.

Framingham News 1 July 1939, 3 July 1939, 5 July 1939.

Frankfurter, Felix. *The Case of Sacco and Vanzetti: A Critical Analysis for Lawyers and Laymen*. 1927. New York: Grosset & Dunlap, 1961.

Freeman, Joseph. "Toward the Forties." In Hart, *The Writer in a Changing World*. 9–33.

Gamm, Gerald H. *The Making of New Deal Democrats: Voting Behavior and Realignment in Boston, 1920–1940*. Chicago: University of Chicago Press, 1989.

Garfield, Curtis F. *Sudbury, Massachusetts: 1890–1989. 100 Years in the Life of a Town*. Sudbury: Porcupine Enterprises, 1999.

Gelernter, David. *1939: The Lost World of the Fair*. New York: Avon, 1995.

Georgianna, Daniel, with Roberta Hazen Aaronson. *The Strike of '28*. New Bedford: Spinner, 1993.

Gill, Glenda E. White *Grease Paint on Black Performers: A Study of the Federal Theatre, 1935–1939*. New York: Lang, 1988.

Goodstone, Joan. *Love Letter to a Small American Town 01776. Excerpts from the Sudbury Citizen*. Sudbury: Beacon Publishing, 1975.

Gordon, Colin. "Governmental Rationality: An Introduction." In *The Foucault Effect: Studies in Governmentality*, ed. Graham Burchell, Colin Gordon, and Peter Miller. London: Harvester Wheatsheaf, 1991.

Gordon, Edythe Mae. *Selected Works of Edythe Mae Gordon*. Intro. Lorraine Elena Roses. New York: G. K. Hall, 1996.

Gorvine, Harold. "The New Deal in Massachusetts." Diss., Harvard University, 1962.

Greer, Jane. "Refiguring Authorship, Ownership, and Textual Commodities: Meridel Le Sueur's Pedagogical Legacy." *College English* 65.6 (July 2003): 607–25.

Guterl, Matthew Pratt. *The Color of Race in America, 1900–1940*. Cambridge: Harvard University Press, 2001.

Gutman, Herbert. *Power & Culture: Essays on the American Working Class*. Ed. Ira Berlin. New York: Pantheon, 1987.

Halbwachs, Maurice. *The Collective Memory*. Trans. Francis J. Ditter, Jr., and Vida Yazdi Ditter. Intro. Mary Douglas. New York: Harper & Row, 1980.

Halter, Marilyn. *Between Race and Ethnicity: Cape Verdean–American Immigrants, 1860–1965*. Urbana: University of Illinois Press, 1993.

Hapke, Laura. *Labor's Text: The Worker in American Fiction*. New Brunswick: Rutgers University Press, 2001.

Happy Birthday Auburn. Presented by Auburn Historical Society. [1977]

Harris, Jonathan. *Federal Art and National Culture: The Politics of Identity in New Deal America*. Cambridge: Cambridge University Press, 1995.

Hart, Henry, ed. *American Writers' Congress*. New York: International Publishers, 1935.

———, ed. *The Writer in a Changing World*. [New York]: Equinox Cooperative Press, 1937.

Heale, M. J. *McCarthy's Americans: Red Scare Politics in State and Nation, 1935–1965*. Athens: University of Georgia Press, 1998.

Henneberger, Melinda. "Something Different at the Arts Endowment: Optimism." *New York Times* 30 August 1998.

Hirsch, Jerrold Maury. "Culture on Relief: The Federal Writers' Project in North Carolina, 1935–42." M.A. thesis, University of North Carolina at Chapel Hill, 1973.

———. "Portrait of America: The Federal Writers' Project in an Intellectual and Cultural Context." Diss., University of North Carolina at Chapel Hill, 1984.

———. *Portrait of America: A Cultural History of the Federal Writers' Project*. Chapel Hill: University of North Carolina Press, 2003.

Hirsch, Marianne, and Valerie Smith. "Feminism and Cultural Memory: An Introduction." In *Gender and Cultural Memory*, ed. Marianne Hirsch and Valerie Smith. Spec. issue of *Signs: Journal of Women in Culture and Society* 28.1 (2002): 1–15.

Hobson, Archie, ed. *Remembering America: A Sampler of the WPA American Guide Series*. Intros. Bill Stott. New York: Columbia University Press, 1985.

Hofstra Library Associates. *Exhibition: "W.P.A.–The Writers Project" Selected from the Collection of Dr. Jen Yeh*. [New York]: Hofstra Library, 1978.

Hogarty, Richard A. *Massachusetts Politics and Public Policy: Studies in Power and Leadership*. Amherst: University of Massachusetts Press, 2002.

"Hurricane Data." *Boston Herald* 25 November 1938.

"Hurricane Souvenir–1938." *The* [New Bedford] *Standard-Times* 1 October 1938.

Hutchins, Francis G. *Mashpee: The Story of Cape Cod's Indian Town*. West Franklin, N.H.: Amarta Press, 1979.

Huthmacher, J. Joseph. *Massachusetts People and Politics, 1919–1933*. 1959. New York: Atheneum, 1969.

Hyde, Lewis. "The Children of John Adams: A Historical View of the Fight over Arts Funding." In *Art Matters: How the Culture Wars Changed America*, ed. Brian Wallis et al. New York: New York University Press, 1999. 253–75.

Irr, Caren. *The Suburb of Dissent: Cultural Politics in the United States and Canada during the 1930s*. Durham: Duke University Press, 1998.

Jackson, Brian. *The Black Flag: A Look Back at the Strange Case of Nicola Sacco and Bartolomeo Vanzetti*. Boston: Routledge & Kegan Paul, 1981.

Jacobson, Matthew Frye. *Whiteness of a Different Color: European Immigrants and the Alchemy of Race*. Cambridge: Harvard University Press, 1998.

Joughin, Louis, and Edmund E. Morgan. *The Legacy of Sacco and Vanzetti*. Intro. Arthur M. Schlesinger. 1948. Chicago: Quadrangle Books, 1964.

Junger, Sebastian. *The Perfect Storm: A True Story of Men against the Sea*. New York: HarperCollins, 1997.

Kammen, Michael. *Mystic Chords of Memory: The Transformation of Tradition in American Culture*. New York: Alfred A. Knopf, 1991.

Kazacoff, George. *Dangerous Theatre: The Federal Theatre Project as a Forum for New Plays*. New York: Lang, 1989.

Kellock, Katharine. "The WPA Writers: Portraitists of the United States." *American Scholar* 9 (Autumn 1940): 473–82.

Kellogg, Grace. *The Two Lives of Edith Wharton: The Woman and Her Work*. New York: Appleton-Century, 1965.

Kennedy, Lawrence J. *Planning the City upon a Hill: Boston since 1630*. Amherst: University of Massachusetts Press, 1992.

Keyssar, Alexander. *Out of Work: The First Century of Unemployment in Massachusetts*. Cambridge: Cambridge University Press, 1986.

Kittredge, Henry C. Review of *Cape Cod Pilot*. *New England Quarterly* 11 (March 1938): 192–93.

Larson, Gary O. *The Reluctant Patron: The United States Government and the Arts, 1943–1965*. Philadelphia: University of Pennsylvania Press, 1983.

League of Women Voters of Massachusetts. *Massachusetts State Government*. 2nd ed. Cambridge: Harvard University Press, 1970.

Le Sueur, Meridel. *Worker Writers*. Minneapolis: Minnesota Works Progress Administration, 1937. Rev. ed. Minneapolis: West End Press, 1982.

Levin, Murray B., with George Blackwood. *The Compleat Politician: Political Strategy in Massachusetts*. Indianapolis: Bobbs-Merrill, 1972.

Levy, Leonard W., and Douglas L. Jones, eds. *Jim Crow in Boston: The Origin of the Separate but Equal Doctrine*. New York: Da Capo Press, 1974.

"A Lexicon of Trade Jargon." *Spinner* 4 (1988): 134–35.

Linscott, Roger B. Foreword. *The Berkshire Hills*. Members of the Federal Writers' Project of the Works Progress Administration for Massachusetts. Boston: Northeastern University Press, 1987.

Loewenberg, Bert James, and Ruth Bogin, eds. *Black Women in Nineteenth-Century American Life: Their Words, Their Thoughts, Their Feelings*. University Park: Pennsylvania State University Press, 1976.

Lucarotti, Alfred. "'Hurricane' in Book Form." *Gazetta del Massachusetts* (Boston) 12 November 1938.

McDonald, William F. *Federal Relief Administration and the Arts: The Origins and Administrative History of the Arts Projects of the Works Progress Administration*. Columbus: Ohio State University Press, 1969.

McKinzie, Katherine. "Writers on Relief: 1935–42." Diss., Indiana University, 1970.

McKinzie, Richard C. *The New Deal for Artists*. Princeton: Princeton University Press, 1973.

Mangione, Jerre. *The Dream and the Deal: The Federal Writers' Project, 1935–43*. 1972. Philadelphia: University of Pennsylvania Press, 1983.

———. *An Ethnic at Large: A Memoir of America in the Thirties and Forties*. New York: G. P. Putnam's Sons, 1978.

Manookian, Stephen J. "New England Hurricane Reappears in Book." *New Record*. [Clipping in Library of Congress Manuscripts Division, Federal Writers' Project, Box A852]

Marinaccio, Rocco. "Dago Christs or Hometown Heroes? Proletarian Representations of Sacco and Vanzetti." *Centennial Review* 41 (1997): 617–23.

Marlboro Enterprise 1 July 1939, 3 July 1939.

Marling, Karal Ann. *George Washington Slept Here: Colonial Revivals and American Culture, 1876–1986*. Cambridge: Harvard University Press, 1988.

Mathews, Jane De Hart. *The Federal Theatre, 1935–1939: Plays, Relief, and Politics*. Princeton: Princeton University Press, 1967.

Melosh, Barbara. *Engendering Culture: Manhood and Womanhood in New Deal Public Art and Theater*. Washington, D.C.: Smithsonian Institution Press, 1991.

Meltzer, Milton. *Violins and Shovels: The WPA Arts Projects*. New York: Delacorte Press, 1976.

Micheaux, Oscar. *The Conquest: The Story of a Negro Pioneer*. 1913. College Park, Md.: McGrath, 1969.

Mitchell, Michael. "The Role of the Writers of the North Carolina Federal Writers' Project." M.A. thesis, North Carolina Central University, 1996.

Moeller, Elsie S. "The Living Conditions of the Portuguese in New Bedford." *Spinner* 4 (1988): 99–105.

———. *Pack a Bag: A Merry-Go-Round of Places, Transportation, and Clothes*. New York: Exposition Press, 1955.

Montgomery, David. *Workers' Control in America: Studies in the History of Work, Technology, and Labor Struggles*. Cambridge: Cambridge University Press, 1979.

Montgomery, Robert H. *Sacco-Vanzetti: The Murder and the Myth*. New York: Devin-Adair, 1960.

Moynagh, Maureen. "'This History's Only Good for Anger': Gender and Cultural Memory in *Beatrice Chancy*." In Hirsch and Smith. 97–124.

Natanson, Nicholas. *The Black Image in the New Deal: The Politics of FSA Photography*. Knoxville: University of Tennessee Press, 1992.

"N.E. Hurricane Book Is Issued by W.P.A." *Brockton* [Mass.] *Enterprise* 1 November 1938.

New Bedford and Fairhaven Directory of the Inhabitants, Business Firms, Institutions, City Government, Manufacturing Establishments, Societies, House and Street Directory, Map, Etc. Boston: W. A. Greenough & Co., 1900–1960.

New Bedford Evening Standard 7 May 1919, 4 June 1919, 12 November 1920, 23 March 1924, 18 November 1925, 20 July 1926, 11 February 1927, 17 April 1928.

New Bedford Standard-Times 10 August 1932, 28 August 1932, 21 September 1932, 7 July 1935, 7 August 1935, 25 November 1935, 24 September 1936, 2 November 1936, 10 April 1937, 20 August 1937, 22 August 1937, 20 October 1938, 3 November 1938, 4 November 1938, 26 October 1940, 6 April 1948, 20 March 1955, 16 August 1958, 17 March 1959, 7 March 1971.

New Bedford Times 11 April 1928, 12 April 1928.

"New Book Sings Fame of Cape Cod." *Boston Post* 10 June 1937.

New York, New England Hurricane and Floods, 1938: Official Report of the Relief Operations. N.p.: The American National Red Cross, 1939.

NYC The Sun 19 August 1937, 20 August 1937.

New York City World-Telegram 21 August 1937.

New York Post 21 August 1937.

New York Times 20 August 1937, 21 August 1937, 29 August 1937.

Nicholas, H. G. "The Writer and the State: The American Guide." *Contemporary Review* 155 (January 1939): 89–94.

1938 Hurricane Pictures from Falmouth to Fall River and New London Areas Mostly in and about New Bedford. New Bedford, Mass.: Reynolds Printing [1938].

1939 Edition Picture Book 1938 Hurricane Mostly new large unpublished before and after photos in vicinity of New Bedford, Cape Cod, Marthas [sic] *Vineyard*. New Bedford, Mass.: Reynolds Printing, [1939].

Nora, Pierre. "Between Memory and History: *Les Lieux de Mémoire*." In *Memory and Counter-Memory*, ed. Natalie Zemon Davis and Rudolph Starn. Spec. issue of *Representations* 26 (Spring 1989): 7–25.

———, dir. *Realms of Memory: Rethinking the French Past*. Vol. 1: *Conflicts and Divisions*. Ed. Lawrence D. Kritzman. Trans. Arthur Goldhammer. New York: Columbia University Press, 1996.

———. *Realms of Memory: The Construction of the French Past*. Vol. 2: *Traditions*. Ed. Lawrence D. Kritzman. Trans. Arthur Goldhammer. New York: Columbia University Press, 1997.

———. *Rethinking France: Les Lieux de Mémoire*. Vol. 1: *The State*. Trans. Mary Troiulle. Trans. dir. David P. Jordan. Chicago: University of Chicago Press, 2001.

O'Connor, Francis V., ed. *Art for the Millions: Essays from the 1930s by Artists and Administrators of the Works Progress Administration Federal Art Project*. Greenwich, Conn.: New York Graphic Society, 1973.

———. *The New Deal Art Projects: An Anthology of Memoirs*. Washington, D.C.: Smithsonian Institution Press, 1972.

O'Connor, John, and Lorraine Brown, eds. *Free, Adult, Uncensored: The Living History of the Federal Theatre Project*. Washington, D.C.: New Republic Books, 1978.

O'Connor, Thomas H. *The Boston Irish: A Political History*. Boston: Northeastern University Press, 1995.

O'Gara, Geoffrey. *A Long Road Home: Journeys through America's Present in Search of America's Past*. New York: Norton, 1989.

"Our New England Guides." *Westborough* [Mass.] *Chronotype* 17 September 1937.

Overmyer, Grace. *Government and the Arts*. New York: W. W. Norton, 1939.

Pawtucket [R.I.] *Times* 28 August 1937.

Peeler, David P. *Hope Among Us Yet: Social Criticism and Social Solace in Depression America*. Athens: University of Georgia Press, 1987.

———. "Unlonesome Highways: The Quest for Fact and Fellowship in Depression America." *Journal of American Studies* 18 (1984): 185–206.

Pells, Richard. *Radical Visions and American Dreams: Culture and Social Thought in the Depression Years*. New York: Harper & Row, 1973.

Pencak, William. *For God and Country: The American Legion, 1919–1941*. Boston: Northeastern University Press, 1989.

Penkower, Monty Noam. *The Federal Writers' Project: A Study in Government Patronage of the Arts*. Urbana: University of Illinois Press, 1977.

Pittsburgh Press 20 August 1937.

Porter, Katherine Anne. *The Never-Ending Wrong*. Boston: Little, Brown, 1977.

Potter, Ted. "Sliding toward a Diminished Culture." In *Culture and Democracy: Social and Ethical Issues in Public Support for the Arts and Humanities*, ed. Andrew Buchwalter. Boulder, Colo.: Westview Press, 1992. 41–46.

Powell, Sumner Chilton. *Puritan Village: The Formation of a New England Town*. Middletown, Conn.: Wesleyan University Press 1963.

Providence [R.I.] *Journal* 21 August 1937, 25 August 1937.

Quincy Patriot Ledger 20 March 1941.

Rabinowitz, Paula. "Margaret Bourke-White's Red Coat; or, Slumming in the 1930s." In *Radical Revisions: Rereading 1930s Culture*, ed. Bill Mullen and Sherry Lee Linkon. Urbana: University of Illinois Press, 1996. 187–207.

Rascoe, Burton. "It Adds up to What?" *Newsweek* 28 November 1938.

Reed, Ishmael, Shawn Wong, Bob Callahan, and Andrew Hope. "Is Ethnicity Obsolete?" In *The Invention of Ethnicity*, ed. Werner Sollors. New York: Oxford University Press, 1989. 226–35.

Renov, Michael, ed. *Theorizing Documentary*. New York: Routledge, 1993.

Rosenberg, Harold. "Anyone Who Could Write English." *New Yorker* 20 January 1973. 99–102.

Rosenman, Samuel I., comp. *The Public Papers and Addresses of Franklin D. Roosevelt*. Vol. 5. New York: Russell & Russell, 1942.

Roses, Lorraine Elena, and Ruth Elizabeth Randolph, eds. *Harlem's Glory: Black Women Writing, 1900–1950*. Cambridge: Harvard University Press, 1996.

Russell, Francis. *Tragedy in Dedham: The Story of the Sacco-Vanzetti Case*. New York: McGraw-Hill, 1962.

Sammarco, Anthony, and Paul Buchanan. *Images of America: New Bedford*. Dover, N.H.: Arcadia, 1997.

Scharf, Arthur. "Selected Publications of the WPA Federal Writers' Project and the Writers' Program." In Mangione, *The Dream and the Deal*. 375–96.

Schindler-Carter, Petra. *Vintage Snapshots: The Fabrication of a Nation in the W.P.A. American Guide Series*. Frankfurt am Main: Peter Lang, 1999.

Schlesinger, Arthur. Introduction. Joughin and Morgan. xi–xii.

Simmons, William S. *Spirit of the New England Tribes: Indian History and Folklore 1620–1984*. Hanover, N.H.: University Press of New England, 1986.

Sitkoff, Harvard. *A New Deal for Blacks: The Emergence of Civil Rights as a National Issue*. Vol. 1. *The Depression Decade*. New York: Oxford University Press, 1978.

Spark, Clare L. "Race, Caste, or Class? The Bunche-Myrdal Dispute over *An American Dilemma*." *International Journal of Politics, Culture and Society* 14.3 (2001): 465–511.

Spinner: People and Culture in Southeastern Massachusetts 4 (1988).

Sporn, Paul. *Against Itself: The Federal Theater and Writers' Projects in the Midwest*. Detroit: Wayne State University Press, 1995.

Stange, Maren. "'The Record Itself': Farm Security Administration Photography and the Transformation of Rural Life." In Daniel et al. 1–35.

Staub, Michael E. *Voices of Persuasion: Politics of Representation in 1930s America*. Cambridge: Cambridge University Press, 1994.

Steinbeck, John. *Travels with Charley in Search of America.* 1962. New York: Penguin Books, 2002.

Stott, William. *Documentary Expression and Thirties America.* 1973. Rev. ed., New York: Oxford University Press, 1985.

Stryker, Roy Emerson, and Nancy Wood. *In This Proud Land: America 1935–1943 as Seen in the FSA Photographs.* Greenwich, Conn.: New York Graphic Society, 1973.

Sullivan, Patricia. *Days of Hope: Race and Democracy in the New Deal Era.* Chapel Hill: University of North Carolina Press, 1996.

Susman, Warren I. *Culture as History: The Transformation of American Society in the Twentieth Century.* New York: Pantheon, 1984.

Szalay, Michael. Introduction. *Lamps at High Noon*, by Jack Balch. 1941. Urbana: Illinois University Press, 2000. [xi]–xl.

———. *New Deal Modernism: American Literature and the Invention of the Welfare State.* Durham: Duke University Press, 2000.

Taber, Ronald. "The Federal Writers' Project in the Pacific Northwest: A Case Study." Diss., Washington State University, 1969.

Terkel, Studs. *Hard Times: An Oral History of the Great Depression.* New York: Pantheon, 1970.

"They Cover the Nation." *Stoughton* [Mass.] *Chronicle* 18 November 1941.

Trachtenberg, Alan. "From Image to Story: Reading the File." In Fleischhauer and Brannan. 43–73.

Tree, Christina, and William Davis. *Massachusetts: An Explorer's Guide.* 1996. 3rd ed., Woodstock, Vt.: The Countryman Press, 2000.

Trout, Charles H. *Boston, the Great Depression, and the New Deal.* New York: Oxford University Press, 1977.

Ulrich, Mabel S. "Salvaging Culture for the WPA." *Harper's Magazine* 178 (May 1939): 653–64.

Vexler, Robert I. *Chronology and Documentary Handbook of the State of Massachusetts.* Dobbs Ferry, N.Y.: Oceana, 1978.

Vorse, Mary Heaton. *Time and the Town: A Provincetown Chronicle.* New York: Dial, 1942.

Washington [D.C.] *Evening Star* 19 August 1937.

Wayland Chronicle 30 June 1939, 7 July 1939.

"We Work on the WPA." *Spinner* 4 (1988): 125–31.

Weeks, Robert P., ed. *Commonwealth vs. Sacco and Vanzetti.* Englewood Cliffs, N.J.: Prentice-Hall, 1958.

Weisberger, Bernard A., ed. *The WPA Guide to America: The Best of 1930s America as Seen by the Federal Writers' Project.* New York: Pantheon, 1985.

"What Boston Is Reading." *Boston Herald* 12 November 1938.

Willison, George F. *Saints and Strangers: Being the Lives of the Pilgrim Fathers and Their Families with Their Friends and Their Foes.* New York: Reynal and Hitchcock, 1945.

Wilson, Alexander. *The Culture of Nature: North American Landscape from Disney to the Exxon Valdez.* Cambridge: Blackwell, 1992.

Wolfbein, Seymour Louis. *The Decline of a Cotton Textile City: A Study of New Bedford.* 1944. New York: AMS Press, 1968.

Wolters, Raymond. "The New Deal and the Negro." In *The New Deal. Volume One: The National Level*, ed. John Braeman, Robert H. Bremner, and David Brody. Columbus: Ohio State University Press, 1975. 170–217.

Worcester Evening Gazette 19 June 1937, 21 June 1937, 24 June 1937, 25 June 1937, 26 June 1937, 28 June 1937.

Worcester Telegram 22 June 1937, 25 June 1937, 21 August 1937, 1 September 1937, 6 December 1937.

"WPA Book Presents Story of Hurricane." *New York Times* 31 October 1938. 5.

"WPA Hurricane Souvenir Book." *Boston Traveler* 4 November 1938.

"WPA Man Winner of Big Award." *Boston Post* 4 April 1938.

"W.P.A. Writer's Cape 'Guide' Wins Him Guggenheim Award." *Boston Globe* 4 April 1938.

Yetman, Norman R. "An Introduction to the WPA Slave Narratives." http://memory.loc.gov/ammem/snhtml/snintro00.html. Consulted June 11, 2003.

INDEX

Page references given in *italics* refer to illustrations or their captions.

CHRISTINE BOLD is a native of Scotland. She received her Hons. M.A. (First Class) in English language and literature from the University of Edinburgh and her Ph.D. in English from University College London. She has taught in the United Kingdom, and in Canada at the University of British Columbia, the University of Alberta, and Trent University. She is currently professor in the School of English and Theatre Studies, University of Guelph, Ontario. Professor Bold has received numerous grants and awards, including substantial fellowships from the Social Sciences and Humanities Research Council (SSHRC) of Canada in support of her work on the WPA Writers' Project and its American Guides Series. She has been president of the Canadian Association for American Studies and coeditor of the *Canadian Review of American Studies.* The author of many papers and articles, she has published two previous books: *The WPA Guides: Mapping America* (1999) and *Selling the Wild West: Popular Western Fiction, 1860–1960* (1987). She is also coauthor of *Remembering Women Murdered by Men: Memorials across Canada* (2006) by the Cultural Memory Group, a collaboration of academics and activists. Christine Bold lives in Guelph, Ontario, with her partner and her son.